FUSILIER

FUSILIER

Recollections and Reflections
1939–1945

JOHN McMANNERS

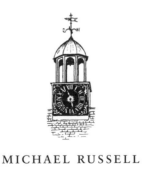

MICHAEL RUSSELL

First published in Great Britain 2002
by Michael Russell (Publishing) Ltd
Wilby Hall, Wilby, Norwich NR16 2JP

Typeset in Sabon by Waveney Typesetters
Wymondham, Norfolk
Printed and bound in Great Britain
By Biddles Ltd, Guildford and King's Lynn

TO ALL WHO SERVED WITH
THE FIRST BATTALION
ROYAL NORTHUMBERLAND FUSILIERS
IN THE WESTERN DESERT,
WITH GRATITUDE AND ADMIRATION

Contents

	Acknowledgements	9
1	Home Base	11
2	Fenham Barracks	24
3	Aldershot	36
4	Fenham, Whitley Bay and the *Pentland*	46
5	Tobruk	59
6	Cairo	82
7	The Great Retreat	95
8	Defence and Attack at El Alamein	109
9	On to Tunis	124
10	Tripoli, Damascus, Jerusalem	137
11	The Greek Army in Exile: Ismailia	151
12	Conspiracies	164
13	Cyrenaica: The Last Conspiracy	177
14	Chairborne in Cairo	187
15	Home Again	203
	Maps	219

Acknowledgements

Advancing years bring a sharp-focused clarity to the memory, just as the colours in a garden become deeper and more vivid as twilight falls. But the pattern is no longer continuous; the recollected details concern highly-selected, isolated incidents. Without access to the Battalion War Diary to provide structure and coherence, this study could never have been completed. My thanks go to Captain Peter Marr, curator of the Northumberland Fusiliers Museum in Alnwick Castle and secretary of the regimental association, who sent me a photocopy of the voluminous War Diary, together with the relevant numbers of the regimental magazine, the *St George's Gazette*. Peter Marr has also helped me by providing information about what happened to various individuals after the time I knew them, and by filling in my sketchy knowledge of peacetime soldiering.

My wife, Sarah, devised and drew the maps. Thanks to Peter Jones, head of the MOD Map Depot, and to Nicholas Hutchins, these are derived from German and Italian maps of the Western Desert, as well as British. My typescript has been read by friends at All Souls College: Professor Robert O'Neill, Chichele Professor of the History of War, John Davis our Warden, and Robert Darnton; to them I owe many corrections and improvements. As ever, Margaret Lord of the College office has typed the manuscript. Michael Russell has copy-edited with insight and imagination, going well beyond the help a publisher might be expected to extend to an author.

Some documentation of GHQ Middle East (Allies) may have been preserved in the Public Record Office, though I doubt if anyone would have thought it worthwhile to keep the files of 210 British Liaison Unit (Greeks). If so, my disconnected memories will remain the sole record of a bizarre series of intrigues and incidents on the fringes of the war, which otherwise would never have found a chronicler.

I

Home Base

I was reflecting what to do after taking my degree at Oxford, when Hitler made the decision for me. In September 1939 I was at the family home in the vicarage at West Pelton, in County Durham; my father had been inducted to the living five years before. In any account of the adventures of a soldier, a picture of his home base is essential to understanding, for this is the recurring flashback in the mind of the exile, progressively idealised in the perpetual anticipation of return. My father had been a miner and my mother a schoolteacher; she converted him to Christian belief and coached him through the years of study required to be ordained. All their savings had gone into paying for him to take a year at a theological college. This background of limited means unfortified by inherited possessions, matched to a working-class down-to-earth practicality and ingenuity, made the vicarage unlike most of its contemporaries, which had an air of gentility and scholarly reserve. Ours, in a knockabout fashion, was more comfortable and more interesting to live in.

West Pelton vicarage was a solid stone late-nineteenth-century house, with lofty ceilings and a spacious hall and broad staircase, a place to live in like lords in summer and like Eskimos in winter. The furniture, bought at auction sales in Newcastle and Durham, consisted mostly of huge Victorian and Edwardian pieces which went for a song as they were too big for ordinary houses and too unfashionable for richer ones – sideboards with vast mirrors, towering arrays of decorative shelves and ornate copings, bookcases that needed the whole family to move them by sliding them along the floor, armchairs in which a small man might vanish. They dwarfed the spindly bits and pieces coming down from our earlier existence. If we were alerted to a saleroom item of more restrained and delicate design, this would be invariably assigned to the drawing-room, my mother's domain, which she made attractive by all sorts of feminine invention. But this was a room used only for meetings of parishioners or great family occasions.

Normally we took our ease amid the overblown and rather ugly splendours of the saleroom white elephants.

Like the furniture, the carpeting was second hand and sufficiently assorted to make some corners of the house look like gypsy encampments, whereas the two main rooms had large, opulent and vividly coloured designs which once had adorned some stately home – and now, with settees and armchairs strategically arranged to cover the worn and faded patches, they still shed an aura of distinction. The auction sales had failed to produce the floor coverings needed for some upstairs rooms, so there were stretches of linoleum with stained wooden borders. My bedroom had a dressing table minus mirror as a desk to work at in the window area, with a bed beside it, then a long stretch of lino running to the back wall. This had two wardrobes against it, one a Victorian mahogany affair of drawers and trays and hanging space, made less ugly by having all the knobs and fretwork on the top sawn off, and a flimsy modern plywood version looking even flimsier beside it. The colliery company sent us loads of coal, a lifeline for winter survival, so in decency towards our benefactors we had to put up with archaic gas lights in the middle of each ceiling, while everyone else had electricity. Finally the gas company went out of business, and in came the electric wiring men sent by the Church Commissioners – much to my mother's relief.

The vicarage had extensive grounds. The entrance from the main road was adorned by two tall pillars with an arch of ornate iron work on top – pitched just too low, as it happened, for the height of our incoming removal van, so that everything had to be unloaded and carried laboriously up the drive. As darkness fell, Father went out with a pocket full of change to enlist a band of children to carry small items in relays, otherwise we'd have still been there in the morning. The drive went round both sides of a shrubbery, and at each side there were tall trees; the church was at the right of the house and on the left there was a lawn – the principal rooms looked out on it. At the back was a kitchen garden and another lawn, which we made into a tennis court. It was ideal for practising; the bad bounces taught the importance of keeping the eye on the ball, and at one end, since the back line was only three feet from the wire netting, every shot after the service had to be a volley. On a strip of waste land near the court, two barrowloads of clay were brought in to form 'clay ends' for quoit

The author's parents

The author: St Edmund Hall tennis team 1938

playing – if you spun the iron quoits properly, they dug in instead of slithering or bouncing.

As these arrangements suggest, ours was a household devoted to the playing of outdoor games. With little in the way of formal education, Father did what he could for his sons by passing on to us his skill in ball games. At soccer he had enjoyed local celebrity as a centre-half, and without any opportunity to learn the techniques of tennis, he had devised his own way of playing based on his instinctive appreciation of the volley as the shot to dominate the court in doubles, and of the lob as the counter to it. For some years, before he became overweight, he had run football teams for boys simply to give me and my second brother, Tom, a chance to become adept at the game, and every holiday had been spent in a rented house at the seaside (at Redcar) with the whole of the day spent either in the sea or on the tennis court. Every night he issued an open challenge to all the local park players, some of whom were not best pleased to be beaten by a big tireless man with a ten-year-old boy as partner, instructed to lurk close to the net and hit anything within reach.

The parish of West Pelton – scattered streets around a centre of the parish church and a few shops, various outlying cottages and, down a steep hill, the populous rural slum of Grange Villa, where almost everyone was unemployed – afforded little social life. Everyday encounters led to cups of tea and gossip, but no one issued invitations; any organised sociability came in the pubs and the church hall. Unlike the bigger mining villages there was no corner-end for idlers to frequent and no parade street for youth at weekends – those who wanted to parade had to take the bus to Chester-le-Street. Normally in the villages of the North-East coalfield, half industrial, half rural, there was a small, exclusive youth group separate from the young wage-earners who paraded at weekends, the confraternity of those who attended the grammar school, bussed in from local areas. They lacked money to spend and would have to delay marriage, but they were comparatively intelligent and well-read, their contacts straddled the smaller village communities, and they continued to fraternise later in their vacations from the university. By the move to West Pelton I had lost this web of contacts and only one or two friendships carried on, and we didn't have many opportunities to meet. In the vacations from Oxford I spent most of the time in study and in keeping fit. In the summer there would be games of tennis with Tom. Once a week there was the chance to join the older men of the church to play billiards on the half-sized table of Harry Rewcastle, one of the church wardens. The 'dole men' who used the church hall twice a week to pay the unemployed had a table-tennis team, and sometimes they would send up to the vicarage for Tom or me to make up their number at a match; there would be invitations to turn out for the cricket and football teams my father had founded. We had some notable sporting occasions. One, sponsored by the dole men, was the table-tennis duel between Tom and Jack Travena in Benny Long's barber shop at Stanley (five miles up the hill). Travena, in his immaculate shirt with flashing cuff links, glaring determination through his rimless specs, finally won, to the despair of the girls who brought in the sandwiches, for they had decided they liked Tom better than the local hero. Another was when our cricket team beat the prestigious Beamish club. They had a terrifying fast bowler called George Mudd ('Slinger', of course) and Bob Dodds the colliery blacksmith hit 100 off him in half an hour, and that included a five-minute intermission to allow those who had parked cars near the pitch to rush them off to refuge under the trees.

The member of our family who faced the most difficult passage to social acceptance in West Pelton was the youngest, Joe. During my first year there I travelled back every day (two hours each way) to my old grammar school at Spennymoor – trapped in the syllabus for the Higher School Certificate examination; thereafter, to Oxford. Tom went straight to the grammar school at Chester-le-Street. But Joe, still of elementary school age, had to go down the hill to the grim school at Grange Villa. The former vicar's two little girls had gone to a private school; one of the vicarage children at Grange Villa was a novelty, and an obvious target for victimisation – but just for one day. 'Lukey' Tinkler, brother of the boxer whose name and picture were on the billboards advertising bouts at the Gateshead Hippodrome, challenged Joe to a fight and was comprehensively flattened. Getting caned by the headmaster for this mayhem left Joe secure in the respect of all the juvenile underworld.

The close-knit family life of the vicarage was variegated by the operation of my father's concept of his station and its duties. At home, he was both gentle and uproariously jovial, but he could be uncompromising and blunt outside, especially where the great were concerned –

as Bishop Hensley Henson (later his friend) found when he spoke at the diocesan conference on 'the poverty of the clergy' (ill-advised in this diocese of dole queues), and Dean Alington when he kept him waiting early one morning on the ground that he never started work until he had 'completed the *Times* crossword'. The toughness was directed upwards and sometimes laterally towards pretentious fellow clergy, but never downwards; though he had no illusions about beggars and never fell for hard luck stories, anyone who was hungry was welcome to share a meal with us, and it really was a meal, for we ate heartily as we had done in the mining days. Once we had a self-styled musician, who played the piano while putting in the tenor to father's bass in a hearty rendition of the Hallelujah Chorus. He dined and was given a bed for the night, but had vanished before breakfast – no doubt on the run from the police. There was the local drunk who would come on days when he decided to amend, would work in the garden and eat a prodigious meal (five helpings of rhubarb and custard – 'It dis yer a power o' good, vicar'). On one of these visits he ruined the front lawn by inspirationally cutting out flower beds in the shape of hearts, clubs and spades, and for a long time islands of weeds bore testimony to his efforts. Another occasional luncher was the ex-bank clerk who had been to prison for stealing the funds; he would write out a neat version of the parish accounts and fulfil his ambition to be a composer by trying out his ideas on our piano.

Very different visitors were drawn to the vicarage by another concept of duty: the parson must be the local leader. If something was amiss in the parish – like wife beating or cruelty to children, whether it concerned the Church or not, Father would be there to negotiate, denounce or even threaten retribution. A scoundrel in Grange Villa ran up debts then fled, leaving his wife facing the descent of the bailiffs to confiscate the furniture. Father went down and organised the hiding of the family possessions in various houses in the street, then when the 'bums' arrived he was there in black hat and full clerical rig seated on the only chair with a cup of tea and waiting for a row. Some visitors came to the vicarage to discuss recruiting for the choir or actually aspiring to join it, so we finished up with a multifarious collection of iron tenors and hoarse and rasping basses and extra boys who would like as not hold their psalters upside down. It was just as well that noise production was reinforced, for another project was the refounding of an almost forgotten village institution, 'The West Pelton Silver Model Brass Band'. Some of their instruments were unearthed in pawnshops and attics, and money was raised to buy more, and in gratitude they came to church at Christmas, Easter and Harvest Festival to blast the congregation out of their seats by accompanying the more dramatic verses of the hymns. And a multitude of people kept coming to the vicarage concerning the famous building project, erecting a 'mission church' at Grange Villa. Concrete blocks from a demolition site were begged from a contractor, a couple of men who had been clerks in architect's offices drew up the plans, and the unemployed of Grange Villa were invited to come and do the labouring for a free dinner and a packet of twenty cigarettes a day. There were difficulties clearing this remuneration with the 'dole men', and other difficulties concerning the exclusion of certain dubious characters who had insinuated themselves among the volunteers. Shopkeepers for miles around were dunned for meat, vegetables, bread and the like, and godly women of the church went down daily to cook vast cauldrons of stew. I was present at the debate in the vicarage on how deep foundations have to be: Father took the average of three opinions and doubled it to be sure. Empiricism reigned on the building site: if a wall looked wrong it was knocked down and re-sited after discussions with all present. I was there on two occasions when momentous decisions were taken. The theatre-stage cum altar area had a lot of space underneath, so a trap door was put in 'in case it was needed by a conjurer'. Let us hope no succeeding vicar has vanished from sight while celebrating the Mysteries. And when the building was finished there was a heap of concrete blocks left over – it was decided to use them to add battlements.

All these bustling parochial achievements and, for that matter, the academic progress of the three sons were built on the self-sacrifice of my mother, who never had a moment's leisure. She rehearsed father every Saturday in the lessons, the Epistle and the Gospel lest he drop an 'h', corrected the spelling in everything he wrote, copied out his business letters in her clear schoolteacher's hand, took the meetings of the Mothers' Union and the sewing party, kept everyone at the vicarage neatly dressed and well fed, listened to everyone's troubles and put up with the continual influx of visitors, welcome and not so welcome. She was happy, asking nothing from life except that 'the boys do well'.

Deeply religious as they were, both parents hoped I would be ordained – as the theologically incorrect cliché went, 'go into the Church'. While Mother had coached Father in theology and allied subjects, I had followed their discussions, joined in, read the set texts, so that when I went up to Oxford I knew my New Testament hermeneutics – the Synoptic problem, the nature of 'Q', the status of the Johannine discourses, the excessive penchant for miracle in Matthew's special source, the arguments for dating the Pauline Epistles and the Gospels. I was *au fait* with the minimalist, reductionist historiography of the New Testament critics, and had historical veracity organised into a believable core. At my college, I was insufferably eloquent in the discussions of the Liddon Society, which grouped together the ordinands. But I had not become committed to going to a theological college. It had looked as if I would get a good degree, perhaps good enough to apply for scholarships and grants to carry on at Oxford for a higher-degree course. After the term ended, with the Finals examination (in history) over, but the results not yet available, discussion about the future was put on hold; I relaxed in unaccustomed leisure and, for the first time, went for a holiday out of England – a daring adventure it seemed at the time, little knowing what overseas adventures really awaited. The opportunity came because of the generosity of 'Jake', my father's curate. The Revd Jack Shannon – known in the family circle for some mysterious jocular reason as 'Jake' – was like my father in that he had been ordained at a later age than usual without academic qualifications, though unlike my father he was well-educated. He was snobbish, but always laughing at himself, pompous but open-hearted, appearing finicky, but an able organiser, a man who was doing a lot of good but would have been surprised to hear anyone say so. A bachelor without ties, he had discovered how to get a free, prestigious holiday by going as chaplain to one of the resorts in Switzerland frequented by English and American visitors, and he was booked that year to look after the spiritual welfare of the wealthy who went to the huge hotel in the mountains at Axenstein. He was entitled to take two relatives at half price, so he declared Tom and I were his 'nephews' – and also undertook to share expenses equally with us.

So, albeit on a tight budget, we managed to go with him. As we passed through France, there were reservists at many of the railway stations, rifles slung on shoulders, with huge packs surmounted by tin helmets on the platform beside them, on their way to report for duty. At

Axenstein, the huge hotel ticked over luxuriously with hardly any clients. The menace of war had kept even the most regular and faithful annual visitors at home. But there was a honeymoon couple from England, George Black the younger, the theatrical impresario and his bride, both enthusiastic tennis players. Tom and I made up a doubles set with them every morning, and in return they invited us to go with them on the sort of excursions by speedboat or car we could never have afforded. One night, a group of half a dozen Germans with a military look about them called in at the hotel to dine; they put a couple of little flags on their table, one their national flag, the other a swastika version. Some Swiss Army officers in uniform came in, sent for a Swiss flag for their table, and pelted the Germans with sugar lumps.

I had to return to England before Tom and Jake for my examination *viva* (everybody, not just the problem candidates on the border line between classes, had a *viva* in those days). After missing a train in Paris I got into Oxford at midnight, knocked up my long-suffering landlady, snatched a few hours' sleep, and rushed off to the Examination Schools for my 9 a.m. ordeal, all sunburnt, the collection of notes I had taken away on holiday unread, and my mind empty of all the useful information it had once contained, like whether the Anglo-Saxon *fyrd* was a mounted force, or what changes in the franchise were made by the 1832 Reform Bill. The examiners said that I looked as though I had enjoyed a well-deserved holiday and wished me good day – no questions. Tom and Jake, on their way home, called at the London Palladium to see the show, by courtesy of George Black, who had devised a whimsical welcome for them. At the end of a number, the chorus came down into the stalls, and Dorcas, of 'the million dollar legs', tried to drag Jake out, dog collar and all, to dance in the aisle. Tom hastened to take his place, a good turn which involved no self-sacrifice.

So back to the vicarage at West Pelton, to await the degree results. All went well, and my parents, in addition to their long-nurtured hope that I'd be ordained, now added the worthy but not-quite-so-Christian hope that I would rise in the Church in a way impossible to my ill-educated father. Oxford was a beginning, maybe in the end the deanery of Durham or the bishop's castle at Bishop Auckland beckoned. All the while, the shadow of war had been drawing nearer, and finally became a terrible, shattering reality. I think that they had half-foreseen that this would mean the end of their dream.

There could be no question about the justice and the necessity of the war. At Oxford we had seen the conflict coming and had discussed it daily. There was the Spanish Civil War, and we never asked for whom the bell tolled, for we knew it tolled for us. When Czechoslovakia went under without a shot fired, we knew its 'fallen bastions' were our bastions, the crumpling of the defences of the West. It was the first and last of the wars of history that were 'just wars' within the Christian definition. We had talked about this at home too and come to the same conclusion; even Father, a pacifist in the First War (though as a miner he was exempt anyway), agreed. But since at Oxford I had been a card-carrying ordinand, the family hope was that I would go on to a theological college, taking exemption from call-up.

From the moment war was declared, the wireless set (we did not then call it radio) became the centre of every household, and the country was run by announcements on the air waves. Among the details about rationing and air-raid precautions, there were directions for those who proposed to join up: university students who wished to be considered for commissions were to write to some board or other, in my case at Oxford. I sent off my letter of application the same day. In my view, you needed a stronger vocation than I had before it could be used as a passport to escape the burden of our generation. And there was a peculiar twist of patriotic feeling involved. Ours was a country which allowed pacifists and clergymen to stand aloof from the national struggle for survival, and that proved, whatever else was wrong with it, that it was a country worth fighting for. It was right that the exemption should be offered, and it was only decent to refuse to take advantage of it.

My parents were stoically heroic; they did not even hint at dissuasion, and while they were proud they knew I'd prefer them not to show it. Writing off to join whatever was going was folly, of course. One could have done one's duty but looked around for some interesting way of doing it. To pull strings to get into the Ministry of Information, as a contemporary at Teddy Hall boasted, would have been contemptible, but to use Oxford contacts to get into a branch of the services requiring intelligence would have been a decent attempt to be useful. In war, even more than in ordinary life, 'It's not what you know but whom you know that counts'. Lord Ranfurly, in his wife's lively memoirs, serves his country, but has more fun on General O'Connor's staff than as a platoon commander on the ground (O'Connor and his staff were taken prisoner, but that's by the way). In the celebrations of the anniversaries of the war during the last few years, Alamein, D-Day, Victory Europe, we have heard universal praise for the spirit of the British people in the dark days of Hitler's onslaught. The heroic unity was real, but it was diversified by a complex pattern of individual reactions to new and terrifying circumstances. Some were pulling strings to get into the more interesting opportunities of serving the war effort, others were doing their best to negotiate their way well back from the firing line. A good deal later I did get strings pulled to get an interesting staff job, and later still I failed to take an invitation to come back into the firing line. This means I understand better now what was happening on the national scale in 1939. It may also explain why I am still around to be writing about it.

The interview with the Commissions Board at Oxford was a three-minute farce. Sitting waiting my turn, my predecessor at the inquest emerged. 'OK?' I asked. 'It seems they want infantry.' One representative of each of the three Services and two comfortable-looking dons were seated at the table, one in a yellow waistcoat that aroused my envy. I have vague memories of white hair and a port-drinker's complexion. 'I see you got a First,' he said, looking at the papers, 'well done.' They asked what my preferences were. In my simplicity, I said, 'Flying, only I had to promise my mother on leaving that I wouldn't.' Perhaps they might try persuasion. 'I think that the infantry is the obvious place for you,' said a voice with the apparent solicitude of one who had carefully weighed my dossier and had found a judicious niche for me. As I went out, a fellow applicant in the waiting-room asked what had happened. 'They have found me a dashing assignment,' I replied, and departed back to Teddy Hall to read the newspapers in the Junior Common Room. Mother had been right, of course. The privilege of sitting down to bacon and egg before going into battle and having a drink in an arm chair after coming down from the clouds was bought by mortgaging the future. Tom, volunteering later, was not subject to the family veto, and he went into the Fleet Air Arm (dangers of sky plus dangers of sea and flying inferior planes against land-based fighters). He was lucky. He crashed at the end of his first solo flight; they sent him straight up again in another plane to rescue his nerve, and he knew, every minute of the flight, that he would crash again. So he did, and was transferred to the Navy, which otherwise was closed to the multitude of volunteers for a life afloat.

The decision of the Oxford Board was quickly clinched. In no time I was summoned to a medical at Newcastle, sworn in and given the king's shilling (actually half a crown). The last hope was gone at home when I arrived back to announce I had been passed A1 – if only I had been found to suffer from some non-life-threatening disqualification, flat feet or defective eyesight. There was an interval with nothing happening, so I went back to Teddy Hall to start research on John, Duke of Lauderdale, one of the notorious 'Cabal' in the reign of Charles II. My supervisor was to be the legendary Keith Feiling of Christ Church. In his book-lined study he sat for an hour hearing me recount my design, the sources I had sampled and hoped to use – and made no comment. We had a glass of sherry and parted. I had hoped to hear words of wisdom, to collect a few flowers of curious information about the Restoration period on which he was so richly informed. How well in his books the picturesque details were piled up: he was the brilliant exponent of the ironies of contemporaneity, presenting the diverse details of incidents that happened simultaneously as each individual followed his interest, lust or personal designs against the backdrop of the national events they heeded so little. Why did Feiling limit himself to small talk or silence? Perhaps he saw no point in learned discourse when I was under starter's orders for war. He may have thought I ought to have been living it up in my last days of freedom. The summons came to report at Fenham Barracks at Newcastle, the depot of the Royal Northumberland Fusiliers, and I took the next train home.

2

Fenham Barracks

On a bleak day early in November 1939 I reported to the guardroom of
Fenham Barracks, at the gates of the vast, ugly, redbrick enclosure, and
was sent across the road to the complex of Nissen huts where the new
recruits were to live. I had a big haversack slung on one shoulder, with
football boots tied to it. As I went towards the hut that was to be my
home, a fat corporal passing by said 'Football boots, the Army likes a
sportsman!' This, I soon learned, was Fatty Fairford, and these were the
last kind words I heard from anyone in authority for the next two
months.

Here was *descensus Averno*, one could but echo Marlowe's Faustus,
'Why, this is Hell, nor am I out of it!' In this time in the recruit company, not a single officer came along to see what we were doing; I
caught a distant glimpse of our company commander, a major with a
highly polished Sam Browne belt and riding boots – Major Tarleton.[1]
There was no sign of a chaplain. We were left in the charge of NCOs,
the chief being a young, red-faced and red-haired sergeant, harsh and
humourless. As I write about him in mostly uncomplimentary terms, I
will not give his real name – just call him 'Sergeant Redhead'. Under
him was Sergeant Lawless, an Irish old soldier called back to the
colours, spluttering, good-natured, and ineffectual, known as 'Windy
Bill'. 'Redhead is a bastard,' he once muttered to me, but he could do
nothing about it. Lawless wore the ribbon of the Military Medal; this
created awe. 'What did he get it for?' I asked Fatty Fairford, the third
member of our instruction team. 'It must have been for fucking,' he
replied.

After endless queuing in the cold for ill-fitting battledress, overalls
and various items of kit, life in our barrack room began. Except for me
and two old soldiers called back to the colours, everyone was a conscript. I was sorry for them, even more sorry than I was for myself.

---

1 The *Regimental Gazette* of 1944, page 27, records Ben Tarleton as being POW in Italy.

They had asked for so little from life, just to be left alone with dull hard work (if you could get it) during the day, and very ordinary pleasures in the evening, the pub and the picture house, the billiard hall and the girls, and to be with their families. Being so young, they were all unmarried, and all except one were from mining villages; the exception was Fram, a heavy ruddy-faced boy from a family of farm workers, clumsy at everything and slow in machine-gun drill. He, like me, and for the same reason, was a target for Redhead's scorn. That first night in the barrack room the whole crowd went to bed in their newly issued Army underwear – the woolly vests with short sleeves and the tight-fitting 'long johns' to keep the legs warm, called 'Bob Fitzsimmons' or 'Jim Jeffries' after the tight-breeched pugilists shown in old boxing prints. There were pyjamas in my haversack but I did not dare to bring them out. The next day my cover was blown by the leisurely ceremony of Sergeant Redhead taking down our home addresses. Everything we said was a target for his wit. The pale young man whose name was Hunter was pounced on as 'Cunter' with appropriate sexual innuendoes – there were tears in his eyes. My address was 'The Vicarage, West Pelton, Beamish'. 'A fucking parson's son, what the hell you doing here?' I was beginning to wonder myself.

The day ended with a ray of light, two late arrivals, both older, both volunteers. One was a well-padded Newcastle solicitor, who was to keep a low profile, and by inviting Redhead and his wife to dinner in his affluent surroundings won respite from bullying. (What was our sergeant's wife like? He used to tell us, gratuitously, with incongruous naïvety and tenderness, and amid his crude slanging, how much he loved her, evidently sincerely. Strange and touching.) The other volunteer rescued me from gloom – Matt Brown, mid-thirties, big, muscular, slow, and reflective, a county rugger player. When the work of the day was over, he laid out his pyjamas, toothbrush, and toothpaste on his bed. If anyone was tempted to be funny, his size deterred them. I pulled out my pyjamas too: what Matt Brown could do, I could do.

With Fram and me, he was on the list to be ridiculed, but his serene and tough indifference was a lesson in how to cope. My rehabilitation was completed after three weeks in this cold and sordid hell by the soccer match between our barrack room and the other rival one, with the NCOs having bets on the outcome. Rarely meeting the time-tests for mounting the gun, let alone technicalities such as remedying stoppages, Matt and I could at least play soccer. It was sad to see how slow the recruits were, even those who had some proficiency at ball control, and those latter, to my surprise, were few – it was a legend that the North-East was a pool of potentially great players. Most of its youth were ill-fed, unathletic, tough in the sense of plodding endurance, but lacking speed and an eye for the ball. Matt played inside left, ponderous but unshakeable, winning the ball with crunching tackles and putting it through to me on the left wing. I got three goals and we won easily. Sergeant Redhead, Bill Lawless, and Fatty Fairford gathered their winnings with glee. At last the two pyjama-wearing sophisticates, the butt of the instructors, had achieved status. It did not protect us from the slings and arrows of the NCOs, but we had secure ranking in the rough and tumble of the barrack room.

Films about army life never have verisimilitude: directors do not dare to give the real-life dialogue, with every significant noun having its four-letter adjective – besides, it would be boring. One of the few things we were effectively taught was machine-gun drill, the actions of the team of five which set up the Vickers gun ready to fire, ferried up the ammunition, and rectified the stoppages, from 'ease, pull, tap' to 'new lock two'. The efficiency of the instruction was solely down to Redhead, and in the circumstances of war a lot must be forgiven to the rebarbative individuals who are effective in the grim narrow purpose of training simpletons in the elementary techniques of killing. He fell into rages over slip-ups, and these were diversified, not only with the four-letter house style, but also with picturesque evocations of sexual parallels. If the number two failed to get the pin fixing the gun to the tripod into the hole at the first try, formulaic obscenities were easily available for inclusion in the censure. No doubt these epigrams were part of the folklore of army training, not the inventions of a single individual. Fatty Fairford had a line in them too, and I learnt from him a few observations sufficiently respectable for saloon-bar use, even if not up to drawing rooms: 'If your brains were made of gunpowder, they wouldn't blow your hat off', and if the aforementioned brains were made of something else, 'there wouldn't be a smell'. The metaphors derived from the bodily functions were further developed in the teaching of the absurdly self-important sergeant who had us shivering on the barrack square learning fire drill. This consisted solely of running out hoses and demonstrating how to direct the spray. The smaller nozzles produce more powerful and further-carrying jets was the arcane secret he revealed. 'When you were young and had competitions who could piss the furthest...' We gave grave acceptance to this piece of scientific information; not for us to admit that we belonged to the unenlightened minority who had never enjoyed this absorbing sport.

The sexual ambience of the barrack room was especially evident when the weary adventurers into town tottered back at night. (I never went out; polishing, 'blancoing' and reading filled my evenings.) Then, there was an exchange of narrations of sexual encounters, real or invented – 'I could have fucked her through her coat', and other expressions of admiration for glamour allied to affirmations of potency. Pat Murphy, a little Irishman with a lined face, an old soldier called back to the colours, was accepted by all as the man of experience and the moral arbiter in these matters. We all felt for him when he recounted his meeting with a 'nice kid' who invited him to go home with her, how he had been tempted but finally refused. 'I should have gone,' he kept on saying, head in hands. His scruples were admired by all and his deprivation aroused deep sympathy. Pat was appealed to as to 'the best way to have it'; the best by far, he declared was in bed, and his audience had to concede that this was unknown territory to them so far, their experience being limited to doorways and alleys in the urban milieu, and haystacks and hedgerows in the country, weather permitting. One night Pat's authority was challenged or, one should say, put in need of more elaborate justification than was usual, for a dour gloomy individual broke his habitual silence to recommend 'having a go' whenever possible, but with the stern proviso, 'Where you fuck you marry.' (Who was this? Was it the same who admired the men manning the launching of the barrage balloons as the elite of the army, thinking they went aloft with their balloons, rifles at the ready, to prang the German bombers?) Pat was able to show, not without instances from his own experience, that this puritanical maxim did not necessarily apply to men who were risking their lives in wartime, especially those of more mature years who had only a limited performance time ahead of them. He conceded, however, that for the young in their home surroundings in peacetime, the austere ideal was to be recommended as counsel of perfection.

We were taught, remorselessly, the drill of the Vickers machine-gun, and we were subjected to square bashing until we became machines, though we were limited to the simple, obvious manoeuvres. That was

about all. There was no question of going out into the country to place
the guns in realistic, camouflaged firing positions and aiming at real targets – true, the weather of November and December was frightful that
year. We practised in the barrack room aiming at landscape targets
about four feet by two. You fix on a feature of the scene (say, the
bottom right-hand corner of a cottage, to be called 'cottage'), then give
orders to the number one of the gun in degrees from that point, using
clock references – 'Range 500, cottage, right two o'clock, two degrees,
streak in hedge, lay!' The degrees were measured by the space between
the knuckles with the hand clenched and held at arm's length. On one
target there was an electric power pylon. Redhead called it 'piling'. A
problem for verbal purists. Almost everyone, the solicitor included, said
'piling', whether from ignorance or subservience. Matt Brown said
'pylon' loud and clear, accent on the second syllable. Master of diplomatic evasiveness, I muttered 'pyl'n' with the accent on the first syllable. Oddly, our NCOs did not seem to notice.

Everyone had to qualify to drive heavy vehicles, so we were sent off
in groups on four or five lorries to take turns driving around unfrequented country roads under the charge of an MT corporal. The NCOs
were much too sensible to let any of us take the wheel, that way lay
trouble. In my particular three-tonner we always went out to the moors
where, on a lonely spur, there was a half-derelict café, unfrequented.
Here we holed in and drank tea, provided free by the proprietor, for
who would charge the defenders of the nation? Outside was always
cold and usually raining, and this enhanced the euphoria of sitting at
the fireside for a couple of hours' respite from Redhead and all his
works. Then off to get back to the barracks at the right time. The final
test came, night driving, and we sat in the back while our corporal
swept us through the darkness. Safely back, he certified us all as passed.

As for firing practice with the Vickers gun, there was no ammunition: we struggled endlessly rectifying the stoppages with dummy
rounds in the belt, but none of us ever fired a live round. Rifle training
was all in the barrack room, lying down with feet properly anchored,
aiming at targets, and each time we pulled the trigger saying aloud
where the shot *would* have gone – 'slightly high', 'edge of bull', etc.
This was supposed to foster awareness and concentration. In the end, a
few clips of live rifle ammunition turned up, and after endless 'going
through the motions' we at last got a day on the range, firing five

rounds each. It was a long day, mostly just standing huddled up in greatcoats, the only fun being when the time came taking up one's turn at the butts – pulling down the targets, pasting up the holes, pushing the repaired targets back up then, after the firing, signalling the number of hits with a disk on a pole. It was a pleasure to award unearned good results to whoever it was who was doing the firing. I dare say half the shots were signalled wrongly, and nobody in authority cared anyway. Then the nuisance of cleaning the rifle with the pull through and a piece of 'four by two'. Once, we went out into the country for a night exercise (twilight actually), and for this we were each issued with a blank round. We looked forward to the fun of lying in ambush in a hedgerow and making a proper bang. Just in time I heard Fatty Fairford saying to Bill Lawless, 'Stupid buggers, they'll have to clean their fucking rifles afterwards.' So I refrained from the pleasure and gave my blank to an eager fellow fusilier who had not heard Fatty's words of wisdom. After all, he had already fired one round so he might as well fire two, for the damage had been done.

There were two subjects concerning morale and discipline on which our NCOs were eloquent. They drummed into us the simple essentials of regimental history – the Northumberland Fusiliers' battle honours, why we wear red and white roses in our hats on St George's Day, the meaning of the regimental motto, 'Quo fata vocant'. They did this with genuine solemnity – no four-letter adjectives, no bolshy asides. We were all serious about it, too: amid the discomforts and futilities of so much that we were doing, we wanted to belong, we were offering our loyalty to our local regiment as we gave our loyalty to Newcastle United football team (or Sunderland or Middlesbrough according to home address). In 1939 we didn't think of dying for our country, just about stopping Hitler; but we wanted to identify with the Royal Northumberland Fusiliers; more and more, the regiment became a tangible intermediary for patriotism, even, in the last resort, something we might die for. Economising governments have trampled on local ties and the Northumberland Fusiliers are no more. If ever we need a large conscript army again, we will regret having destroyed the allegiances of local pride.

Something else drummed into us by the NCOs was the necessity, the overwhelming importance of saluting officers, and doing it correctly, 'longest way up, shortest way down'. You had to recognise badges of

rank, of course, but for the quick and instant decision to salute the recognition sign was the officer's collar and tie showing through the open top
of his battledress. (When the Canadians came over, all wearing ties, the
old certainties were eroded, but this was later, when I was an officer cadet
at Aldershot, and was never a problem for us: the Canadians were the
ones wearing carpet slippers or co-respondent shoes as well.) In the
exhortations of our NCOs on saluting, one would look in vain for any
hint of hostility to officers, or irony, or reservations. I could guess and
later confirmed that the bar of the sergeants' mess was the place for critical glosses. But none of this showed. The NCOs were moulded into an
hierarchical system, and their arbitrary authority over us was matched
by their own acceptance of arbitrary authority upwards. Yet it was
always 'on parade on parade, off parade off parade'. Nothing was quite
what it seemed in the iron front the system presented to the world and to
those novices who aspired to be accepted in it.

Our stint in the recruit company amid the Nissen huts, puddles and
duck-boards ended without ceremony – no officer looking in to see us,
no touching wind-down of the reign of terror, with Sergeant Redhead
and Corporal Fairford, moist-eyed, wishing us good luck in going off to
fight the Hun. Not so. We went off on leave, the weekend and a couple
of extra days, then came back to report to the guard room to discover
our individual destinies. I found that I had to lug my kit to a barrack
room in the main brick buildings; I was the only one, the others going
off elsewhere, the conscripts to a unit, Matt Brown and the solicitor to
an Officer Training Unit, OCTU. I never heard of them again. As I later
discovered, I was on the list for OCTU but the bureaucracy had lost the
documentation, so I was shunted off with various other 'odds and sods'
(as the phrase went) until it was found. The idea of asking to see someone in authority never occurred to me. I had no ambition, I had joined
'for the duration' to fight and I would wait until I was sent to do it. I
had, however, been recognised, being put up to lance corporal, acting
and unpaid, but a rank none the less. Mother sewed on the stripe when
I next got home, with a great deal of fuss about exactly how to place it.

The story of life at home, and of those wonderful weekends when I
could escape and forget the barracks must be largely excluded from
these recollections. As Chateaubriand said about heaven, 'No one can
be interested in beings who are perfectly happy.' What can I say to
interest the reader? Once I had left the recruit company, I could get

away on Friday night, rather than midday Saturday, an enormous extra ration of heaven. It was important to be dressed correctly, boots 'bulled', cap badge polished, for you had to present yourself at the guardroom to be inspected before being allowed out. Anything wrong and you had to go away and put it right, and that not too quickly – time must elapse so the reason for the guard corporal's displeasure was not being treated as trivial. Walk down from the barracks to Newcastle bus station (twenty minutes), take a bus to Chester-le-Street, then wait there on a bleak tarmac island on the road for the half-hourly service to Stanley. There would be a gale howling down the dark, deserted main avenue of Chester-le-Street, and generally rain with it. The bus was always crowded at night, full of the smell of damp clothing and cigarette smoke. In long johns, battledress, and great coat, one became insufferably hot. Outside it was pitch black, the blackout having suppressed the street lamps and compelled householders to ensure that not a gleam of light escaped, while the bus windows were misted up. The bus ground along by twists and turns, everybody asking everyone else where we were. I was usually the expert, having travelled this route twice a day for a year as I went back daily to my old grammar school at Spennymoor. Misery, calculated to intensify the pleasure of escaping into the fresh air and walking up the street to the vicarage, stumbling in the shrubbery in the darkness, then suddenly blinking in the bright light of home.

Home as a refuge. This sentiment was a reversion to the times of ten years ago before I went happily to grammar school then to Oxford, the days when I had to go to the primary schools of Durham County, the schools from which the conscripts I had been living with were drawn. These were a sub-world which could only be likened to the barrack room; here, order could only be maintained by methods which would bring down a criminal prosecution now; several times a day boys would be lined up for savage canings on the palms of the hands – six on each side was a common occurrence. Going home in the afternoon at 'tea-time' was a magic experience, entrance to a refuge, an island of culture and civilisation. Escaping from Fenham Barracks was much the same experience. It baffled the imagination to understand how those two worlds could exist alongside each other, and made one reflect how few in number are the people, and how fragile the circumstances, on which our happiness depends.

Not long after reaching the dizzy rank of lance corporal, I found a girl friend. Within the parish, this was a daring initiative. I had female company at Oxford, but – unlike today – those who were dependent solely on scholarships had a limited social life, they could not afford commem balls or dining out, and they worked much harder (and played games more) than the undergraduates of today. There would have been girls for company had we stayed at Ferryhill, where my father had been a miner, then a curate – the confraternity of the young people who had been brought together by the grammar school. But now, away from both Oxford and my original roots, there was just the social group around the parish church. Here, the rules governing relationship of the sexes were much the same as those prevailing in a cruder form in the mining village generally – segregation with interaction between male and female groups, until it became it became possible to make a move towards a particular individual on the other side – then, this was public news, and was significant. For a vicar's son, the situation was near impossible, my father's relations with his flock were involved. Companionship must come from outside the system. The chief engineer of the colliery and his family lived aloof from the village down a tree-lined drive, they rarely darkened the doors of the church, but they had a seventeen-year-old daughter, Joan, a newcomer to the local social scene since she had been going every day to a private school in Newcastle. We began to meet in town when I could find a free afternoon with not enough time to get home, and when I had a fortnight's leave before going to OCTU we went to lunch and dine in Newcastle. There was not much to do in wartime for those who wanted only respectable pleasures, but we could drink coffee in Carrick's, where a string quartet played, and find somewhere to linger over a meal. To escape from the coarse atmosphere of the barracks, one thing above all else gave happiness – civilised conversation, and if it was with a good-looking girl, so much the better. Joan was attractive and sympathetic and life then had an urgency; we belonged to a world which, for all we knew, was coming to an end.

Being in a brick building, my new barrack room was warm, and as we were just filling in time, the tensions of Army life slackened. A corporal who slept in the room was in charge, and we talked a great deal. From him I got a sight of the training manual for the Vickers medium machine-gun. This revealed the *arcana imperii* – up to now there had been no admission that such a source of information existed, for this would have broken the unspoken assumption that our instructors had received a direct revelation of the secrets of gun drill from on high. An hour or two with the book and all was clear – 'beaten zones', 'fire in enfilade', 'fixed lines'; in a flash I leapt from fumbling neophyte to master of strategy. One of the technicalities we had been taught concerned the 'canelure groove' or just the 'canelure'. This was the groove around the gun barrel at the point where it fits into its housing, and through which it moves with the recoil, and it is kept airtight by being packed with asbestos string, tapped in carefully with slight oiling. In the book, there was no 'canelure'. The phrase 'channel or groove' had been transformed by successive generations of instructors into this new and splendidly technical sounding word.

I can remember only two occurrences from the ensuing weeks in limbo, one reassuring me about my personal future, the other, trivial as it was, disillusioning about our prospects of winning the war. For the first time, an officer came into our barrack room, a newly-commissioned second lieutenant, tall, pale, blonde, sympathetic, the sort of appearance that is typecast in war films for the predestined early casualty, too decent to survive. Our corporal had me talking to the class explaining how the explosive energy of the gun and its recoil was harnessed to running through the ammunition belt in automatic fire – this sort of thing, as against practice, was my line. Afterwards, the second lieutenant urged me to apply for officer training, and finding I was already on the list undertook to follow up my case. That was how the missing documentation was unearthed and I was put down for the next intake at the Machine-Gun OCTU at Aldershot.

The other incident was being summoned to accompany a group of Territorial Army officers onto the Town Moor outside the barracks as an orderly to carry the demonstration kit; a regular major was in charge. One hapless lieutenant, dark hair plastered down in the style of the Brylcreem advertisements, was unable to fathom the workings of the 'director', a little telescope on a disk with degrees from 0 to 360 marked round it, the whole thing mounted on a tripod. He was supposed to measure the angle between two bushes on the skyline. 'Corporal!' roared the major, 'get hold of that director and show him!' I did it without turning the dial to zero, just doing the subtraction. 'That's too difficult for this lot,' raged the major, 'show them how they can start at zero.' Luckily, I didn't meet any of those Territorial officers again. I wondered, was our army really as bad as this? In public houses everywhere there were posters on the walls, 'We are not interested in the possibility of defeat: for us it does not exist – (Queen Victoria)'. I had always thought this was stupid. A little reflection on the possibility of defeat and we might have been better organised to avoid it. I remembered the name of the lieutenant who could not use the director. Just before I joined the 1st Battalion in the Western Desert he died heroically covering the rearguard on the sandhills at the narrow neck of land at Agheila. Later, when we advanced westwards along the coast again, my colonel went to the spot and found the sand littered with empty bullet cases where the guns had been overrun by the German tanks, firing to the last.

My final move at Fenham Barracks was agreeable. Together with two other candidates for OCTU, who had arrived in the recruit company after me, I moved into a tiny room with a fireplace, the three of us in the charge of a heavily built Scottish corporal. We became friends with him, and when we returned from our weekends at home, he shared in the good things we brought back with us. We made the place a den, adorned with pictures of female film stars, our rifles hanging up crossed on the walls as in a hunting lodge with tin hats as the centre-piece; we always had a big coal fire and we left our beds ready to sleep in, instead of arranged in military fashion with our kit spread out for inspection. When we went out we locked the door, hiding the key above the jamb, to preserve the secret of our lair. The idyll was finally broken. I was the first one back one Sunday night to find our corporal sitting hunched up on his bed, head in hands. 'Youse fellers have dropped me right in it!' There had been an inspection in our absence, and the blame had fallen on him. We mollified him in the end, home-made cakes and scones began the process and whisky completed it. Once he had held out his mug for a second swig from the bottle, relations were restored, but we now had to lay out our kit properly and do without a fire in the daytime. Things were never quite the same, but the summons to the OCTU came soon and we went off home for a fortnight's leave before reporting to Aldershot.

Going home! That is what had kept us sane. And now home for a whole fortnight. Except for going to town with Joan, I did virtually nothing during that time, perhaps going to the parish hall to play billiards or table tennis with my brothers. Otherwise, I just sat enjoying the blessed ambience, the friendly faces, the deep concern, the intelligent talk – things in short supply in Fenham Barracks. On Sunday morning there was church. It was obligatory to sit in the front row; the churchwardens would have been offended if the vicarage family did anything else. We three brothers walked up the aisle with my mother; it was a great thing for her to have a son in uniform – it made it easier for her to talk to the women of the parish as their sons were called up and they came asking for sympathy. Perhaps she was almost reconciled to my decision to put ordination on hold.

3
Aldershot

Fenham Barracks, higgledy-piggledy buildings in drab red brick, run-down and dirty, seen through winter gloom and pelting rain, was the antithesis of the Machine-gun OCTU at Aldershot. Here there were clean huts banked with newly-filled sandbags, rectilinear tarmac roads criss-crossing through them from the entrance marked by the standard whitewashed stones at one end, to the vast parade ground at the other, seen through days of endless sunshine – a magic summer for anyone with leisure, a commodity in short supply for officer cadets. They gave us brand new battledress, making sure that it fitted, and white bands to wear around our side hats; the whole place was a scene of purposeful movement, walking (or rather, strutting), everywhere we went; on errands or non-errands, we rattled along erect and crisply, always ready to offer quivering and muscle-wrenching salutes. It was a moot point what to do if sent in overalls (rarely worn) on some menial task – how to get there and back in reasonably impressive order. Once I was put in command of a detail of half a dozen to clean out the guardroom (something odd must have happened there, for this was not normally a task for cadets). I marched them with brooms at the slope like rifles and buckets swinging rhythmically ('Come on that man, get that bucket moving') while I marched at the front. I had decided that if we met an officer, I would salute while giving the command, 'Squad, eyes right!' (or left, as the case demanded). Luckily, no one in authority saw us, for this might have been taken as a send-up of the system; on the other hand, shambling along would have been a terminal offence. I ought to have devised a middle way.

The cadets were a strange assortment, diverse in every way but lumped together and cooperating desperately in a tense confraternity united in striving to survive on the list of potential officers. So far as I knew, I was the only one to come directly from a university; those who had volunteered at the start of the war would have gone on ahead of me, thanks to the inefficiency of the company office at Fenham. At this

distance of time, those who remain in the memory are the unusual ones
– with one exception, my particular friends, those I went out with at
weekends, are no longer clear to me.

In one corner of the barrack room was a bizarre trio. One was a
seedy Irish actor who had toured the length and breadth of the country
and had tales of lodging houses and landladies, and prostitutes, including one with a wooden leg. He was tall, thin, rigidly erect with a bald
head surrounded by a tonsure of black hair, and sporting a bristling
little moustache. He was acting the military role now, the personifica-
tion of 'bull' and briskness, a lesson to all of us how to do it. His
panache was matched by his ally, another ex-actor and ex-boxer, big,
with an excessive Bismarckian moustache and a dewlapped blood-
hound countenance, as if auditioning for the role of Colonel Blimp. The
pair were caught one night by the military police outside the permitted
boundaries for weekdays, having removed the white cadet bands from
their hats. Yet they escaped unscathed. According to their own account,
they reminded the commandant that he himself had laid down the
maxim 'not to shit on your own doorstep', and being engaged on a
dubious quest they had gone further afield and in disguise. Was it true?
Probably, for they were adepts at playing the system. Strangely, the trio
was completed by a slight, bespectacled architect, Wilfred Hillman, a
South African. Why had he volunteered instead of going home to the
veldt, sunshine and safety? He was a loner, and drifted into being a
satellite of the other two. Among other unusual characters was Keith,
who kept us laughing – portly, with triple chins that wobbled as he
stamped on parade. He did everything effectively, but with the air of a
comfortable man trapped in uncomfortable circumstances, which
indeed was his case; this gave him the adopted persona from which he
launched his wry observations. Very different was Lever, lean, dark
with steel-rimmed spectacles, desperately intense, standing so rigidly on
parade that kindly Sergeant Self urged him to relax lest he collapsed.
For our lawyer, we had Hodges, a solicitor: he must have been forty,
small and overweight, bespectacled, with a faded moth-eaten moustache and a shambling gait. An improbable soldier, but he had volunteered and was, as we discovered, a man of determination. There was
also a courteous and melancholy ex-colonial servant, obviously fallen
on hard times and penurious; he consoled himself with memories of
sexual encounters in the waves of tropical beaches with men-hungry

ladies of the white establishment (where had he been?). Finally, there was the handsome cad of the barrack room. One morning, a group of us were on the back of a truck being wheeled off into the countryside on an exercise. Letters had been handed out just before we left, and as most of us had not got one, this character undertook to read out his to entertain us. Someone, mother, maiden aunt or whatever was reciting the chronicle of life behind chintz curtains amid flower pictures and coffee-table books. 'Oh, how naughty! Tiddles was coming in from the garden with ever so dirty paws! "Tiddles," I said, "I don't think you deserve your milk today", and she gave me *such* a look! But she really is so nice and always seems to know when you are coming – though she did spoil Aunt Elsie's knitting' and so on. After a while, and a great deal of mirth, someone said 'I don't think you ought to be reading all this to us.' 'Oh, it's not my letter,' said the cad, 'they gave me this one by mistake.'

Smartness of dress and bearing is something any fool can assess, and assess it they did. The morning inspection parade before work began was terrifying; it was impossible to guess what minor point would be the issue to be seized on by the inquisitor of the day. Those like me with cadaverous features and lantern jaws were in perpetual danger of being accused of having had an inadequate shave. There was a method of insurance: always, very slightly, cut oneself. Wherever we had been on the previous day, in dust or in mud, our boots had to gleam like mirrors. A few old experts resorted to 'burning', that is, rubbing in meths and setting a match to them, thus smoothing the surface ready for polishing. But if the boot was damaged, it was irretrievable disaster. The formula was – literally – spit and polish, applied inch by inch and 'boned' with a toothbrush handle for hours, thus laying a foundation for the briefer daily polish. Nail varnish applied to the perfected surface was tried by some, but it would crack and a major rescue operation would have to be mounted.

The system was ruthless. The threat of RTU (Return to Unit) hung over us, one slip and you were out. A regular NCO who had come proudly to the course, 'knowing all the lurks' and thunderously efficient at square bashing, in a rush one morning laid out his kit in regulation style but failed to clean the inside of his mug. While we were at lectures, there was an inspection. When we returned to the barrack room, all that remained in his place was the forlorn iron bedstead, nothing more.

A few days before the course ended, another cadet managed to place a Vickers gun in a ridiculous position, facing the wrong way for the exercise. No one saw him go, but he vanished, like the Psalmist's description of the eventual fate of the wicked man: 'I went by and he was gone, I sought him but his place could nowhere be found.' These sudden departures, with no time for commiseration or leave-taking, alarmed us into extreme efforts.

On two occasions, however, the system was outwitted. On a hot afternoon we were drilling on the parade ground under Sergeant-Major Fletcher, lean and atrabilious, but all bark and no bite. Suddenly, the air-raid sirens sounded. All in a fluster, the sergeant-major, normally so phlegmatic, bellowed, 'Take cover!' No doubt he had visions of our precisely aligned ranks being swathed down by a strafing Messerschmitt. As one man we fled to our barrack room, put our kit away, made up our beds, took our boots off and laid down to snooze. There was no hope of getting us back on parade again; it was a collective escape for which no individual could be blamed, for all were equally guilty. The other occasion was a single heroic individual openly defying the rules on principle. On our first morning inspection parade, trousers creased both vertically and horizontally to form the 'box crease' above the brilliantly blancoed puttees, our boots below gleaming like dark mirrors, the pattern of the front line was interrupted by the sight of Hodges's boots, dull and dubbined. The attendant sergeants were thunderstruck. One rushed off, and with stamping heels saluted the inspecting officer and muttered to him in a low voice. Hodges stood there at what passed with him for attention, his eyes meek behind his bifocals. When the officer came round there was no sensational outburst, but what was more sinister, a brief glacial observation: 'This man to report at the commandant's office after parade', addressed to the sergeant as they walked past Hodges in the line. What happened, or rather did not happen, beggared belief, though the evidence was there for all to see next morning and every subsequent morning – Hodges in his dull greasy dubbined boots. He said not a word to anyone, just carried on, as they say, 'regardless'. Apparently, when hauled up before the commandant he gently pointed out the paragraph in Army Regulations laying down that in wartime boots were to be dubbined, not blackened and polished. When I was an adjutant, my colonel once said to me, apropos of a disciplinary matter, you could do anything you like in the

Army provided it could not be brought up as a question in the House of Commons. It looks as though his was just such a case. Anyhow, Hodges knew the law and would not be moved.

What did we learn at the OCTU? Drill, to be sure, extending even to 'pile arms' (could anything be more useless?) and bicycle riding – 'Prepare to mount', 'Mount!' (which was ridiculous). There was machine-gun training, extending now to more interesting things like night shooting with the aid of pegs and the aiming lamp. But there was no ammunition for actual firing, whether of the Vickers gun, rifles or pistols: we 'went through the motions'. With the pistol, we at least found out by going through the motions that the drawing and firing we had seen in Western films was no good (every one today, of course, knows how from the police procedures on TV). There were lessons on how to inspect motor engines to check if they had been properly maintained; though there was a single engine there on display, it served only for the identification of the various parts – no one actually took it to pieces or did adjustments to it. There were no route marches and, as far as I remember, no PT. What was useful and interesting was going out on TEWTS (tactical exercises without troops) in the desolate training areas around Aldershot, endless vistas of sandy soil in odd configurations, slight wind-blown trees and struggling bushes, with plenty of broken ground for covert manoeuvres and ambushes. As the scenario of an imagined military operation unfolded, individual cadets would be pounced on: something unexpected has happened, what do you do? I believe I got some credit for a 'cool' answer on one occasion. 'Enemy plane overhead, what action?' 'Directly overhead, sir?' 'Yes!' 'Nothing, sir.' 'What?' 'Too late to fire at it, sir, too late to avoid being seen. Just keep a quiet eye on it.'

Another time we moved on from the TEWT to do a practical exercise, and at this I flopped so badly that I ought to have been RTU-ed had not luck intervened. It was on night exercise, and small groups of cadets were to try to slip through an observation screen set up by the others. I had been nominated to do various leadership tasks over the last few days and I supposed I'd not be asked yet again: but after listening in a perfunctory fashion I found myself given a compass and the command of one of the teams. In consultation with my group I decided to outflank the whole screen and operate at the double. Two hours later, we were lost. We ran into a tank crew brewing up over a small fire in a hollow; clearly, we were on someone else's territory. In fact we had been told of boundaries to our exercise but I hadn't been listening. An hour later we emerged from the undergrowth in a clearing where the trucks were waiting to take us home, hurricane lamps burning as beacons. 'Cutting it fine', said the officer in charge; the other three commando groups had been caught by the screen and their adventure had come to a premature end. There was an assessment session next day. The screen commander could not believe we had slipped through undetected. Oddly enough, no one said that we must have gone outside the boundaries, no doubt because they would not have suspected that we had given ourselves time to do this by running all the way. Did my record bear a commendation for a fine stealthy patrol, or was I down for a slippery customer? Certainly, if I had not got back in time, I'd have been on the next train back to Fenham Barracks.

When there was a problem-posing TEWT the standard correct answer was always the simple one: obey the order implicitly, come what may. Once it was an assignment as a rearguard platoon: a bridge had to be blown up before the enemy could get there; your truck has been left on the enemy side of the river, with a pile of equipment, and there are two wounded soldiers lying nearby; the truck cannot carry the equipment and the soldiers together. To take the platoon back over the river and fight off the foe until the truck completes one or two journeys is the wrong answer; the correct course of action is to blow the bridge immediately the enemy are sighted, leaving truck, equipment and wounded to fall into their hands. You complete the vital task, whatever the suffering. A parallel case of bias towards the simple, decisive action came in practice when, at last light one day an enemy plane actually flew over. The cadet commanding the detachment in the guardroom whipped out the Bren gun onto its tripod and blasted away into the heavens. It was obvious to him and to all of us that the plane was too high and too far past to be hit, but the guard cadets were officially commended. Again, this is doing the standard Army thing – 'for heaven's sake, *do* something!' One Monday morning on a TEWT in blazing hot sunshine, cadet Langley was asleep on his feet, nodding, the beer of the night before befuddling his senses. 'An enemy machine-gun opens up on your left flank. What do you do? Langley!' Suddenly waking up, Langley, in his confidence-inducing Scottish accent, gave the correct answer, 'Push on, sir!' Subconsciously he had absorbed the psychological bias of our indoctrination. I suppose that I had too, for two men were to die because I pushed on.

Above all, we had to be taught map reading and the use of the compass. This was taken by the major in overall charge of us, always splendid in service dress and Sam Browne belt, a Grenadier guardsman. He was a kindly soul, and his attempts at censure, collective or individual, never managed to achieve a tone of severity or menace. I dare say more than one of us survived the course because of his shrewdness in judging character and his innate decency. But at a certain point, the compass – or, at least, instructing us about it – defeated him. He got through the problem of the magnetic variation, and in spite of the shortage of compasses, got us all taking accurate bearings. But when it came to adjusting the lid and the use to be made of it, he drifted into an impenetrable haze. His name was George Repton and we called him, inevitably, 'Compass George'. I couldn't have guessed that I'd have to serve on a battlefront where everything one did depended on compass bearings.

There was one astonishing, unforgettable lecture on our course given by a major coming in from outside – battered and hard-bitten, though his medal ribbons showed only routine service. He gave us a morale-boosting hate lecture against the Germans: 'Wait until you see the piggy gleam in his eyes, then let him have it – get in with the bayonet and hear him squeal!' (We did have a session of bayonet practice once, stabbing away at sacks on frames, but neither the sergeant instructors nor ourselves had our hearts in it.) There was consternation at this tirade, silent and open contempt almost slipping into laughter. It was insulting. We were a rum lot at the OCTU, here, no doubt, for assorted motives, but we had all volunteered and therefore, for one reason or another, we were undertaking to kill. To try to impose gratuitous hatred upon us was outrageous. My heart sank to think of the Army I had joined. Someone in authority had authorised this vicious old dig-out to orate. I was always afraid to appear as a 'Holy Joe', otherwise I think I could have mustered the courage to protest. We all came away from this lecture laughing, but also feeling tainted; pitch had been thrown at us, and we were defiled.

Our spare time was half day Saturday and all day Sunday, provided guard duties did not interrupt (there were no church parades), and provided we managed to do the tasks of cleaning out the barrack room, lavatories, showers etc., and setting out our kits in glittering order in a fixed pattern for the week's final inspection. It was continual summer weather, and out we would wander to a few chosen places. There was the Blue Pool at Camberley, where we would lie on the grass watching the girls in bathing costumes showing off their figures; I don't know if they swam much – we were always too tired to try. There was a village with its welcoming pub and its municipal bowling centre with half a dozen greens. The trouble was that after visiting the inn our bowls sometimes were given the wrong bias and went whizzing off into the games on either side, to the despair of the venerable experts in panama hats and white trousers. Just once or twice a group of us went to the theatre on a Saturday night. Once, when there was an invitation for a volunteer to join in a 'play', I rushed onto the stage beating the planted actor in the audience. This got wild applause, but I felt rather a cad when I saw how nervous the cast were. The girls, with their pale, heavily-made-up faces and thin dresses hastily tried to coach me in what to say. They needn't have worried, for one thing I was expert at was remembering words, indeed, embellishing them a little, and finally I delivered my punch line with éclat as I knocked off the policeman's helmet, 'You can't arrest him, he is my mother.' It struck me afterwards that the management of the OCTU might call me to account for this escapade; did I take the line that it was a momentary impulse that I regretted, or was it a test of initiative that I had deliberately imposed on myself?

There were some Saturday afternoons when I played tennis; there were half a dozen perfect grass courts and never a soul competed for the use of them. My opponent was a fellow cadet, Harper – alas, I have forgotten his Christian name. I had the stronger service, but he generally won – a machine player with every shot executed with perfect technique. Sometimes he was not free to play because his girl friend came to Aldershot – she was petite, pretty, charming and always smiling. There were wonderfully in love: I could only wish that I had found such a happy complete relationship. More than almost anyone I knew I wished the war would spare them, not leave one of them alone. I will never know, and I cannot bear to picture how it would be if one of them received the news that the idyll was over.

It was at the OCTU that I first met a padre. It was night and in the barrack room we were all polishing away at our kit, battledress tops off and inglorious in braces, when a chaplain in Sam Browne and service dress appeared, accompanied by a huge man in some sort of khaki outfit, rather like that worn by First World War soldiers, the jacket topped by a thin rim of collar and buttoned up to the neck. There was confusion as we struggled to our feet – a padre, maybe, but an officer, three pips on the shoulders. With embarrassed shyness he told us to carry on as we were, he just wanted to say some prayers. Upon this, his escort, an 'Army Scripture Reader' (the only one I have met and the first time I had heard of one) broke out in *basso profundo* singing 'Rock of Ages'. This over, the chaplain said a few prayers, and the Scripture Reader, to the chaplain's evident chagrin, pronounced a word or two to remind us there was a Judgement, then sang the last verse of the 'Rock' and they departed. 'My God, Mac,' said one of my friends, 'this chap is in your department.' So he was, and I rushed out in pursuit. Luckily, the Scripture Reader had stalked on ahead, so I was able to nobble the padre on his own. I begged him not to go round with this archaic evangelist and just call on us by himself and chat to anyone who seemed interested. Apparently it was not as easy as that; I had the impression that this sort of fraternisation was frowned upon from on high – not from heaven, of course, but from an intermediate authority vested with a similar infallibility. A few evenings later, the padre came back and invited me to have tea with him on the following Sunday afternoon at the Queen's Hotel, just outside the barracks (officers only, of course, but it was a rule he could transcend). He was shy and gauche and finding his ministry well-nigh impossible, but he helped me enormously by listening. From this and from later experience I would testify that a macho padre who can mix it toughly with the soldiery is not as good as a mild and holy one who in the promiscuous mêlée of the barrack room and amid the horrors of war represents the decencies of home.

On Sunday mornings I got up early and crept out of the sleeping barrack hut to go to communion. So far as I could see, no one else turned out early in the whole OCTU. It was quite a walk to church, but I had permission to have breakfast late, after the official cut-off time. Hardly anyone got up to breakfast on the Sunday, but everything was cooked all the same. So when I went in the cooks were enjoying their gargantuan meal and I helped myself and emulated them. There were trays full of fried bacon and others of fried eggs, these latter now being solid sheets of white with little bumps indicating where the yolks were. Those were the days when one had an appetite; I would have a dozen rashers and half a dozen eggs, sliced out in a single strip – all this in severely rationed England!

News from the battlefield was the background to our brief pleasures and harsh life-style. Then the fighting surged into our conscious minds with dark immediacy. Some cadets were sent off to the main railway stations and staging centres where the soldiers evacuated from Dunkirk were passing through, to act as orderlies for carrying stretchers, dispensing tea, running errands. They came back shaken by the impact, not only of reality, but of defeat.

Under high pressure testing, you find out about yourself. After the OCTU I knew that I'd not be a good leader, and that in practical matters of command, I'd be indecisive and unsure. To get through, I'd have to put up a façade; I'd be best as an ideas man for some stronger character who could take responsibility easily on his shoulders. But I also found that I'd be an able teacher. We had to give lessons to a group of fellow cadets and I remember offering a comic and convincing discourse on the night aiming lamp. 'Now listen to that,' said good Sergeant Self, 'he made it interesting.' Towards the end of the course, he took me aside. 'I don't know if you'd fancy it,' he said, 'but in case you would, keep your nose clean, they are talking about taking you on as an instructor.' Quite rightly they didn't, though I'd have been, in a way, effective, exemplifying the saying about 'Those who can, do it, and those who can't, teach'.

But a distinction did come my way and I was proud of it. The intake chose me to give the after-dinner speech when we entertained our two chief officer instructors to dinner after we had qualified. The only thing from the speech I can remember is reminding Major Repton how he had compared us to a Chinese labour battalion, 'he found the chinks in our armour'. There was no passing-out parade. We had to put our names down for the regiments in which we wanted to serve. Naturally, I chose the Northumberland Fusiliers and, to my surprise, Wilfred Hillman and his two actor friends opted for them too. There was a rush to put in orders with representatives of various military tailors who gathered at the barracks, armed with their catalogues, exhibits and tape measures – from your chosen firm you ordered the full set, uniforms, Sam Browne belts, shirts, ties, shoes, etc. Then off home, where the kit we had paid for arrived surprisingly quickly. Then off to Fenham Barracks in the splendour of brown shoes, ties and a pip on each shoulder, to see the other side of that grim institution.

4

Fenham, Whitley Bay and the Pentland

At last, with a pip on the shoulder as passport, I gained access to the arcane sanctuary at the heart of Fenham Barracks, the officers' mess. Amid solid Victorian surroundings, comfort reigned, and exquisite meals were served. These were the work of Mr and Mrs Profit – their names still remaining with me when so many others are forgotten. Profit, after long service with the regiment, had become the mess steward on retirement, and he had married a wife who was a culinary genius. Wartime rationing might never have existed for those who were privileged to lunch and dine in their Lucullan grotto. The organisation of a mess is the responsibility of an officer, the PMC (President of the Mess Committee). Our permanent PMC, a major, might have served as a model for Siegfried Sassoon's 'scarlet major at the base'; 'you see him with his puffy, petulant face, guzzling and gulping' and 'speeding young heroes up the line to death'. But in fairness, he had nothing to do with the young heroes, let alone speeding them anywhere – he did not fraternise with non-regulars. He was unpleasant with a peculiar affectation of sarcasm and superiority, in a cut-glass accent that accorded ill with the banality and, at least on one occasion, the coarseness of his conversation. He would declaim openly against newcomers who never drank at the bar: the mess and its comforts were financed by the profits from the sale of alcohol, and in his view we all had an obligation to swill it down to boost the catering fund. It was the logic of the old couple in the Monty Python sketch complaining of their son's treason to the family by failing to make purchases to augment their hoard of Green Shield Stamps. However, a character like this no longer disillusioned me with the Army. The useless reservists and the ancient dug-outs brought back to the colours ran the transit camps and holding units – the worthwhile officers were wanted by their battalions.

The chief occupation of soldiers in wartime is hanging around doing nothing, though preferably purposefully. We had nothing to do at Fenham and nothing to do it with, no maps, compasses, binoculars, slide rules, ammunition, training manuals. We were six junior officers staying at the barracks (Wilfred Hillman and the two actors were three of them.) A civilised old captain looked after us, and prescribed a few duties, chiefly walking around and watching the squads of recruits doing machine-gun training. There was some point in this – as I remembered, never seeing an officer had been a disheartening feature of my own experiences as a recruit. On one of these tours I came on Sergeant Redhead; his language was moderated in the presence of an officer, but I was obviously just a nuisance. It was sunshine now and the squad was out of doors on the edge of the barrack square, two fusiliers sitting behind the gun rectifying the stoppages, and the rest standing round on the tarmac awaiting their turn. I tried to relieve their boredom by asking a few military conundrums picked up at the OCTU of the kind, 'You fire your rifle with the bayonet fixed, how does this affect your aim?' (The answer concerns not the pull of gravity, but the effect of increased recoil.) As I departed, Redhead was asking his squad what I had been saying. I didn't do anything like that again, for by now a certain sympathy for the brash and disagreeable sergeant had crept into my mind. It was unfair to come as a superior figure and push into his private little world of competence.

Would that in all this period of wasted time we had been given a chance to learn something. If only we could have gone out in a truck with maps and compasses and remedied one of the defects of our OCTU education. This was impossible, but why could we not have been shown how the whole Army system is administered? – how to run a company office, a battalion office, a quartermaster's store, how to render returns, strength slates, equipment lists, especially the mysteries of the G1098, charge sheets, court martial procedures.

At the end of each day we had to turn out at last light for the 'stand to'. The fusiliers in our particular building in the barracks paraded with rifles, the six junior officers in the van. Since there were no pistols to issue to us, we had to have rifles and wear the belts, cross braces and ammunition pouches that went with them. This was a vexation. 'Proper' officers would leave their belt with pistol in holster in the mess and walk straight over after dinner, we had to go to the armoury every time to draw the webbing and rifles, and the sergeant in charge was liable to be dilatory, making us late and a bad example to the troops. After receiving a rocket from our long-suffering captain we henceforward gulped down our pudding and omitted the coffee for the dash to stand to.

One night, the 'balloon went up', the invasion alert came. The recruits stayed in barracks, but the whole permanent staff was bussed off to the coast to man the defences. For some reason (reliability, because I never touched alcohol, or more likely just chance) I was left behind, as it were, in charge, with a couple of phone numbers I could ring. Being left like this was a treat: the glow of *schadenfreude* at being comfortable when everyone else was wandering in the driving rain on the beaches, the sense of importance in being responsible for the vast echoing barracks and the recruits in the Nissen huts across the road, lingering over meals without the curse of the stand to, reading the newspapers at leisure in the mess emancipated from the disapproving stares of the snobbish PMC. But after about thirty hours they were all back, cursing and mud-stained and with no confidence that the coastal defences could keep out Hitler's raiders. It was odd that in all this upheaval, just as in the routine days preceding it, we had never seen whoever it was who was in command of the place; Fenham Barracks seemed like a great multi-chambered hive in which everything was kept going by the forces of routine and primeval instinct.

At least Fenham was near home and I could get off every weekend, while on the odd weekday afternoon I could meet Joan in Newcastle. Having put up with a scruffy lance corporal in ill-fitting battledress, she was now in the more interesting situation of being accompanied by an officer in gleaming brass and burnished leather. Her friends were envious and nicknamed me 'the colonel'. Then suddenly, we were warned for overseas duty and told to buy 'tropical kit'. Foolishly, all six of us junior officers did what we were told, and signed cheques for pith helmets and khaki drill: the helmets were never worn and the light-weight clothing could have been bought more cheaply in the NAAFI shops overseas. Our final destination remained a mystery but, together with about 100 fusiliers newly trained in the recruit company, we were sent off forthwith to Whitley Bay to await our movement orders. This was a little holiday resort on the coast about fifteen miles east of Newcastle. There was a fair-sized hotel, the Rex, where we had our officers' mess, and a row of derelict houses in a street running down to the seafront where we were billeted, without heating or hot water. The beach could not be frequented because it was mined and festooned with coils of barbed wire, but there was a spacious promenade suitable for drill parades. The kiosks on the front were boarded up but still displayed the signs advertising ice cream and lemonade, bringing melancholy reminders of days of sunshine, buckets and spades and the shrill joyful cries of children. Three or four concrete pillboxes dominated the coast line with their wide fields of fire. Out on the point was a lighthouse, blacked out now, of course, as was every window in town. A minor duty that might come one's way was to go round the pillboxes at dusk with an NCO of the permanent establishment, unlock the pillbox doors, and check if the machine-guns were correctly laid on the prescribed fixed lines. I forget how the drill worked, but the correct procedure after checking involves pressing the trigger to relieve tension on the spring; those foolish enough to go by the book might find that, somehow or another, a round had got into the breech and a shot would echo out – with awkward explanations to follow. About one night of every three a streamlined bullet of the special new long-distance ammunition went skimming over the dark waves under the louring winter skies. Another duty you could be rostered for was to preside over the weekly pay parade. Each soldier was marched in, gave his name, the pay sergeant repeated it and stated the amount, the officer counted out the sum, the soldier with some difficulty collected the money, saluted again, smart right turn and departed. It was absurdly time-consuming for everybody and insulting to the soldier; why couldn't the cash be ready in pay packets, if necessary, without all the marching and saluting, the soldier to check the amount in the presence of the pay sergeant? There were many to be paid and the affair lasted all day. When all was over, the officer and the pay sergeant added up the record, the officer signed it and took it, with the cash left over, to Lieutenant Hollingsworth, a member of the permanent staff at Whitley Bay. The money was never right, one just gave up trying to reconcile the figures and the cash in hand, and signed and handed over. Hollingsworth never said anything, at the time or afterwards.

Among the ancient officers on the establishment at Whitley Bay were two august characters, Major 'Flossie' Flower of the Northumberland Fusiliers and Captain Alexander of some other regiment. Alexander was indeed ancient and wore the blue and white of the Military Cross on the service jacket which his batman pressed newly for him daily. He was given to drink and had a frozen non-expressive lined face with bleary eyes. He was always courteous and agreeable, though rarely with anything to say. Major Flower was big and bumbling and appeared to care only for the minutiae of soldiering – we junior officers put him in our category of boring old dug-outs. In this we were mistaken, as we later found from conversations with those who had known him. He had been a first-rate regimental officer, strict, but genial and an agreeable man to serve under. And, though it was long before I found out about it, his later career during the war was remarkable for both courage and administrative ability. For long I had assumed that Flossie – his real name was Henry (Harry) – must have lived out the war ruling Whitley Bay transit camp. Not so. For most of his soldiering days he had served on the imperial fringes – India and the Royal West African Frontier Force – and not long after I left Whitley Bay to go to the Middle East, Flossie was sent out again to the Empire's far-flung battle line – an Empire now facing collapse. He was posted to the 9th (Territorial) Battalion of the Royal Northumberland Fusiliers as second in command – an unlucky battalion which was sent to Singapore just in time for the capitulation. The lieutenant colonel was ordered to leave and Flossie took over. For the next three years he achieved the great ambition of a regular soldier, to command a battalion – but this time in a Japanese prisoner of war camp. His obituary in the regimental gazette describes how he kept up the morale of his men and won the reluctant admiration of the Japanese, no doubt helped by his stubborn observance of protocol and his mental resilience. I had supposed that his towering stature would have impressed the guards, but apparently this was something that the Japanese particularly resented.

There was a gap of sympathy and comprehension between the amateur soldiers and the regulars, but as our failure to appreciate Flossie Flower shows, the fault was far from being on one side. We could not picture the milieu of the regulars before we arrived to disrupt it – a community which included wives and families, a round of social events set apart from civilian society, a strict hierarchy in which promotion by seniority precluded manifest rivalries, an odd but agreeable relationship with the parallel communities of warrant officers and other ranks strengthened by social get-togethers and athletic and sporting competitions, at once friendly and feudal, at the worst a 'Well done that man' patronising attitude, at best seriously interested and concerned. It was a world that can be evoked by reading the regimental publication, the *St George's Gazette*, for the years before the war. Here, the officers figure by their Christian names – Derek, Tommy, Dick, Alastair: the readers

knew who they were without the need for surnames – they constituted
an exclusive confraternity. During the war years the *Gazette* continues
in this familiar way, while the newcomers, the amateurs, have surnames
only. It may look like snobbish differentiation, but it was inevitable, for
the readers of the magazine had never heard of them.

There was a further reason for the irreverently critical attitude of the
newcomers to the Army we had joined. Until we reached our final destination, the fighting battalion, we were being passed through newly
created camps and billets and subjected to hastily devised courses of
instruction and mental conditioning. It wasn't the Army as it had been
that we came into, but a former organic unity disrupted to function as a
vast ramshackle training organisation for largely reluctant conscripts.
At Fenham, the Nissen huts had been rushed up and a course of
machine-gun instruction cobbled together just before we arrived; for all
its façade of order and precision the machine-gun OCTU at Aldershot
was a school of warfare only by external appearances, its course bits
and pieces with inadequate intellectual content and very few practical
demonstrations – it fell short of being even a poor man's Sandhurst; the
commandeered hotel and houses at Whitley Bay constituted a transit
camp that must have been well-nigh unmanageable. Once one tries to
picture the multifarious business that must have passed into Flossie's
office every day, it becomes clear that he would never have been able to
do anything about the transients but keep them up to the mark in turnout and discipline. Whitley Bay was a miserable, disillusioning set-up;
what we forgot was that it must have been so for Major Flower and
Captain Alexander as well as for us.

For the first time the new officers had a chance to do something for
the men, who were divided into two platoons, one under Wilfred Hillman and the two actors, and the other under the 'three Jacks', myself
(christened John but always called Jack), Jack Watson, a young Newcastle surveyor, and Jack Marshall. Jack Watson was solid, bespectacled, red-faced, light-hearted, lively and ebullient, with a wonderful
sense of the comic – and beneath the hearty exterior, a quietly convinced Christian. Jack Marshall was dark-haired, reserved and reflective in temperament. They were the most genial and friendly
companions one could have hoped to find; Whitley Bay, that cold, dead
place, was rendered enjoyable by their presence. There was no equipment for training, but we would take our men on route marches,

enlivened with the usual songs (it was the sentimental ones with a hint of sadness that were the favourites, the 'long, long trail a-winding to the land of my dreams', and not the ghastly 'Pack up your troubles in your old kit bag'). Since we had a complement of decent voices to put in the parts, we impressed the good citizens we happened to meet on the way – unless their sympathetic looks were inspired by pity for our youth and for our probable fate. We had fun putting on a camouflage demonstration. It is the man who simply sits in the shadow of the open doorway of a house who is never spotted, and Jack Watson offered half a crown, recklessly upped to five shillings, to whoever found him. I hastily gave the game away before he got up to ten and had to fork out – it was no mean sum in those days. Wilfred and the actors did much the same with their platoon, and such was the entertainment value of the exaggerated game of soldiering that they played, their men probably had more fun than ours. The trio put on a wonderful variety show in the local theatre, which did us a world of good with the local citizens. The highlight was 'The Green Eye of the Little Yellow God', with Wilfred as the narrator and the other two in pith helmets and tropical kit, with rows of false medals, the interruptors – who had been to Katmandu and knew the terrain and the persons; whatever happened to versification, their expert knowledge had to prevail.

We inflicted drill on our platoons, reluctantly, Major Flower prescribing it. This took place on the promenade, with the all-too-healthy sea breezes blowing. And here I got into trouble. Flossie Flower arrived and after a while asked who was the senior officer. I admitted to this, though not expecting commendation, for his countenance was grim as if news of another lost battle had just come in. The cross bracing of the men's webbing at the back was not uniform, some left over right, the others right over left. Thereafter, Major Flower viewed me with a severe eye. Worse was to come. I did not own a peaked hat, a 'cheese cutter', but had two side caps, one of superior khaki cloth with the Northumberland Fusiliers' metal cap badge gleaming in it, the other the special 'dress' hat of the regiment, the inside a pale gosling green, the outer flaps of black velvet with a woven badge of silver wire at the front. I met Flossie one day when I was wearing the khaki side cap. 'You can't wear that,' he roared, 'you must wear either the regulation peaked cap or the regimental dress side cap.' I assured him I had one and would wear it henceforward. Shortly after this, when I was wearing the gosling green and black version, Captain Alexander nobbled me. 'What on earth is that?' I explained, but he had never heard of such a thing. 'You must wear either the regulation peaked hat or a khaki side cap.' Henceforward, I wore one of the caps and kept the other down the front of my battledress, making a quick change as required. The inevitable happened. There was a lecture, attendance obligatory. (Some academic from the Newcastle branch of Durham University came out and lectured to us on current affairs; what he said seemed to me to be left-wing meanderings, and if Major Flower had understood him aright he'd have been looking down the G1098 equipment list for 'horse whips for chastising, subversives, officers for the use of', instead of ordering all of us to attend.) As I was returning from this miserable lecture along the seafront, I found I was overtaking my two senior officers, who were walking along together. I hung back, but Captain Alexander looked round and courteously waved to me to walk with them to our mess at the Rex Hotel. As I was wearing the khaki hat he was happy. But Flossie exploded when he saw it, and was not mollified when I pulled out the other one, demonstrating that I had it all the time, and that vexed the good captain as well. 'You're struck off all duties tomorrow', said the major, 'to go to Newcastle to Bainbridge's to buy a proper hat.'

By starting very early next day I left myself enough time to get home for three hours – important, for when the order to move came there'd be no getting away for farewells. The hats on display at Bainbridge's were of wartime austerity manufacture, but when I told the shop staff my story, a virtuous civilian soldier persecuted by a couple of regulars, someone recollected a better hat from long ago surviving somewhere, and a search for it began. So I didn't just get a hat, but a 'Herbert Johnson hat', the last one available in Northumberland Fusilier land – even Flossie hadn't got one. It had a softer top than the others, and went up rather high at the front above the peak, with something of the sombre panache of the hats General Rommel was later pictured as wearing. It looked better than all the cheese cutters in creation; and it was a tough hat. In all my wanderings in the desert, and through all my intrigues with the Greeks, it lasted as good as new: a photogenic hat, and indestructible.

During our time at Whitley Bay, the three Jacks had some magic evenings, incredibly happy times, but so simple the formula that it is nigh impossible to describe how it could be so. Jack Marshall had an ancient car, and in it we would go out to a country pub, the Red Lion at Earsdon. He had persuaded the landlord to let us have a little room separate from the bar entirely to ourselves, where we sat round a huge fire. With us was Jack Watson's fiancée, Dorothy, a charmer if ever there was one. She would come down from Newcastle and go back on the last train. One night when Jack had to rush off early to guard duty, I escorted her back through the dark streets to the station. She told me how they had been in love since school days, and made me promise that 'if anything happened to Jack', I would write and tell her about it. When it happened, I let her down. And I had as my companion an astonishingly beautiful girl, Joan Allen, an art student whose home was at Whitley Bay. We met in the Rex Hotel, for the officers, who took all their meals there in a private room designated as the mess, had the run of the public rooms, including the ballroom, where there was dancing every night. We became friends; she told me that she did not want to form an attachment, having just been rendered very unhappy by one, and I told her of my indecision about ordination and lack of any clear immediate purpose but to serve in the war. She was so attractive that it was almost impossible not to lose one's heart to her – but what future could there have been; at any minute I'd be going on shipboard to a destination as yet unknown. But she always came out with us to the Red Lion. Jack Marshall had a pint; the rest of us did not drink alcohol, and the landlord brought us coffee and sandwiches. We talked incessantly around the blazing fire in the darkened room, of home, of religion, of the war, of the past and our hopes for the future. But would there be a future? The grim news from the battlefields gave deeper meaning to these idyllic occasions; we had found an oasis in the desert, a shelter from the storm, but our happiness was doomed to be ephemeral. The attractive girls, Dorothy dark and Joan fair, gave the atmosphere a sort of fragrance compounded of desire and tenderness. Jack Watson, after desperate adventures, got through and married Dorothy: what happened to Jack Marshall, what happened to Joan? As I write this, I wish, without hope, that we might meet again.

We were still at Whitley Bay when Christmas came, the Christmas of 1940. No question of being allowed home, we were on a few hours' notice. There was an officers versus sergeants football match in the morning, a rather drunken party, then a Christmas dinner at the Rex –

not a happy Christmas. For a second time, soccer rehabilitated me. The sergeants were tougher, but even slower than the recruits at Fenham had been, the ground was icy, but just beginning to melt, and nothing counted but sheer speed. From then on, Flossie Flower almost approved of me, even if I didn't know if it was right over left or left over right, and though I had deceitfully worn the illegal hats; while Captain Alexander's face unfroze for a moment in a smile.

Then immediately after Christmas, the movement order came. Dorothy had come down on Boxing Day and thus, by sheer chance, saw Jack just hours before we left. There was no time for me to contact home or to say goodbye to the two Joans in my life. Packed in a dirty, unheated train, grinding and jerking slowly as trains did in wartime, we were off to the Firth of Clyde. Jack Marshall was not sent with us; Jack Watson and I travelled together, and after just leaving Dorothy he needed a great deal of cheering up. During one of the many halts during that endless night, a station platform became – almost – visible, and here was a trolley with a tea urn. There was a rush out to monopolise it by a group of officers, not of any regiment we knew. An angry major roared at them from the train, 'Horses first, men next, officers last', the first time I'd heard this famous dictum of military moralising. It was received with shivering incomprehension. It was a pity to lose one's self-respect for a mug of NAAFI brew.

We boarded the Dutch vessel, the *Pentland*, an old cruise liner, early in the morning. We made a brave sight as we sailed: merchant ships galore manoeuvring to take up station, until outside harbour the convoy formed up, fifteen destroyers covering the flanks in arrowhead formation, and at the back, in the centre of the base of the triangle, an immense battleship, squat in the water. Sky and sea were a metallic grey, and so long as we were near land, RAF fighter planes swooped and roared over us. Conditions on board were terrible. Officers, at least junior ones, were three to a single berth cabin. In the holds, the men were packed solid so when they lay down they covered almost every inch of floor space. The ship was totally and permanently blacked out, so the atmosphere was mephitic; this was in our cabins, so what of the holds where the troops were confined? The officers took their meals in the restaurant in two very crowded sittings. Yet, in spite of the hellish conditions and the desperate confusions faced by the waiters, breakfast, lunch and dinner rolled on for us as if the *Pentland* was still on one of its luxury cruises, printed menus, lavish courses, recherché dishes (this, of course, for the officers). Presumably, the huge freezers of the ship were filled up at various ports around the world far from rationed England.

Jack Watson and I shared a cabin with Ronnie Jacobson, a master of wry Jewish humour, ridiculing everyone in a fashion that was unexceptionable because his chief target was himself. He undertook to tell us two jokes at dinner every night, and in due course increased the number to three, then four – it would have taken a much longer journey to exhaust his store. His specialities involved parsons, old ladies or parrots, and his masterpieces were an irresistible combination of all three; the parson's presence creates the necessity for decorum, the old lady strives to ensure it, and the parrot shatters all her delicate contrivances. Apart from the six Northumberland Fusiliers (the three of us in one cabin and Wilfred Hillman and the two actors in another) many of the officers on board were a disillusioning sight. There were a whole lot of railway men going to build a line in the Sudan, jumped up into ranks from lieutenant colonel downwards without serious military training. They were awash with money, drank the bar dry every night, and after dinner ran a poker school with vast wagers. One of our actors, subsidised by his two friends, was sent into the game with high hopes of teaching them a lesson and winning a dividend in the process; but he simply did not have the funds at his command to last out against them. This phoney cohort of 'station masters' (Ronnie) monopolised the company of a band of nurses, plied them with grog and had their wicked way with some of them – or so they said, but how was it possible to find fornicating elbow room on board? The nurses were mostly battleaxes, but a younger one, good-looking in a solid complacent fashion, had the time of her life. Ronnie had a nickname for all of them, and she was 'Wardrobe'. When the convoy pulled into Sierra Leone for a day, the senior railway men, Wardrobe and a few other nurses and some of the ship's officers went ashore in a lighter, to the jeers of the soldiery crowding the rails in a brief escape from their Black Hole of Calcutta below. Having steamed far out to the north and west, almost to Newfoundland, then raced across the Atlantic to Sierra Leone (where the battleship left us), our convoy now set off again round the Cape to Durban, where we stayed for a week. It was a beautiful town, bathed in sunshine; unlike Cape Town, it was enthusiastically pro-British, and there were no signs of racial tension. The three of us hired a car one day to go out to see 'the valley of a thousand hills' and the scenery all the way to Pietermaritzburg. Our driver was a young woman; when we asked her if she felt safe driving in the lonely countryside, she pulled up her skirt and showed us a revolver in her garter. We thought we had discovered evidence of racial tension, but she said it was not blacks she was afraid of. The town feted the soldiery; rich families kept open house for officers and the Durban Club made us honorary members. Astonishingly, Jack, Ronnie and I were so shy and naïve that we did not dare to go there, in contrast to our two actors, who had a permanent station booked at the Club bar and graciously accepted the alcohol and the admiration.

When we cast anchor at Suez, the first lighter coming out to meet us bore testimony to the absurdity of the tropical kit we had been conned into buying in England. There were a couple of second lieutenants on board, clearly part of the military organisation running the port; they had shorts and shirts of a lighter khaki hue than ours, and they wore greyish, long-sleeved pullovers with cloth-edged slots at the shoulders to let the epaulettes on the shirt go through, and they wore Sam Browne belts with the cross brace running under the shoulder piece. Their hats were the flat, peaked 'cheese cutters'; our pith helmets were the only ones in Egypt.

Once ashore, we were driven off to the most melancholy spot in the Delta, the Infantry Base Depot, a forest of marquee-style tents along the shore of the Great Bitter Lake in the centre of the Canal. It was an institution of mindless discipline and highly organised boredom, designed to ensure that even the terrors of war would be preferable to being stranded here. Possibly, there were those who preferred to stay there nonetheless, because it was safe, and there were stories of NCOs who had dodged their movement order by seeking out a hapless wrongdoer to put on a court-martial charge requiring their presence as a witness. But I have only one authentic tale to tell of the IBD. The first morning there, while I was walking through the forest of tents, I was nobbled by a captain of the permanent staff, notable for his pendulant jowls and vast bushy moustache unsupported by chin. He took exception to the belt I was wearing, a black leather job with a purse concealed in its structure, given to me by Mother who wanted to ensure that the oriental pickpockets she had heard so much about did not filch my pocket money. Apparently, the only belt I could wear was the Northumberland

Fusiliers version in dark red and dull yellow (I can't remember ever seeing anyone in the battalion wearing one, though I did later on, get one). I took the offending belt off and kept up my trousers by auto-suggestion in the interminable two days we had to spend in this miserable place. Long afterwards, I met this man of discipline again in the foyer of Shepheard's Hotel in Cairo: he had a painted lady on his arm and wanted a room, and there weren't any. His choleric countenance became livid and his moustache drooped in despair. I recounted the story of my meeting with him in the IBD to the Greek officer who was with me: 'Let not his adultery be consummated,' I concluded, devising a Homeric curse.

We were not allowed to linger by the Great Bitter Lake, for the 1st Battalion, the regular battalion of the Fusiliers, was short of officers. The triumphal advance through the desert was over, the Germans had arrived in North Africa, and retreat was imminent. With four other second lieutenants, I hauled my kit into the back of a covered three-ton lorry, and we trundled away along the desert coastal road westwards to the battlefront. There was Wilfred Hillman and I cannot remember who else – Jack Watson and Ronnie Jacobson were left behind, that is certain. When we reached Tobruk we were dumped in a transit mess, a little tent in a rock crevice in the pseudo-shade of a withered fig tree. The news of the war was desperate, it looked as though the Germans would break through to the harbour at any minute. A truck from battalion HQ came to collect us, and we were sent at once to fill the vacant slots for officers – I was given a platoon of Y Company. Fresh-faced and smart in battledress, I took over a group of weary, battered men, faces dark with the sun and sunken with fatigue; they had taken part in Wavell's victorious onslaught and were bitter and dejected at being in retreat – and it was the Germans who were coming now, not the despised Italians. They had fled down the coast road through the green Jebel hills, then debouching into the desert had dug in astride the Mechili track – this was the 'devil's causeway' along which mobile forces raced to cut off the circuitous and crowded coastal road. Now they were pulling back towards Tobruk; there were sounds of artillery fire quite near now, and while we were there a single shell fell nearby without exploding. We were scheduled to stay as part of a garrison in Tobruk, while the rest of the army went back to regroup east of the Sollum pass.

5
Tobruk

War is about killing. This is the elementary reality, so obvious as never to need stating, but impossible to accept as part of one's individual thinking until the decisive moment of experience. While we were hanging round dejectedly on flat, endless desert under an iron-grey sky, trucks all packed and ready to move as the sound of firing drew nearer, I was sent on my first reconnaissance. Together with an Australian infantry captain I was to go to a speck on the far skyline to find out what was there, and was there any sign of the enemy? The captain's truck took us part of the way – this was somewhere just west of the road running southwards out of Tobruk to El Adem. I was a complete novice, and he was hardly battle-hardened. Between us, we had neither map nor binoculars. Cluelessly we set off together to have a look, in the Arabic-inspired jargon of Eighth Army, 'have a *shufti*': no orderlies with us, no one to cover us, and walking upright. The feature turned out to be a sandbagged post, and on realising this we started crawling. When we looked over the parapet there were about a dozen dead Germans, slashed to bits with grenade fragments and bayonet thrusts.[1] That night, I took out one of my few Forces letter forms and wrote to John Brewis, my old tutor at Oxford and now Principal of St Chad's theological college at Durham, near home. It was to say that, if I ever got back, I intended to be ordained, and I wanted him to remind me.

My platoon's first assignment was to provide defence in depth behind the south-west segment of the defensive perimeter of Tobruk, Ras el Meduar on the map. It was known as the 'Salient', for the Australians had early on pushed out from the old Italian concrete defences and captured the strategic Hill 209 with its observation post. Soon it would be known as the Salient for a different reason, inwards, not outwards, facing. It was about 27 April when my company commander, Dick Hensman, took me here on a recce. The approach by

---

1 It seems to have been Post 33, and the Germans had been killed by the Australian corporal Jack Edmonston, who died of his wounds and was awarded the VC.

vehicle was dicey: you drove along a flat plain with the escarpment on your left, and all the way the dust of your passage was visible to far distant observers, who might decide to call down shellfire. Then, tucking the vehicle close in to the escarpment, you climbed up a wadi, rocky and twisting, perhaps twenty feet deep, and out at the top where the ground sloped down the other way as a featureless hump of rock. Looking south-west, if you had binoculars, you could discern the outline of our infantry emplacements, running just below the crest so as to catch an attacking enemy as they came over. I was to site my HQ at the top of the wadi and put the two sections (there were two Vickers guns in each) on the forward slope facing across to our defence line, perhaps a mile away. Since this was my first assignment in real warfare, Dick took pains to tell me what I had to do: if I had been on the perimeter, I would have been encouraged to blast at any target presenting itself, but back here it was a waiting brief in concealment. (I now see in the battalion War Diary a copy of the operation instruction of 16 April that sums it up: 'Guns allotted to penetration tasks must remain SILENT and concealed until a major attack by infantry takes place. The object of these guns is to stop a successful attack through the FDLS [Forward Defensive Localities], stabilise the situation and gain time for the counter-attack troops to come into action. To achieve this, fire must be withheld until the enemy are at close MG range.')

The gun site was unpromising since it was solid rock, but the engineers were to come to blow holes for us. That night I brought my gun trucks up, and we carried the weapons, ammunition and other essential kit up to the head of the wadi, and sent the trucks off to company HQ in a distant ravine near the sea. On the following day we moved rocks around to protect our future gun emplacements – clearly the forward slope was not under enemy observation, no doubt because hill 209 was still ours. On 29 April, in the afternoon, the engineers came, drilled holes in the rock and fired their charges, creating a mass of rubble into which the sections burrowed all night to set up their gun positions. If the enemy came, I would probably be undetected peering out from the old rocks at the head of the wadi, but it seemed unrealistic to suppose they could fail to notice the newly blasted white rocks sheltering the sections. (As it turned out, they didn't, perhaps because we paid a lot of attention to trying to construct hideouts looking as natural as possible.)

ON ACTIVE SERVICE.   2/Lt J McManus
145626
Y Coy
Royal Northumberland
Fusiliers
To Lloyds Bank   1st Battn
Collingwood St   Middle
Newcastle   East Forces

I bequeath all my
goods to my pater, Rev J McManus
Vicarage, Kerryhill, Co Durham in
event of my decease.
If I am "missing" or
a prisoner, I empower him to
administer all my deposits
J McManus
2/Lt RNF
31st May '41

Witnessed
J. E. Richardson pte AIF
J Martin Fus. R.N.F. 31/5/41

The author's will, written on active service 31 May 1941

Photograph of the author taken during the siege of Tobruk

As dusk fell that night half a dozen divebombers attacked the perimeter in front of us, and a barrage of shells fell, filling the twilight air with dust. After an hour, silence, though far off to the left there was small arms fire. At dawn there was more movement than usual along the perimeter defences, a truck drove up and a few tiny figures gathered around it. The thought struck me that the enemy might have broken through in the night. Had I possessed binoculars, I would have known at once, either way. The corporals commanding the two sections were no better off than I was. This is how the British Army was equipped in the fight for survival against Nazi Germany – heavy machine-gunners without technical aids to recognise targets. But it seemed unlikely that the enemy were there. If they were, it must all have happened very quickly, and why had they not patrolled farther? There were no more defences, no infantry, no mines, no machine-guns other than our four to hamper them from going through, over the escarpment and across the empty plain towards the harbour. I crawled over to the sections – mercifully no one here had started to move about, they were still wrapped up in their blankets. I told them about my fears and ordered them to be ready to fire if an advance towards us began, otherwise no movement of any kind.

Away below us a battery of 25-pounders was stationed, down on low ground well to the left of our feature in the gap between it and another rocky rise, the guns so well camouflaged as to be virtually undetectable. About noon, I looked across and saw the camouflage nets coming off, and suddenly the guns opened up, it must have been over open sights, firing straight at the perimeter. They got off a single salvo and counter-battery fire hit them directly. There was a terrible pause, then a gun or two fired again – then their whole position vanished under a cloud of dust as shells crashed into them. Thereafter, silence and stillness. Perhaps they got the guns out that night. There must have been many casualties.

So the question was settled. The enemy had broken through. If we were spotted, artillery would have made an end of our sections in min-utes. At night, we were vulnerable to patrols; we had no answer to trained infantrymen appearing in the darkness with grenades and machine pistols – we had neither. On the other hand, if there was an attack towards the escarpment, we could take a heavy toll of advancing

infantry. That night I told the sections not to stir and not to fire unless
the enemy made a major display of movement.

We stayed where we were all the next day without being detected.
The following afternoon my company commander came up the wadi
to check on us. He half expected to find we were annihilated. He said
there were complaints, from outside the battalion, that we were not
firing. Although he appreciated the folly of doing so, he told me to
blast off at the Germans at last light so we could say we had done
something – it was at that time of day that movement would be taking place in the enemy positions. He went off to visit his other two
platoons and from the plain behind us came the crump of shells; they
had seen him on the way up and had been waiting to have a go at him
at the next sighting. I crawled to the sections, not welcome there, for
anything, however minor, might give their positions away, and told
them of my orders to fire at last light – but only on my signal: I
wanted to see movement among the enemy first. Twilight came and I
could see nothing stirring on the perimeter. I got the panic feeling that
I was lying there disobeying orders, so I raised my hand for the guns
to open up. As soon as I did so, I wished that I hadn't. Thank God,
nothing happened. Had the section corporals not seen my hand in the
gloom, or had they decided not to commit suicide by opening up? I
realised the folly of what I had been about to do: I was obeying an
order which I knew was nonsense, a public relations exercise. I
crawled over to the sections and did not do what I could easily have
done, that is, got the guns firing; instead I repeated my old instructions, keep in hiding and only fire on major movement. A couple of
days later Dick came back, cursing because he had been shelled again.
He had tried driving at top speed across the flat instead of creeping
along the edge of the escarpment, and he'd been lucky to get through.
'How did the shoot go the other night?' I should of course have muttered, 'Fine, fine', or 'Not so bad', but I merely said, 'I didn't do it; no
suitable target.' 'Damn it!' said Dick, with the utmost cheerfulness, 'I
reported that you'd given them quite a pasting.' Look it up in the official war histories: this is what they record happened.

The next day an Australian captain came up the wadi on a recce:
he was to bring a company of infantry to hold the ground in front of
us, a belated sealing of the gap. (Apparently, to the left of us the
Germans had tried to force through with tanks, and had been stopped

by anti-tank guns and the Australian infantry, who had let the tanks through then shot up the forces following behind them. We were on the flank of what had been meant to be a much bigger salient. The low ground in front of us was firm, but not rocky, and that night the Australians dug in. We had agreed that they should site their trenches so we could fire in enfilade across their front, by observation in daytime and on fixed lines at night. These infantrymen were astonishingly efficient; when morning dawned, their positions were virtually invisible, and they were never shelled. The next day the captain told me that he was going to go forward again at night as near as he could get to the enemy – so he did, with astonishing stealth and effective concealment. So my splendid theoretical fire plan had lasted but twenty-four hours.

My passive role facing the enemy breakthrough on the Ras el Meduar sector is a point at which one of the standard war histories gives a full account into which I can fit my memories. Professional historians conflate a mass of documentation to present a global view, a wider picture unknown to the actors in the frame presented. It is fascinating for a fellow historian to observe the working of the technique and the outcome when you have been one of the multitudinous cast yourself – seeing how little you really counted, but appreciating some of the reasons for the way things happened as they did. The detailed Australian war history, *Tobruk to Alamein*, by Barton Maughan, has not had access to the war diaries of the few British units concerned, principally ourselves and the Royal Artillery, but it skilfully uses the massive documentation from the Australian side, together with a vast collection of reminiscences by individuals. My impression of being alone on the hillside is strictly true, but what I did not know was that various Australian units were operating to pinch in the flanks of the enemy salient – the Germans could not have moved forward further, as they were threatened laterally, especially from the east, by the forays of the most aggressive infantrymen they had ever encountered. (There is, however, a mistake on the sketch map of the salient given in the Australian account: the minefield shown on the flat in front of my platoon was put in afterwards, when the infantry company dug in to seal off the salient completely – they were unconstrained by mines when they sited their trenches, then pushed them forward again.) *Tobruk to Alamein* also solves a problem that had worried me. Why was my platoon sited on the exposed forward slope facing flat on to the perimeter, when heavy machine-guns should be tucked away in re-entrants or on reverse slopes, firing in enfilade to hammer down their pencil-shaped beaten zones of lead across the path of any enemy advance. I was puzzled that Dick Hensman had put me there. Later, I realised that this was just one instance of a problem that dogged the battalion all through the Desert War. We were divisional machine-gun troops; our companies were detached to work with brigades or similar units, and the platoons were then delegated to give supporting fire to various infantry groups. The company commanders had to do their best to ensure that we were given reasonable fire tasks and were properly sited. I know now from the War Diary that Dick Hensman had protested to his Australian superior in command of that sector, but had been overruled; I was put there at the orders of someone who did not appreciate our long-range capacity, but was thinking of us as Bren-gun auxiliaries. It also appears from the Australian history that I was pulled out of this unsatisfactory position in the first instance to do a shoot from further along the ridge and in the process some shellfire came our way. Try as I may, I cannot remember this; suffice it to know that once the platoon moved off that barren forward slope Dick must have ensured that we did not have to go back there. Students of the processes of memory or novelists of the Proustian kind may be interested to know that I remembered the first time when I was supposed to shoot at the enemy but didn't, while I have forgotten the first time that I actually did.

From experience in the salient, I had learnt – at least half-learnt – a crucial lesson. The machine-like obedience drilled into us at the OCTU must give way to common sense and your duty towards your men. Immediately afterwards there was a chance to put the lesson into practice. Somewhere on the central sector I was sent to work with an Australian battalion. The colonel told me there was danger of an enemy tank breakthrough – there had been a lot of shelling and isolated shells were still coming in from time to time. I was therefore to put my guns down on the flat stony plateau ready to fire at tanks and force them to close down so his infantry and anti-tank weapons could attack them more easily. I did so, putting the machine-guns in exactly where required. Immediately, shells came down, creeping nearer. Promptly, I got the guns out and sent them well back behind a declivity out of sight and left them there. With my batman driver I went back to the Australian HQ dug-out and stayed outside, lying on the ground – if the guns were needed I'd send back and have them whizz up in their trucks and set them down to fire. No one seemed to care either way. We were not part of the Aussie plan, and we could join in if we liked, it was a free country. Martin (my batman) and I lay wrapped in our greatcoats just outside the dug-out and waited. There were no alarms and finally the battalion stood down.

After this, we hung around waiting for a new assignment. We were stationed along the 'safe' side of the escarpment well to the east of the Salient, with the trucks hidden in the entrances to various wadis. My HQ was in a cave high up on the steep face, occupied by an Australian doctor and his two orderlies; he had a phone, so I could be summoned to move off at short notice. Two odd things happened here. One night, in a random bombardment, a stock of ammo in one of the wadis was hit and the ensuing fire filled the air with cordite fumes. Fusilier McArdle of my HQ rushed in, shouting 'Gas!' I went off with him to investigate, and while we were away the doctor rang up his command HQ, causing a universal alert to go out to the garrison, and everybody wore gas masks for an hour or so – except of course my platoon who knew better. The Australians subsequently were sure this was a trick of the higher command to compel us to look for our gas masks; I have an idea that the story of this alert (without the information of how it began) comes somewhere in the war histories. The other strange event, eerie almost, came from my custom of walking around, partly to keep fit, and partly to get to know the terrain around us in case of a crisis. On the endless plain at the foot of the escarpment there were old trenches and dug-outs here and there. In a superior dug-out, on a shelf cut into the wall, there was a stack, six inches high, of leaflets newly printed. They urged the Australians not to fight for selfish Britain, to think of their wives and children far away, and ask themselves who was now comforting their girl friends. I gave them to Dick Hensman who reported to battalion HQ where everybody annexed a souvenir copy – something I'd not thought of doing. Had a German agent infiltrated and gone across there by night? If so, why leave the propaganda in a place where there was so little chance of its being found?

The Australians regarded themselves as the best fighters in the world. They were. This was not by dint of discipline, to which they were recalcitrant; they were held together by 'mateship', refusing to let each other down. Nor was it by organisation; their deficiencies in this respect were

atoned for by initiative and reckless improvisation. At night patrolling
they had no equals. The Fusiliers got on well with them and were
accepted as honorary Australians, not starchy Brits or stuck-up Poms.
Later, when we were in defensive positions on the 'Blue Line', an Australian unit we had for our neighbours used to lift mines to get the
explosives out to go fishing. At night they would send out a foraging
party to raid the DID, the big ration dump, where tins of goodies we
rarely saw were stashed away. After one of these raids, they would
always send some one across to give us a share. But our regular officers
found them hard to take. Dick Hensman never quite got over his
encounter with a bronzed character in shorts and boots and nothing
else except his identity tags on a tarry string round his neck, who
offered to buy his cap badge: 'Name your price, Squire'.

My platoon's next task was a peaceful one, but enlivened by two further chapters in the Hensman-Digger feud in which, surprisingly, Dick
came off best. We had to construct our gun emplacements on the edge
of a minefield, covering it with fire. The work done and the sections
installed, I went round the next morning to see them. One of the sections was completely cut off. During the night the Aussies had laid
mines all round them to supplement the existing field. 'She'll be right,'
they told the expostulating sentries, 'Stuff your officer', and the like.
My batman, the ever ingenious Martin, went off looking for a pole or
plank for us to push ahead of us to test the dangerous ground. At this
point, Dick arrived. He was enraged, but saw no problem. 'You can
always tell where newly laid mines are,' he said. The only reply to this,
if the phrase had been invented then, would have been, 'You could have
fooled me.' He prodded gently with the toe of his desert boot until we
had a thin path through, and the hungry section got out to make themselves a belated breakfast..

The second crisis was the descent of the phantom gunner upon us.
He was an Australian private driving a captured lorry towing an
immense Italian artillery piece; he stopped just beside my mine-belea-
guered section, unlimbered the gun and fired an immense shell off over
the crest. Immediately he fired, he rushed up to the top of the rise to see
where the explosion was, then back down again, gave his gun an
adjustment, and let loose three or four more shells, then in a wild rush,
hooked up his tow bar and drove off like mad. No sooner was his dust
vanishing in the distance than down came the counter-battery fire

remorselessly, the bracketing rounds dead on where the sniping can-
non had been minutes before. There was shrapnel all over our section
post, though mercifully no casualties. On his next visit, I told Dick the
story. He went off, and was back again shortly with the huge breech-
block of the gun wrapped in a sack. 'Don't let him have it back unless
you are sure he'll keep away from you,' he said. With the breech-block
at my feet in the truck I set off to look for the phantom gunner, and
finally ran him to earth in an underground concrete chamber, lying at
ease on a stretcher, his huge naked stomach drooping over his khaki
shorts, and deep in the study of *Pix*, the magazine devoted to risqué
photographs of their girl friends sent in by Aussie troops. His gear all
around proclaimed his speciality; he was a cook. He welcomed me
with antipodean geniality, without striving to rise; when I told him my
section had been shelled, he conceded that this indeed had been the
case. 'There was a lot of shit flying when I left the place, I'll grant you
that, cobber.' I don't know if he'd have been very helpful, however, but
when he saw the breech-block of his cherished weapon he leapt up in
alarm. To get it back he promised that we'd see him no more, nor
did we.

The enemy attempts at a breakthrough were not renewed, and the
garrison settled into a siege routine. My platoon then got a more established home on the Blue Line, the second line of defence. The outside
perimeter arched from the deep ravines running into the sea on the east
and on the west, in between taking the higher ground where possible,
though just below the crest. The Blue Line of minefields and wire was a
mile to two miles behind this, on the flat. It was astonishing to us that at
the OCTU we had not been told anything about the art of constructing
gun positions; however, in this case they were ready made for us. Each
section had a pit for each of its machine-guns and a slot in between with
a loophole for the corporal to observe from, with narrow drainpipes
inserted on either side for him to talk to the firing posts. The whole was
roofed in, beams and iron poles holding up sheets of corrugated iron
with two layers of sandbags on top – 'mortar proof'. There were two
problems. Would orders through these drainpipes really carry to the
guns in battle? Also, where did the officer set up his command post? I
assumed he stayed free to move around to liaise with the infantry (who
would presumably come in a crisis, whether falling back from the front
line or coming up as reinforcements) and also to be able to visit both

sections. But in the height of the attack, he'd have to dive in with one of them.

Fortunately, there is detailed contemporary evidence about our life style on the Blue Line: a journalist, J. L. Hodson, visited my platoon, and chatted with us for a couple of hours. His account, in *War in the Sun*, is a model of precise observation and sympathetic understanding:

September 28th 1941

I spent the remainder of the day with the Northumberland Fusiliers, who've been in the desert over a year: they set out on a three-days' exercise in September, 1940 – and they're still doing it. The Colonel laughed over that; both his trouser-legs are patched, for they set off with little kit. During this time they've lost about 200 men, but fifty are now back, recovered from wounds. "Round my last office, dropped a score or two of bombs. One 600-lb bomb hit my truck – the truck disappeared, but only one man was hurt; two others lying with the protection of a few sandbags escaped altogether." I hear a saying: "Lie down in the desert, turn round about three times and you're dug in a few inches and nothing but a direct hit'll do you much harm." The C.O. said that boredom and discomfort during the summer were the worst enemies, but the men have stuck it very well. 'We've had a camp by the sea to which the men have gone for three days at a time.' This regiment went to Benghazi and came back into Tobruk. They wear trousers as distinct from shorts, partly so that they are easily distinguished and partly because the red-hot cartridge cases from their machine-guns have a trick of shooting into shorts, with uncomfortable results. I visited some of the gun positions and met a young second-lieutenant who was a research history scholar at Oxford (got a First there). His father's a North-Country vicar and he himself was going into the Church – a tall, brawny lad with fine grey eyes and hair on the cheek-bones. He took me down into the gun-posts – we slid down a narrow hole and crawled along a trench; into the gunpit comes a pipe-end – a drainpipe, which has become a speaking tube; excellent, too. They've got a dining-room underground, also. They're lucky altogether at this post. The men were quite chirpy – several hail from Hull, others from

Newcastle-on-Tyne and neighbourhood. Among their badinage
was:

"If our password is 'boat' again, I'll dot somebody one …"

"Mussolini is the best quarter-bloke we ever had …"

"You ought to try our bully. It's like chicken – it is, straight …"

"We're just waiting for Jerry to come over …"

"At night we tell fortunes by cards – we're always going out on
the 20th …"

Their spirits were fine, but they don't compare with the Australians for good teeth and physique. One lad had a wide gap in
his teeth at the front.

A cricket match was going on nearby – against the Australians.
We had provided two bats (previously given by another batch of
Aussies) and the Aussies found the ball. It was the sort of cricket
played on brick crofts – rough pitch, no grass, and the ball had to
be clouted in the air to get runs. The Aussies had made eighty-
seven, we hit up about forty, and they put the Northumberlands in
again. As I watched, an enemy aircraft was seen and the waiting
batsmen were told to take cover; but the match didn't stop and the
aircraft didn't trouble us. The Second-Lieutenant said: 'I was
doing a thesis at Oxford on a seventeenth-century chap – doesn't
seem so important now.' I said that if he went into the Church
after the war he'd find all this useful in meeting the men on level
terms. Yes, he said, he knew that – that was partly why he's here.

Monotony was the disadvantage of the comparative safety of the
Blue Line. The cricket match with the Aussies was a one-off, a lot of fun
for once, but not repeatable. On two occasions I was allowed to send
the platoon, in successive groups, to swim at the coast. There was a
peaceful cove, the sky and the sea vivid ultramarine, the war forgotten.
The story went that one day a German plane had swooped to strafe the
bathers: if so, it was a breach in the veneer of chivalry which sometimes
overlay the sheer cruelty of war in the desert, where the desolation
formed a sort of arena for battle without killing women and children
and flattening homes. The bathing parties would return, the boost to
their morale offset by envy of the men of the various technical units leaguered up near the ocean, their naked bodies glittering bronze as they
took their daily sport in the cooling waves. A German pilot baled out of

his stricken plane one day, fairly near to us and falling well within the
perimeter, so he was bound to be taken prisoner. Even so, the whole
Blue Line erupted in rifle fire against him. It was as a break from boredom and in exasperation at the total air supremacy of the enemy, rather
than savagery. I stopped my nearest section from carrying on firing –
captives were superior to corpses as an argument to bring the enemy to
give up, I argued, but I only half believed it and they did not believe it at
all. Mercifully, the tedium was relieved by pretty substantial meals; the
commissariat at Tobruk, once the initial chaos was overcome, was
effective, and when the platoon sergeant arrived every night with the
rations, everyone wondered what novelty there might be this time. And
apart from a grim fortnight early on when the water was down to a pint
a day per man, for all purposes, there was a reasonable drinking ration.
My HQ was better off than anywhere else, for Martin built a distillery
from old car radiators and other parts from wrecks, gathered fuel and
produced, from unspeakable liquids, a strange, harsh-tasting pure
water. He also washed my shirts in petrol, which was fine so long as
they hung a while in the sun until they were no longer combustible.

It was astonishing what enthusiasm greeted the issue of a rum ration.
Someone possessed a small pewter measure, and I would go round with
the platoon sergeant seeing each man got his tot. There were always
two or three inches left in the bottle, and I saved these up until we had
enough for a private issue under my own authority. This system did not
last, for the ubiquitous barrack-room lawyer protested that it should
all be dished out at once, so I spun a coin to decide which section
should be the first to get an extra half tot each. Splendid! It was the
other one. I didn't drink alcohol, which was an advantage when equi-
table distributions had to be made. It also endeared me to my company
commander. Dick was astonished when he brought round a bottle of
whisky from the NAAFI for each officer, and I told him he was welcome
to mine.

Once or twice I went back with the platoon sergeant, 'Darkie'
Sutton, when he went to draw the rations, so I saw Tobruk harbour
with its sunken ships and quayside ruins. Once we picked up a rein-
forcement newly come in on the destroyers (they brought stores and
men only on moonless nights and got away again quickly before day-
break). It was another Fusilier Martin, authentically from north-east
England. I had forgotten the incident, but long after the war he

recounted it. He was dropped off at the ration point and told to ask for Sergeant Sutton, who would be expecting him. He was directed to a truck and beside it, on an ammunition box, two weary, hatless figures sat, head in hands.

'Sergeant Sutton?'

'Yes, Fusilier Martin, put your gear in the back and we'll be off'.

'What's the officer like?' asked Martin.

'Oh, Lieutenant McManners, he's a right bastard.'

When the truck finally stopped at our position on the Blue Line, the sergeant and I got out of the front. 'Welcome to the happiest platoon in Tobruk,' I said to Martin, 'and the first lesson is, not to believe everything Sergeant Sutton tells you.'

Once we were stirred out of lethargy by battalion HQ. We were told that, to prevent us from growing stale, there would be a training day, and together with a couple of other platoon commanders I went to an OCTU-style TEWT. A scenario was given for 'Withdrawal' and we were asked to position the machine-guns in a suitable place to form part of a final defence line for the harbour. The official solution was the obvious one, to take up a hiding place amid the massive ruins of Fort Pilastrino, the last high ground before the downhill slope to the coast. Oddly, we never guessed that this was for real – a plan for a pull-out by sea had been devised, and we were to be rearguard.

While on the Blue Line, I was sent on a series of independent shooting missions, five in all. The first was a success, if that is the word for it, though my own part in it was inglorious. I took the four guns on a long carry (no use of trucks for fear of raising a tell-tale dust) to a hollow near the perimeter, and set them up for an indirect shoot on an enemy strongpoint sketched in on the map. It was afternoon, and with the heat haze hampering visibility, some incautious Germans might be venturing out of their trenches. I was to climb up the steel scaffolding poles that constituted one of the artillery observation towers (about as high as a three-storey house) and shout down fire orders to my batman who was manning a phone down below, and he would relay them to the corporal in charge of the guns (we had run out a signal line and put on telephones for the purpose). Dick Hensman loaned me binoculars for the operation. Almost at the top, I found that I dare not go up further. There was a box up there covered in sacking to hide the presence of an observer, and it jutted out all round, so to get into it meant swinging away from the struts then hauling oneself over the rim. I had discovered vertigo. I tried to rake the horizon with the binoculars, but not very profitable when you are hanging on with one hand, and trying to peer round a pole and you have still not managed to get the binoculars focused. Then a voice came from the box, 'Don't come up here if it's too hairy, sir, have a go and I'll observe for you.' It was an artillery sergeant, with no hint of contempt, or of complaint lest my presence on the tower would draw the attention of the enemy. I was thankful, and gave the order to fire. Four guns blasting away together put down a terrific barrage of lead. 'You got one,' said the sergeant, 'stretcher bearers are running out.' 'Stop!' I yelled. Where did duty lie? To go on and kill more? I turned the guns through a couple of degrees and lifted the range somewhat. A salvo, but a waste of ammo now surprise was gone; we were not going to get another hit. Apart from the artillery sergeant, no one knew I had panicked at the climb. The gun crews were a long way off in the hollow, and my batman had no idea that I had meant to get right up into the box. Looking at the battalion War Diary, I see that this machine-gun shoot making use of the Italian-built observation towers was not the only one – there was a repeat performance, a more effective one. Jack Watson, though I did not know it at the time, had finally come up from Alex on a destroyer, and been allotted a platoon. On 17 September he ran an indirect shoot on enemy working parties at first light and at dusk – this is described as having been 'highly effective'.

The other shoots were night operations. From the OCTU, the whole drill of pegging out the firing point and using the night-aiming lamp was familiar, but what of practicalities? No one had told us that in an exposed position we needed to fire through a screen of old blankets to conceal the muzzle flashes from the enemy. And we knew nothing of moving around in darkness: our only nocturnal foray at the OCTU had been the game of Cowboys and Indians in which I nearly got lost. The first shoot taught me an invaluable lesson. The desert looks entirely different by night – the streaks of colour gone, the once barely noticeable rocks or war débris suddenly looming large, tracks and wheel marks crossing and recrossing in confusion. If the compass bearing doesn't get you there, its no good looking back and trying to see where you came from. This is what happened to me – I tried to find my pegs by compass bearing and where were they? In the end I got there and opened fire later than agreed, but this didn't matter, as it was just harassing fire, though everything of course had to be spot on for range and direction, to avoid hitting our own trenches or patrols. Thereafter I found the way by different methods. I would leave my batman on the pegged position with a shaded torch, establish a trail of desert junk, war débris or stones at twenty yard intervals to the turn off from the main track, with my orderly there as traffic director. If necessary a third man would be left on the route at a tricky point. These three I called the 'wrecking squad'. a title they enjoyed. These devices are not in the military manuals, and I did not reveal to my company commander the secret of my unerring skill at night manoeuvres. True, if the enemy had broken through to the Blue Line during the six or seven hours between the recce and the shoot the platoon would have been two or three men short. The next shoot went like clockwork and we had the satisfaction of seeing Very lights and of hearing ragged fusillades all along the enemy line. As we lugged the guns and gear off to trudge to the trucks and make for 'home', a mighty crump of mortar fire fell dead upon the position we had just vacated.

Our last shoot was a particularly testing one, for it was part of a precisely organised operation. It was not long before the break out, and a party of British commandos had come in to alarm the enemy with night raids. This one was on the quiet western sector. Every night the Germans put out a screen of four or five Spandau machine-guns ahead of their defences to fire across their front; they were sure to open up once the raid began, and we were to blast them from about a thousand yards' distance. Dick Hensman took me on foot on the recce that afternoon, no one else with us on this flat expanse of desert close to the enemy. After he had gone, I put in the marking pegs, and Martin finally joined me, having laid down direction markers on his way. He stayed there alone, and Fusilier Stagg, my orderly, was left on the turn off from the main track, while I went back to the Blue Line to get the guns loaded on the trucks to move at last light. At about one in the morning we were all set, with the four guns cheek by jowl behind their blanket screens. Dead on zero, Very lights went up, shots rang out, then the German machine-guns opened up – there was no mistaking them, they were firing tracer. We blasted off at once; virtually immediately the sound of the Spandaus ceased and the tracer streams stopped, abruptly and finally. We had annihilated them, but we kept on firing relentlessly. One number one put a whole belt through without pause. Another was

furious because a stoppage intervened; he rapidly remedied it and rattled on to catch up with the other three. It was one of the few occasions
when you knew you'd been effective. A note of congratulation was circulated to all concerned with especial mention of our accuracy. There
were dead men out there, but it was in the darkness and a thousand
yards away, and that does not qualify for the hauntings of remorse.

While on the Blue Line with the Aussies, I met Padre Parry. He was a
caricature of the clergyman lost in the confusions of war, bespectacled,
pottering and clueless, but a saint, and his sincerity shone through and
gave him authority. He came visiting in the afternoon, tin hat anchored
by its strap on his shoulder at the ready (we did not wear them normally); he had Forces air-letter forms and cigarettes to hand round, and
he issued an invitation to his Sunday morning service in one of the great
caves back at base which were earmarked to serve as hospitals. I was
the only taker for his service: it was nine o'clock on Sunday, since an
enemy attack would come either at last light or dawn, when it would
have been unwise to leave one's post. It was a communion service, with
many well-known hymns and – surprisingly – a large orchestra, mainly
brass, the players brought together from all sorts of units by Parry's
ingenuity. In the vast cave, their music was deafening. After the service,
Parry told me that he had a concert party, and offered to bring it to the
Blue Line for a performance, after dark of course, for the German
planes ruled the skies. My platoon and the Aussies provided some of
the turns, and the padre's party the more professional ones, and an
orchestra. I had edited my platoon offering in deference to the dog
collar, but I need not have bothered; the night air of the desert was blue
with the obscenities of the visiting comedians. My contribution for the
thespians of my platoon was an operatic version of the poignant drama
memorialised in the Army ditty

> 'Please don't knock our shit-house down,
> Mother is willing to pay,
> Father is over the ocean blue,
> Sister is on the game,
> Brother dear has ...' and so on.

One of the Aussie contributions was a version of 'Cheer up my lads,
bless 'em all' sung with Sunday school solemnity in deference to the
padre, then finally, in the last verse, vehemently resorting to the four-

letter verb that was usually used to replace 'bless'. Parry had a scattered flock, so we saw him only occasionally. But he was round again after the Aussies had been pulled out and sent home, and the battle of the break-out was near. He knew that our platoon was for over the top, so he came to ask if we wanted to write farewell letters home, which he'd post if we were killed. A few of us wrote them. But what could you say? Afterwards, before we left to go back to Egypt, he came round again to give us our letters back. How inadequate mine seemed. I tore it up immediately.

For a short time, our platoon was pulled out of the Blue Line and sent to do a job on the west perimeter near the sea – not all that far away from the area where we had given the commandos covering fire on their night raid. An Indian battalion held this section, the rocks and ravines being ideal terrain for their peculiar expertise. My guns were of little use in this rugged area where a field of fire could rarely be more than thirty yards; as I remember, the guns were left on the trucks hidden in clefts awaiting some contingency that never came. (I think, perhaps, that there was a possibility of an enemy breakthrough further round the perimeter and in that case we would have formed a defensive flank to keep the rocky fortress of the Indians from attack from the desert plain behind them.) I ate and socialised in the officers' mess tent (only one of the officers was actually Indian.) The commandos had gone, but their liaison officer was still there, Admiral Sir Walter Cowan, seventy-five years of age and determined to die with his boots on. We all dreaded having to go with him on a recce, for there was a choice of walking alongside him waiting for the sniper's shot, or crawling alongside like a dog being taken for a walk. In the mess he could sometimes be persuaded to recount adventures from his early days commanding a gunboat on the Nile – 'We smashed the mosques like egg shells' – or recounting the initial careers of some contemporary admirals – 'I knew he'd go far, young Cunningham.' I asked him about Evelyn Waugh, who had served for a time with his commando unit: 'Writer feller, good man, drank bottled beer with his breakfast.'

One of the officers of the Indian battalion was Lieutenant Cook, who could always be recognised from the wide-brimmed Australian hat he wore. When senior people were away from the mess, he would recount his amorous adventures before the war, when he had been a commercial traveller. He could grade the counties of England in accordance with the facility of the girls, my own county, Durham, being the worst – 'Very difficult to get your greens'. One evening, five or six of us were sitting on deck chairs outside the mess tent enjoying cooling drinks as the heat of the day declined. Cookie came along the track on the opposite side of the ravine – it ran down to the bottom, then there was a steep climb up the other side to where we were sitting.

Occasionally, the enemy would harass us by dropping a mortar bomb in the wadis, assuming, rightly, that some of them would be used for living, stacking stores or ammunition or whatever. This night, out of the silence a single mortar bomb fell with a crash, apparently right on Cookie, who vanished in a cloud of débris. We all remained seated. 'Poor old Cookie,' muttered some one. The dust cleared and the poor old victim emerged, red-faced and dusting the desert from his trousers. When he had climbed up to the mess, someone in a deck chair said 'Hello, Cookie, what's happened to your hat?' He took it off and paled when he saw that all one side of the brim had been sheared off by shrapnel. A tirade of oaths began, cut short by Admiral Cowan: 'This won't do, Lieutenant Cook, we can't have language like that in the mess.' Afterwards, back in Egypt, I read in the English language newspaper in Cairo how the old admiral's Army career had finished. On the Great Retreat, he was rounded up by an Italian tank. He refused to surrender and emptied his pistol at it; fortunately, they bore him no malice and took him off to a POW camp. As the phrase went, he 'was put in the bag'.

A platoon commander lives in a narrow little world, concerned only with his own men and observing only a tiny segment of the battlefield. A momentous change took place, but we knew little of it. During the moonless nights of August, September and October, the Australian Division was ferried out of Tobruk and replaced by the Polish Brigade and the British 70 Division, an astonishing feat on the part of the Navy, costly in ships and lives. The change over was complete by 19 October, when General Morshead ('Ming the Merciless' to his own troops) departed, and General Scobie took over. We knew the change was happening, but had no idea of how it was organised. Apparently, our CO, Tubby Martin, had insisted that we must remain in the fortress, giving the assurance that our morale was fine; there was a dust up when a padre (Quinn, I think, the name – brash and courageous, winner of the MC – and nothing to do with the battalion, for we always avoided having one) told the higher command that the Northumberland Fusiliers were worn out and dispirited and ought to be relieved. Nothing of this came to our ears at the time; in truth, we never expected to be taken out and were no more dispirited than any men in our situation naturally would be. One change was very obvious to us and a great subject of speculation – a whole lot of brand new tanks had been imported into the fortress. Long before they arrived, when we were on the ration run or going on a swimming party, we had seen plywood dummy tanks covered in camouflage nets spread around in the open; the enemy gunners regularly shelled them, and by the time the genuine articles arrived they had given up and left them alone.

Operation Crusader, the move up from Egypt to take on Rommel in a set piece battle and relieve Tobruk began on 18 November. There was to be a breakout by the garrison to link up with Crusader, drilling through the enemy line to the south east of the perimeter and going on to Ed Duda, a huge flat-topped hill designated as the meeting place. My role was to take the guns through once the tanks had returned from their mission and set them up ready to fire at any counter-attack. Every event and detail of that day is clear in my memory, yet I cannot recount it. I was reckless in my decisions and cowardly after them, and two of my platoon were killed. There was Fusilier Stagg, the gentlest and kindest of men, who took the full force of the bullets while I escaped with minor wounds, and Fusilier Paget who grabbed a medical kit and was fatally shot when he ran to help. I can never forgive myself. I hope the dead have forgiven me and I pray for God's mercy.

The Battalion War Diary for 20 November records:

06.33 hrs. Phase V (capture of Duda) under command of 32 Army Tank Regiment. Success signal put up for capture of BUTCH (i.c. an enemy defensive position, so nicknamed). which gave 11 Platoon Y Coy their cue for ... starting and taking position on BUTCH for the purpose of supporting attack of King's Own on to JACK. On arrival at what was held by K. Own to be BUTCH, 2/Lt McManners in the leading vehicle went up over the crest and was immediately engaged by machine-gun fire from very close range. It appears that the area and extent of BUTCH was far greater than had been appreciated. 2/Lt McManners and five ORs were wounded and two ORs were killed. The rest of the Platoon

halted below the crest and was unaffected. Further forward movement was impossible and finally 2/Lt McManners decided that an
indirect shoot was the only method, but by then, JACK had
already been captured ...

The fighting was still going on when I got out of hospital and I got
onto Ed Duda and stood on its summit. We held the northern side of
the hill, the south side, looking across an empty desert plain to a far
escarpment, was in dual occupation, some wadis and re-entrants held
by Germans, others by ourselves. A section of fusiliers with two Vickers
guns had been stationed in one of them ready to fire at movement on
the plain; it had been overrun, and I was sent to see if any equipment
was left or any evidence of what happened to the men. The only way
was to go across the top, where the rock in the centre was pitted by
broad shallow blast scars and littered with jagged shards of metal – a
huge Italian coastal gun had been shelling it from miles away. The first
wadi I tried was the one, a litter of pieces of minor equipment, but no
guns and no bodies. Then the first mortar bomb landed, obviously from
a near hiding place and descending vertically. I wedged myself between
two rocks and hoped, as the explosions rapidly followed each other. It
would have taken a direct hit in my slot to get me, but they got within a
couple of feet. After about ten rounds, silence. Instinct said run, but
common sense dictated stay: let them think that they had got me. I gave
it an hour before setting off back across the summit. But the naval gun
was firing again. It was not dangerous to cross, but frightening all the
same. The shells were crashing down at roughly the same point every
time and there were identical intervals between them. The trick was,
move immediately after a shell burst and once the shrapnel stopped
raining, get to the edge of the fall-out zone and lie there until the next
explosion, then run like mad until the crump of the gun firing in the far
distance sounded, and throw oneself down again. The assumption had
to be that the place of aim and speed of reloading remained constant.
    When I was going down the other side of Duda, twilight was closing
in and a minor *khamsin* (sand storm) was blowing. At the foot of the
hill, a figure loomed in the grey sand-filled darkness. I lay down and
drew my pistol, still never fired. This was it, I would have to kill an
enemy directly. It never struck me to give a chance to surrender. I would
let him draw near, and as soon as I was sure he was a German, I would

shoot. I took off the safety catch and moved the cylinder so the first, the empty chamber, was past the firing pin. As I was levelling into the aim, the gun went off into the ground, making the most miserable of pops. The approaching figure did not hear it. When he was about ten yards away he muttered 'Bugger it' with heartfelt vexation. I stood up and he never saw the pistol. He was an RASC officer who had got hopelessly lost and was glad to be given a compass bearing.

My siege of Tobruk ended with the acquisition of an indispensable property. I bought binoculars from a soldier who had taken them from an Italian prisoner. I might also have had a German automatic pistol instead of my antique issue revolver, had I not been a naïve wanderer on the battlefield. On the last day of fighting in the Tobruk area, I was going forward at night, accompanied by Corporal Shaftoe, a solid, imperturbable regular whose rock-like presence more than once had kept me from faltering. We passed through a small group of enemy dead and one wounded man, a dark handsome officer who had been shot in the foot. I paused to reassure him, telling him we could not stop but the medics were following us – he seemed grateful. Later, Corporal Shaftoe showed me a wicked-looking automatic. 'I took this from him,' he said darkly. I did not ask if the German had appeared about to use it, though it sounded as if he had. Shaftoe must have thought me a fool, but he gave no sign of it: his voice showed only genuine friendship and concern.

6
Cairo

It was a great day – in mid-December 1941 – when the whole battalion moved out of the Tobruk defences to begin the drive down the narrow strip of coastal road back to the Delta. We had been under siege for seven months, and the battalion had been in the desert ever since Wavell's offensive had routed the Italians. The trucks and equipment were worn out, some of the gun barrels distorted and unserviceable, hair was long and full of sand, faces burnt by the sun. To the disappointment of the regular officers and all the old hands, who knew Alexandria so well, we were to go to Cairo, so we cut off the tarmac and went diagonally across the desert to hit the Alex–Cairo road at Half-Way House, a huge, crude café: had it been smaller it could have been used for a saloon in a Western film. Our trucks were parked all around, keeping well spaced, for dispersion had been the key to surviving air attack in the desert. I sat down to drink tea with the platoon. It was a peculiar social occasion, for we had rarely been all together, the two sections and headquarters were independent units for eating and each truck was self-contained; there was no central cooking. Each section elected its own cook (Corporal Shaftoe's section had Fusilier Jennings in this thankless office, until they discovered that he was keeping a jerboa – desert rat – as a pet). As we sat there, Dick Hensman, swarthy and saturnine, as ever wearing dark glasses, came up and winkled me out: he already had his other two platoon commanders in tow. 'Officers and men separate now,' he said, and we went into Half Way House for an indifferent coffee at an unreasonable price – though we were able, for the first time, to fraternise with him and with each other. This was to be the pattern of the future: apart from a few formal events, inspections and the like, in barracks officers and men were segregated, and only met again when it was time to pack the guns onto the 15-cwt trucks and ride back to the battle line or for training in the desert.

We were initially stationed at Abassia Barracks, neat one-storey brick buildings. Here, we had an Army Christmas; but there was no football match between officers and sergeants and no joint parties, though the junior officers had to turn up for a few minutes at the men's Christmas dinner, as if to certify the fare as worthy of the occasion; then we hastened to retire to our own, much to the relief of both parties.

After this un-Christian Christmas without a nuance of home, we were sent on leave by companies. The regular officers all went off to join their old friends in the upper social circles of Alexandria, and the non-regulars were inclined to urban pleasures. I went off to Luxor (at Dick Hensman's suggestion) with Robert Marshall, a fellow platoon commander in Y Company; we travelled on the overnight sleeper train. Our hotel, just opposite the vast pillars of the temple of Karnak, was almost empty, no tourists, no Forces people on leave other than ourselves – just half a dozen ageing permanent residents and a naïve Hungarian girl who was companion to some old lady. So we ate heartily, saw the sights, reminisced about home, but had no social conversation. Only the Hungarian girl would talk to us, but she was sad company: 'Why you talk to me when you have plenty of soldier girls in Cairo?' One wondered what in the end her fate would be. We hired a guide for the week, and three donkeys, and every day we rode off to explore the Valley of the Kings. The felaheen working in the irrigated fields always waved and shouted cheerfully to us, an appealing contrast to the degenerate urban proletariat we had met in Cairo. Once, riding along an embankment between two canals, we met a group of two or three peasants escorting a camel laden with long reeds jutting out on either flank occupying the entire width of the causeway. The one party could not stop the camel's majestic progress, and the other could not slow down the donkeys' cheerful trotting, so we had to lie low on the backs of our steeds and let the reeds rasp over us. This sight reduced the felaheen to helpless laughter which was still echoing over the watery flats as they vanished out of our sight. We must have seen more of the Valley of the Kings than any modern tourist, and we had the haunting experience of being alone, as if we were the first explorers who had stumbled upon the temples and the tombs. But one thing we resolutely refused to do: we would not stay up to see Karnak by moonlight, or get up early to see the sun rise over its immense columns. In Tobruk, we had had our fill of wandering around during the night, and seen the sun come up all too often over desolate desert landscapes. Then back to Cairo, getting out of the sleeper onto the station platform with miserable characters fighting each other to carry our luggage, and the vendors eternally shouting 'Gazzuza, Gazzuza!' (*eau gazeuse*) or 'Eggs-a-bread, limonada!'

The 1st Battalion RNF had been stationed in Alex for three years before the war, and the officers had become friendly with the exclusive Anglo-French segment of society, entirely separate from the immensely rich upper-class Egyptians, the Greek community bound together by the observances of the Orthodox religion and commercial links, and the bourgeoisie of diverse Levantine origins owning so many of the shops and night clubs. (The vast mass of the Egyptian population of the city did not come into any sort of reckoning: from the weary patient policemen and the reliable domestic servants down to the multitude of rogues and riff-raff, they were just a picturesque background to existence, though if defeat had compelled us to start pulling out of the Delta, they could have become menacing.) The exemplars of good form in the Anglo-French social group were the family of the consular judge, Judge Holmes, whose son was our adjutant, and its wealthy patricians were the Finneys and the Barkers, active in the upper reaches of international trade and cotton-broking. (This sounds a judicious sociological analysis – it is just a historian trying to make something of a few naïve observations recollected from over half a century ago.) When the war broke out, some of the girls of these families, diverse in background but educated at the English school and the French *lycée*, were formed into a concert party to entertain the troops. The organiser was Mrs Barker, known to us, though not to her face, as Gabriella; she ruled her flock with a rod of iron and prevented unsuitable attachments. At every performance she appeared in splendour on the platform to announce each item: 'And now, Vivian will sing for you'. She looked like the majestic Mrs Teasdale in the Marx Brothers' *Duck Soup*. The shows put on by the concert party were sophisticated: the girls good-looking, graceful dancers and wearing a succession of lavish costumes; the star was Vivian, a singer of satirical songs in a deep voice of the kind much later made fashionable by Nancy Sinatra. Not long after Christmas the party came up from Alex to Cairo to perform in various camps and depots, and since our regular officers knew them, a celebration was naturally held in our own mess. Here I met Betty, very young, English and Greek, who could have auditioned for the part of a Hedy Lamarr look-alike. We went to coffee at Groppi's next morning (Mrs Barker, of course, having rung battalion HQ to find if I was reliable and no doubt discovering that I was almost disappointingly so). Thereafter, in intervals of the desert war and Greek liaison wanderings, when I was in Alex, if she was free, we would dine together. She was a charming companion and good friend, and I remain deeply grateful to her – feminine company means a great deal to a soldier shaken by the traumas of war.[1]

The appearance and atmosphere of most of the places where we could socialise when back in the Delta have gone from the memory; I cannot picture any of the restaurants or hotels (except that fearful 'Long Bar' at Shepheard's) or the cinemas. As for the night clubs, I never went to them unless there was socially no escape. But Groppi's at Cairo and Pastroudi's at Alex stay in the mind: there is a splendid decadence in having morning coffee and éclairs amid gilt mirrors and all the kitsch of affluence. Three cameos from the Abassia epoch linger with me. One was going to an air-conditioned cinema to see *White Christmas* and the stifling heat striking up from the pavement as we came out. Another was receiving a hesitant salute from a private in REME – Harold Taberner, a friend at Oxford and a fellow soccer player (when he had time to spare from playing rugby). He complained he was dying of boredom as a storeman, with no hope of promotion, let alone a commission; no one gave him credit for intelligence, his good degree in Classics went for nothing in REME. We agreed that I'd call on his commanding officer to ask to see 'an old Oxford friend I'm told is in your unit', a subterfuge to draw attention to his intellectual qualifications. The charade was played out, but nobody was impressed. The moral: don't join a technical unit, for here no one can get on by pretending to be an engineer or a mechanic. The commercial travellers and estate agents were awarding themselves phoney degrees and rising in the Education Corps.

Finally, a vivid picture in the mind concerns the meetings of what one might call the 'John Meikle support group'. Meikle, an engaging handsome subaltern, an ex-Palestine policeman, had won the Military Cross early on in Wavell's rout of the Italians. Immediately back from Tobruk, he had been in charge of paying the fusiliers of his company before they went out to sample the delights of Cairo; then he had sampled those delights himself, spending – or just losing – the money that

---

1 Soon after the war Betty married an American and went to live in the United States.

was left over. In the morning, his company commander, a super-efficient regular, put him on a charge for a court martial. This meant he was confined to quarters under arrest, and the other junior officers had to take turns staying with him as escort – arrayed in Sam Browne belt and cross brace and side arm. Every night, some of us – some one time, some another – would gather to keep the two of them company; it was, in a way, a subversive assembly of non-regular officers. At these sessions, 'Guts', Lieutenant Gutteridge, would entertain us with brilliant mimicry of our senior officers. He would start with our colonel, Tubby Martin, generally depicted in one of his rages at breakfast back home in Ireland after the war. The effect of this impersonation was achieved by comic exaggerations; others were depicted by the slightest of touches, a mannerism, an affectation. Meikle's company commander had the peculiar trick of asking questions in a very low voice, then asking supplementaries, until the process appeared menacing; Guts always put him in a reenactment of John's arrest, each time inventing a different and absurd charge for the occasion.

'Meikle, I looked in at your platoon this afternoon' (this very soft and sinister).

'Yes, sir!' (brash and forthright).

'Do you realise there was something amiss there, Meikle?'

'No, sir!'

'Think hard, Meikle, was there some detail you had overlooked?'

'Certainly not, sir, can't think of anything.'

'Well, let me give you a clue; I looked at your gun tripods.'

'Sir!'

'Yes, Meikle, I looked at the tripods. Did you realise that one of your tripods only had two legs. How do you account for that, Meikle?'

While at Cairo, the battalion was required to take a turn in sending junior officers to the provost marshal's office, to be sent on a 'disciplinary patrol'. You would walk smartly around followed at a discreet distance by two military policemen; if a soldier failed to salute, the red caps would put him on a charge. In theory, you were looking for other sorts of misdemeanour as well, but as the patrols were in the mornings, these rarely came to light. The patrols were simply an enforcement of saluting. Who was it in authority who had decided that it was decent to use holders of the king's commission in such a scheme of entrapment? I turned up late for my assignment, and every area had been allocated except the Sharia Wag el Burka sector. 'I don't think we'll send you there,' said the captain in the provost's office in a kindly, patronising way, after eyeing me balefully up and down to see if he could detect any fault in my turnout. Wondering if having been late would in some way be held against me, I said I didn't mind doing it. The captain hesitated; clearly he felt that this was an opportunity to have an insalubrious quarter of Cairo looked at by a naïve officer who was ignoring the Army maxim never to volunteer. Finally, he decided he'd send me, and handed me the list of duties that went with this tour, which was an especially long one.

There was a delay until a double-strength escort could be mustered: two redcaps and two Aussie military police; it was then that I realised I'd have done well to take the chance of escaping and go to Groppi's for a coffee or Shepheard's for a lemonade. The Burka was a reasonably attractive street with Western-style buildings but an atmosphere of colourful oriental seediness; practically every door gave entrance to a brothel. This was the authorised red light district, where the army sent medical orderlies to check if the women were free from VD (Monty ended all this when he arrived in Cairo). In a little square set back from the street there was a high blank wall, and against it a hundred or so Aussies were running a gambling school: the noise could be heard all along the Burka. My sheet of instructions from the provost marshal's office said all organised gambling was to be suppressed. 'Am I expected to enforce this order?' I asked my escort (a sensible question among sensible men, but not in the Army). 'You are the officer, sir,' said one of the redcaps. Stupidly nettled by this strictly correct reply, I did just that, and ordered the crowd to disperse. As soon as I had spoken, I realised the folly of it: there was an astonished silence, then a murmuring tide of incredulous anger. Then a gigantic figure said, 'He's all right, mates, we're gonna do what he says; put the fucking dice away.' We hastened off at a brisk walk and if we heard laughter and the noise of starting again, none of us chose to notice it. 'Good on you,' said one of the Australian policemen. 'You just put years on me, sir', said one of the redcaps.

Having invited trouble, we now found trouble thrust upon us. There was a tumult in a brothel with the sound of breaking glass, and the disturbance spilled into the street. A huge fat muscular Arab, the chucker-out, was wrestling with two black soldiers – no doubt from one of the pioneer battalions from East Africa. A monstrous 'madame', wearing the load of jewellery you would imagine went with the job, appeared demanding the intervention of duly constituted authority, in this case myself. This was the sort of 'discipline' my escort were qualified to exert, and we stalked inside to restore order. There was a long narrow hall, with curtained alcoves all the way down each side. A group of girls in tatty exiguous costumes were in a cluster at the far end waiting for clients; they seemed to accept a sort of hierarchy, the two better-looking ones rushing up to greet the officer, lifting their skirts in unambiguous invitation. One or two soldiers walked around naked, except for their boots, which were valuable and would be stolen if left unattended for a single moment. A couple of little girls aged between five and seven were around to bring drinks for the customers; they were dressed as devils in tight-fitting outfits of fish-scale design and carried little black pitch-forks. I stood aloof, a symbol of order in polished leather and bur-nished brass while the military policemen restored a lustful tranquillity by turning away all black troops. No doubt they moved on to unofficial establishments and caught VD – that is, unless their money was taken away by other Egyptian entrepreneurs first, like the dentists who per-suaded them to have their glittering white teeth encased in gold. These Pioneer Corps soldiers were from East Africa. Forbes-Watson had served there and knew the language. I was with him once when he stopped to talk to some of them, and was greatly amused when they referred to the Cairo dentists as '*danganya waru*'. Like all good curses, it was untranslatable.

We fulfilled a similar peace-keeping mission in an adjoining brothel, then set off out of the Burka. As we left, a smart sergeant-major marched into the street, and as I returned his salute I could not resist saying, 'Rather early in the day for this, Sergeant-major.' 'On the con-trary, sir, it's fresher now.' That was how it was, no human beings involved, just commodities that were fresher.

Soon the battalion was moved from the neat simplicities of Abassia Barracks to the Citadel, a gloomy castle dominating the old quarter of Cairo; next door was the Blue Mosque, with two of Napoleon's cannon-balls lodged in the wall above the arch of the gateway. Though the Citadel was notoriously bug-infested, it was a fine setting for the game of soldiering – put a guard at the postern gate, drill on the bar-rack square, enjoy a mess with old-fashioned heavy furniture, including a full-size billiard table, and sleep in high-ceilinged rooms with only two junior officers to each. My days were enlivened by sharing with Jack Watson. He had come up by sea to join the battalion; before that, he had been in Alex, where he was befriended by the two charming Holmes girls, daughters of the consular judge and sisters of Hugh, our adjutant. They had commissioned him to take up a case of whisky to their brother and, not surprisingly, it went missing on the destroyer. When Jack handed over the letter he had brought without the grog, he innocently referred, as he had been doing, to one of the girls by her nickname. Hugh Holmes's reaction at the time is recorded in his memoirs and is a pointer to the difficulty some regular officers found to adjusting to the amateurs who had joined them for the duration of the fighting. When, long after the war, the memoirs were published, Jack wrote to Hugh and friendly greetings were exchanged, so no bitterness remained in these old memories of mutual incomprehension.

There was an alarming accident in our room that could have been a tragedy. Every day our batmen came to the room to polish, iron and generally turn us out like field marshals. On one of those occasions, Jack's man drew his pistol from the holster where it was hanging up over the bed, and pointed it in jest at Martin, my batman. The trigger clicked on the empty chamber, then with the gun pointing to the floor, the trigger was pulled again. A bullet drilled a hole in the floorboards. Jack had not unloaded it and only the custom of leaving the first chamber empty had saved Martin's life. At the OCTU we had been taught – for a mere hour – how to use a pistol in the days when there was no ammunition, and no one had mentioned the importance of unloading.

At the Citadel, I was promoted to second in command of a company, at that time something of an achievement for a non-regular in a regular battalion, though the elevation was only temporary and there was no change in rank. This was under Andrew Bonham-Carter, big, broad-shouldered, straightforward and uncomplicated, easy to work with. (Alas, he was killed in the fighting in France much later.) As it happened, the job of second in command turned out to be demanding. Someone on high thought it would be edifying for us to march to the Anglican cathedral for a service of thanksgiving for Tobruk and to impress the Egyptians at a time when King Farouk was meditating an undercover understanding with the enemy. For two days I stood with the company quartermaster sergeant in the steaming heat of the *dhobi* (laundry) supervising the ironing of the shirts for the parade. One by one the fusiliers presented themselves, and the colour sergeant, armed with a long wooden ruler, measured the standard width of the sleeve turn-up and the correct distance from the shoulder to make the end of the sleeve fall exactly on the elbow joint. The *dhobi* man pressed in these folds with steamy, intent accuracy, then the fusilier presented the finished article for my inspection, saluted and stamped off briskly.

Another ordeal awaited me on the day of the parade. Each company had its commander in the van, and the second in command alone at the rear, giving the order 'Quick march!' This had to be done in step with the company in front. The formula is to keep saying to yourself in time with them, 'Left, right, left, right, quick march!', then, when the right distance has opened between their tail and your head, yell 'Quick march!' aloud. If you let the gap get too big, the formula breaks down and the abyss of the unknown opens before you. You may have to call 'Change step!', notoriously difficult to get right. But at the crucial moment, the mouth goes dry. 'W Company!' you bellow, then the 'Quick march' does not come. They are getting away from you – pray heaven I can overcome this paralysis. I will resign my commission, I will volunteer to assassinate Hitler, I will atone for this somehow, I will go into a monastery. 'Left, right' and 'Quick march!' thunders out. Crash, thump, it's all right, they are off! Arms are swinging shoulder high, dead on time – there's a party scheduled in the mess tonight. We were the very last company, the rearguard, and the second in command of the battalion marches at the very end of the whole show, so is alongside the second in command of the rear company. Thus, Major Forbes Watson was my companion. The streets were lined with the usual motley crowd. Forbes kept muttering to me, 'Mac, we are last, they'll close in on us; we must sell our lives dearly to let the battalion get through ... Stick close to me, Mac, I'm wearing my sword, you can rely on me.'

After the march we had tremendous festivities, and the officers' mess became a scene of riot, the only time in the battalion when I saw its staid decorum thrust aside. One of the games played early in the evening was jousting on horseback, the officers in pairs, one the horse, the other the rider, moving around the room and trying to pull down the others. Forbes and I won this one; I was the rider, he was the horse, being big and solid and knowing the tactical secret – keep alongside the walls; he also circled anti-clockwise so my stronger arm, the left, was free to pull others down. Our essential secret, however, was simple: neither of us had been drinking, from principle on my part, from an abstemious temper on his. Later on the night turned to vandalism with the playing of 'billiard fives', hurling the balls onto the slate to be caught on the opposite side on the rebound. We all had to fork out subsequently for cracking the slate – the real scandal being that it was probably not replaceable. The fusiliers, needless to say, went out to paint Cairo red, and on the following morning every company office had its queue of delinquents, with the military police there to give evidence against them. Andrew presided at our hearings, his hat pulled down low and to one side to try to hide the black eye he had collected in the riot in the mess.

A strong moral dilemma was put to me shortly afterwards. A dozen or so Italian women, camp followers of Mussolini's defeated legions, had been made prisoner, and to our colonel's rage we were ordered to look after them in the Citadel until a more suitable place was found for them. They were a dubious lot, of course, but not bad looking. They were imprisoned in a spacious room, and a small room at the entrance to the building was made into a guardroom; a sergeant and half a dozen men were rostered in turn for duty there every night – for obvious reasons. Before breakfast one morning an officer of our company, Lieutenant 'Dusty' Miller, called on me. He had been duty officer the night before and in the course of his rounds he had inspected this whore guard and found the sergeant and his men engaged in enthusiastic sexual activity with the women whose long deprivation had made them untowardly enthusiastic themselves. Dusty had read the riot act and sent the men back to their guard room, ticked off the sergeant, but told him that 'for this once' he would not report him. Later that night, he had ill-advisedly gone back and found they had all resumed where they had left off. What was he to do now? If he reported them, his own foolish leniency would come to light. He was afraid to go to Andrew Bonham Carter, as a regular might lack sympathy with the weakness of a commissioned civilian. As second in command of his company and as a friend, would I give him advice? It seemed to me that in such circumstances it is pointless to try to distinguish between what you say as a friend and what you say in your official capacity: there is complicity, and you might as well accept it. The sergeant had let Dusty down, but there was no sense in allowing anger at the betrayal to dictate the choice between two evils. The court martial of the delinquents would not do the battalion any good, and Dusty would not do much for his image as an officer. I told him to say nothing. Eventually the women were trundled away somewhere (the refugee camp at Kabrit?), travelling in a covered-in three-tonner with the floor made comfortable with mattresses (a lot of debate as to whether these were advisable). Long afterwards, when I sat in the councils of the great, Tubby Martin and Forbes Watson were talking about how well they had coped with the problem of these whores of the declining Roman empire – no scandal or trouble, thanks to their judicious arrangements. I did not tell them otherwise.

The Northumberland Fusiliers were old desert hands, indeed, the most experienced of all the units in the 8th Army, for they had been in Egypt for some years before the war. While we were in Cairo, Forbes Watson was nominated from on high to represent our desert expertise and test the sun compass to report on its feasibility for general infantry use. The old-established method of desert navigation was cumbersome. As a preliminary to a long journey you selected recognisable features on the map and joined them by doglegs to form a journey pattern to the final destination – you could be a long way out if you tried to do fifty or a hundred miles on a single bearing. To get started, you walked a hundred yards from your vehicle (to avoid the magnetic pull of the mass of metal) and took your first bearing, picking up some feature on the horizon – a hump, a streak of colour say; then you told your driver to use this for direction (granted, he would have to swerve to avoid rocks, clumps of camel thorn and the like). Well before the driver's target mark was reached, you chose a new feature by the same process. All the while, you held your compass duly set to be a rough check on your driver's fidelity to instructions; also, you kept an eye on the truck's mileage clock to see when the end of your dogleg was due. And if when the clock ran out you didn't find what was supposed to be there, then what? Much of this rigmarole was eliminated by the use of the sun compass. It was screwed onto the mudguard on the driver's side, and its plate, marked in degrees, was adjusted so that the shadow of an upright pointer fell on a particular notch when you were on the right bearing. The driver simply had to keep the shadow on the mark. After half an hour the plate would have to be adjusted to fit the changed position of the sun. There was no chance of mistaking a point on the horizon, and no jogging away for a hundred yards to take a new bearing.

Forbes Watson loved vast spaces, strange and wild scenery, and lonely forays, and he made the test of the sun compass an excuse for a romantic venture of desert exploration. (His correct Christian name was 'Reg', but his friends and the regimental *Gazette* always called him Forbes, as if it were his first name.) I was lucky to be sent along with this excursion as back-up officer. We had three jeeps – the two of us with our batmen drivers and a spare jeep with the driver and an expert mechanic on board, and plentiful supplies of petrol and water. We raced off south-westwards, past the mirage haze over the Faiume extension of the Nile's waters, until we came to the Great Dunes. These were about a hundred feet high, their ridges in knife edges with a slight haze of breeze-blown sand. The dunes ran in parallel lines with fast corridors of hard going between them, about half a mile wide or more; each dune line had gaps at irregular intervals where you could slip through into another corridor and race along again looking for the next opening. When we emerged into open desert with the vast dunescape behind us, we seemed to have left the whole world we knew behind us. When we next stopped for the night I made a point of asking Forbes just where we were on the map, for if he for some reason keeled over, I'd have to get this party home again. Now we were racing over an endless plain, tiny shells and pebbles crackling under our humming tyres. The map we had got on to was empty, except for a dotted line marking 'Bagnold's track'; we had left behind the barrel track to Siwa long ago.

Our objective was a solitary feature on another otherwise empty map, 'Conical hill', a great black cone with steep sides at about 45 degrees inclination. We reached it late in the afternoon of the third day. After the evening meal, Forbes and I went up the steep slope to a ledge where our batmen had put a folding table, two deck chairs and a lighted hurricane lamp. They stayed with the jeeps which were tucked away out of sight around the cone, sufficiently far away so we could not hear the drivers talking. The faint wheelmarks of our journey were on the opposite side of the hill. It was as if we had been whisked there and dropped off by a magic carpet. Before us, as the sun went down, there was a vast desert prospect. The twilight rapidly faded into darkness. Forbes had a glass of whisky, not the bottle, on the table. We put out the hurricane lamp – it was an absurdity. The stars were myriad and brilliant, glittering in a fashion unknown in northern latitudes. A slight, cool breeze blew across from the far end of the world. We talked of friends, family and home and hopes for the future. But what future could there be? The German-Japanese alliance was racing to triumph everywhere, the wishful hope of a Russian counter-attack had faded, and the Germans were moving east again. Would we ever get back to England, or was our destiny to retreat out of the Delta to hold the line Baku–Batum or to fight a rearguard action along the Golden Road to Samarkand, perhaps eventually to be lifted off by some American rescue force to find refuge in the New World. The emptiness and silence engulfed us. Talk became impossible. We sat there in silence, conscious only of the breeze, the stars and the velvet blackness. There was a haunting background of comradeship: the two of us there on the pinnacle and the four men below, allied in a common purpose, its grimness forced out of the mind by the serenity of the night, dwarfing us and every human endeavour. In the strictly religious context, I have never had a mystical experience, but here was the peace passing all understanding, the nearest I can ever hope to come to experiencing the eternal serenity at the heart of the universe, an infinity of reconciliation in which I yearn to be enfolded. We sat there for two or three hours, silent. Forbes and I never mentioned this moment to each other afterwards, though we often reminisced about everything else.

7
The Great Retreat

We left the Citadel for the battalion's old haunt, welcome to all who had served there, the permanent tented camp at Sidi Bishr, just outside Alex. It was here that a circular came round: applications were invited to join a new organisation being set up in London to start compiling a history of the war; a good degree in history and actual battle experience were required, and commanding officers were forbidden to withhold the names of any who were qualified (a most unusual stipulation). The idea nagged me for a couple of days; few could be as eligible as I was, and I would get a flying start in academic life as well as escaping the hazards of war. How would I ever be able to explain to my parents at the vicarage that I had refused the opportunity? Tobruk had been an effective converter to the concept that it was possible to serve the war effort without deliberately courting danger. Anyhow, in the end I wrote an application and sent it off to battalion HQ. Within ten minutes I had been summoned by Colonel Martin. He was bristling with anger and spluttering – as I found when I knew him better, he had a vividly lucid incoherence at command – 'Out of the question. It's for fellows in all sorts of units but not First Battalion RNF. Never be able to face your old colleagues. Job here to do. We'll win and they can write it up. Look here, I'll throw this away and never mention it again, tear it up, what!' And he matched actions to words and threw the pieces in his waste tin with the magnanimous air of having done me a special favour. So much for commanding officers forbidden to withhold names. Yet when I got outside I was conscious of a feeling of elation. I belonged to the battalion and I'd be devastated to leave it. Within the next few days an instruction came to me: 'As from today and until further notice Lieutenant McManners is acting in command of X Company' with Tubby's initials, copy to etc., etc. Here was 'the job you have to do'. It was only until a regular officer came back to take over, of course, but I was gratified. Then the thought struck me, what if we moved back to the battlefield before the replacement came? I doubted if I could handle it and my elation ebbed somewhat.

And now, to take over command of the company. Next morning I found that I had to sign a wodge of paperwork, lists of all the equipment down to the spare lock springs. 'It's all here, sir', said the colour sergeant brightly and briskly. I was no longer taken in by the standard 'bull': perhaps, like John Meikle's platoon in Guts' legend, one of my tripods only had two legs. But life was manifestly too short to begin checking. The outgoing regular said, 'To tell you the truth there is a range finder missing, lost on an exercise in Northumberland long ago. Company commanders have signed for it ever since.' I signed. Then off to see Charlie Dipper, the Lieutenant-Quartermaster of the battalion, risen, as usual for his office, through the ranks, large, square, bald, severe to regular officers and considerate to the amateurs. 'Charles,' I said, 'I have taken over X company and have signed for the kit, including a missing Barr and Stroud.'

'That doesn't surprise me, I wondered when I'd be told.'

'What do I do next, any suggestions?'

'Do nothing. Seeing there's a war on, I'll write it off.'

It was as simple as that.

During our stay at Sidi Bishr, so socially agreeable to so many of us, Colonel Martin decided that we had been softened by our four months in the fleshpots of Egypt, and were not being significantly improved by the desultory training programmes we were – officially – running, and that something must be done to get us into trim for war again. So two of the companies were ordered into the desert on a three-day exercise, with Tubby himself inspecting how things were done. Off they went gloomily: Tubby went along taking Jack Watson with him as personal assistant, the mess corporal, the drivers, the mess tent, a couple of deck chairs and a table. All officers on the exercise were given a pep talk: 'Get rid of the flab', 'too much easy living', 'think tactically', 'get to know your platoons again', 'no comforts on this trip, live hard, hard arse, hard arse'. Setting off early they got well into the wilderness and had a day's exercise in recce, making camp, action in air attack, siting gun positions. After a hard day touring round, as the sun was setting, Tubby got back to his mess tent, alone in the emptiness; Jack Watson staying by the truck to put the gear away. Slumping into his chair, Tubby called, 'Corporal Baldock.'

'Sir.'

'My whisky.'

'We haven't brought it, sir.'

'What?'

'Lieutenant Watson said to leave it behind.'

'What! Watson, Watson!'

'Sir.'

'Where's my whisky?'

'I put it off the truck, sir, seeing you said we had to go hard arse.'

'Hard arse my foot,' yelled Tubby, mixing his anatomical metaphors.

As dawn broke next morning Jack Watson was trundling back from Alex anxiously consulting map and compass to find that bastion of enforced temperance, the Colonel's HQ. How had Jack had located a couple of bottles of suitable whisky in the middle of the night? Knocking up the Union Club, touring the bars trying to find whisky that had not been made in the Delta from rotting dates or with colourful Chinese labels on the bottles, or going out to Sidi Bishr and waking up someone in battalion HQ, perhaps even Hugh Holmes the adjutant, an earlier victim of Jack's inability to deliver where whisky was concerned? And what were relations with Tubby like for the rest of the exercise? From my later experience of Tubby, I'd say that Jack would have found him agreeable company, as after the day's work they sat in their deck chairs under the stars.

Oddly, we didn't know much or think much about the state of the desert battle line. We didn't listen to the wireless. The local English-language newspaper, the *Egyptian Mail*, told us more about the Russian front than the Libyan one. The Germans had advanced, but in early February we had stopped them at Gazala, and there was a stalemate until the end of May. Meanwhile, to my relief, a regular arrived to take over the company and I reverted to second in command. The new man, Major Tommy Hamilton, had come straight from being an instructor at the Staff College, and didn't know the desert. He was tall, thin and stooping, going bald, perpetually smiling, genial and approachable, a genuinely Northumbrian Fusilier, being of one of the old county families, a good Christian, emancipated from pride and self-importance. I was lucky: we immediately struck a rapport, deepening into friendship. No sooner was he installed and, presumably, had signed for the equipment, minus the written-off range finder, than orders came and the whole battalion was off westwards along the coastal road.

An account of what happened next to our company, as seen from the vantage point of battalion HQ, is given in the War Diary compiled by Wilfred Hillman, the Intelligence Officer. The CO's recce party had left Sidi Bishr for the Egyptian frontier on 26 May, and when X Company came up it was put into a defensive position covering Halfaya Pass, one platoon on the pass itself, and the other two on the beach. I cannot remember this deployment, and in any case it was a defence role far to the rear, and did not last more than a day or two before we were called up to the Gazala Line. It appears that on 3 June Tubby Martin agreed to detach X Company to go under the command of the South African Division in Tobruk, and General Klopper had decided we'd be used in a mobile role as divisional reserve. All this went for nothing, for the Diary records that on the following day we were put under the command of 9 Indian Infantry Brigade as part of a composite force to attack the enemy tank line, break through to the Sidi Mustapha feature, and consolidate and hold it. The record describes the force as crossing the 'start line' at 0415 hours and our tanks going forward at first light. But everything went wrong. The infantry had all its transport shot away, and they were stranded; our tank attack ground to a halt. At 1900 hours our battalion HQ agreed with the brigade HQ that it was necessary to retreat; there was no tactical reason to try to hold the piece of desert we occupied, and we had no anti-tank weapons to face the coming German tank attack.

My own recollection of the happenings of that 5 June will fill in the details of this outline in the Diary, and if it shows that to X Company the battle was not as lucid and purposeful as the headquarters' account suggests, that is what one would expect. Before the operation of that day began, Tommy had arranged with the tank commander that we would be available at his call to come forward – if German infantry were following up their tanks, we would shoot them up, so too if they had anti-tank guns following on. At that time we had no radio communications, so the only way to receive orders from the commander of our armour was to be up there with him. So Tommy did what one of the RNF company commanders[1] had done in an earlier battle: he went forward with the tanks in his little pick-up truck, driving just behind or just alongside the leader. The armour was forward of a ridge, and Tommy left the gun platoons below the ridge crest, comparatively safe.

1 This was James Jackman, who was killed and awarded a posthumous VC.

My instructions were to drive along keeping him in sight awaiting his signal to bring forward whatever platoon was needed. All hell broke loose once the two forces of tanks came within range of each other. The solid shells flew past with terrific velocity, or bounced by on patches of rock and hard ground. I cruised up and down just below the ridge line, nosing higher from time to time, standing up in my truck to observe Tommy through binoculars, then slipping back again to avoid the flak. Tommy was standing up all the time, observing the battle and waiting for orders; presumably, the lid of the command tank would be lifted and someone would tell him when we were to intervene. It was as heroic and absurd as the Charge of the Light Brigade. The firing would stop and start and all I could see was a haze of sand, wisps of smoke from burning and a few great looming shapes of tanks, and amid the chaos, Tommy trundling around. This went on all day, until in late afternoon the noise of battle became less strident and insistent. Tommy emerged from the maelstrom and joined me; he was sorry we had not been asked to do anything, and he was as clueless as I was as to the import of the battle where we had held front seats. We went off to find the platoons. Two men had been wounded by fragments careering over the top of the ridge; one had been badly hit in the leg and had lain there at the wheel of his truck and not been noticed by those who had dug holes and kept out of the flak. I can remember helping to lift him out. What I cannot recollect is (as the War Diary states) having two of our trucks damaged in a minefield – certainly, all of our platoons emerged from the day's non-event intact as fighting units.

We went back to the battalion area. It was peaceful there, though the sound of battle rolled in the near distance. Tubby Martin was driven past and asked me about the day, and I told him of Tommy's heroism. He said he'd want the details later. I was full of admiration for my company commander's performance; coming fresh from the Staff College and never having heard a shot fired in anger, it was astonishing.

The sun was setting and Tommy said we must dig ourselves slit trenches, get something to eat, and rest. 'I'm not digging another hole,' said Martin, mutinous semantically but not in tone. 'Don't,' I said, 'just get brewing up while I have a shave.' Somehow he had got hold of two tins of McConaghy's (that was the brand name for mixed meat and veg, much preferred to bully). I told him not to heat mine up until I was smart and clean, so he dined while I shaved. Just as I was stowing mirror and razor away, a thunderous noise came rolling towards us, like the Hollywood sound effects for a cattle stampede, and a host of vehicles swept through, missing our trucks here there and everywhere by a few feet on either side and raising a hurricane of dust. We didn't know it yet, but the great retreat had begun. Tommy drove off to battalion HQ to get instructions. Being an old hand by now I passed the word round the platoons to pack up. Tommy came back with the order to move. 'We must be off in half an hour.' 'Now, if you like,' I assured him.

I cannot remember much about that night as we ground our way eastwards. It was impossible to keep together, for there were trucks on the move everywhere, but I kept the HQ vehicles trundling along while Tommy was leading the gun platoons. Then a smart soldierly figure emerged from the darkness waving me down. It was a brigadier – could I be mistaken about this high rank? My memory is clear but it seems impossible that he could be so elevated in rank. For *vraisemblance* sake, I must demote him to major. He appeared to be in charge of a large fleet of three-ton lorries. 'Absolutely disgraceful! Somebody has to make a stand somewhere. I order you to stay here and man the defences.' And there were his defences, the lorries drawn up in a big circle, like covered wagons awaiting the charge of the Indians, the drivers at the ready with rifles. This is why the British lose every battle but the last, both the continual losing and the final win are here explained. Did I say that I already had my orders, that a single armoured car would finish off all his cowboys, that it was his duty to preserve all these vehicles for transporting the infantry? I didn't say anything, but I told Martin that now was my chance to have that tin of McConaghy's. It would take too long to heat, so I ate it ingloriously cold at that most dismal time of all, the hour before dawn. 'You're not going to stay here, are you?' said Martin in his most irreverent mood of censure. 'Future generations will come on pilgrimage to this spot,' I replied, 'to see the monument for McManners's last stand.' When I had finished my dinner-cum-breakfast, after a look around the fringes of the waggon circle for our bellicose major, I passed round the word to move and we glided slowly away towards the grey crack of dawn. We steamed along at a steady pace, the stream of fugitive vehicles long vanished, but innumerable ruts and tracks running parallel as far as the eye could see were evidence of their transit. Later on, far off to the left, we saw a procession of three-tonners driving at racing speed eastwards leaving a plume of sand behind them. I expect that the pale light of dawn had revealed to the major his vulnerability.

The desert is endless and a retreat is endless confusion, but we caught up with the rest of the company without difficulty. You get an instinct where to look, for the Fusiliers, mobile in their 15 cwt trucks, pulled off the main tracks and 'bomb alleys' and leaguered up away from others with their vehicles well spaced-out. We knew that the obvious place to make a stand was Tobruk, and this indeed was the official plan. Tommy came back from battalion HQ to tell us this was so; however, we were not to go back into the defences we knew so well, for the South African Division was settling in here, but to join the 29th Indian Infantry Brigade in holding the 'box' at El Adem, a strongpoint surrounded by mines a few miles to the south. The Indians were dug in around the extensive perimeter, and we positioned our machine-guns to give them protective fire in enfilade. The enemy were soon moving across our southern flank, out of range, though the dust of their vehicles darkened the horizon. The Indians had a battery of Bofors anti-aircraft guns, and I was walking between them and the infantry trenches when there were urgent shouts of warning – the guns were being lowered to fire flat trajectory. I dived into a hole as they loosed off a few rounds, no doubt at the by-passing enemy transport. One had to be careful among the Indians, for they obeyed orders literally. If the order to fire was given, there'd be no allowances made for innocent pedestrians. We had got along without bothering what the password was – lists came round and nobody passed them on; but you were in danger in the El Adem box if you hadn't got it on the tip of your tongue.

The sound of battle now rolled to the north of us, and we rightly surmised that the Germans were concentrating on Tobruk. We remembered the defences there and felt complacent, but the Germans remembered them too and knew what to do this time. Then the order came to us, 'Last round, last man.' This was chilling. It was curious to see that this legendary phrase of heroic finality could still be used: presumably it was supposed to install a steely resolve, and in Dr Johnson's words, about the prospect of being hanged, to 'concentrate the mind wonderfully'. But being interpreted, it meant that there was no hope for Tobruk and that we were being left to our fate – the very reverse of morale building. Once the gun platoons had been installed in their firing positions, the trucks had all been brought back to company HQ where they were dispersed and camouflaged, Tommy ordered me to wreck them. I dare say that this was officially laid down as part of the drill to comply with the 'last round, last man' order, to deny the enemy the use of the vehicles and, possibly, to prevent us using them to disobey orders and flee. Every instinct of my desert experience told me this was folly, and I begged him to reconsider. I promised him that I'd ensure the trucks were disabled by having all the distributor arms gathered in, and when the enemy attack really came I'd have the engines comprehensively ruined. After all, I'd be back in HQ and Tommy would be with the platoons when battle was joined, and I'd have the leisure to perform this fell task. Tommy agreed reluctantly. I talked to the MT corporal, treacherously, I fear. I told him to be ready for urgent action in two contingencies. One was to rush the trucks back to pick up the platoons at a moment's notice. Two was to remove the distributor arms, but only when I specifically told him to do so. The notion of future wrecking measures I kept to myself – best not put it into his head. Tommy was too busy rushing around on what was supposed to be the eve of battle to bother himself with what I was doing. In the middle of that night, the last round, last man order was cancelled and we were told to get out if we could. The wretched Indians were dependent on three-tonners to be moved; I didn't see any spare vehicles about, so I expect they were all made prisoner. Tommy told me to reinstate the transport and he rushed off to tell the platoons to pack up. He must have been surprised to find that the drivers got their trucks back to the platoons before he arrived himself.

Everything seemed confusion as we got moving, but only apparently so; when you are running for your lives it is astonishing how everyone cooperates. I panicked at one point. Finding the company sergeant major and the company clerk forlornly standing, with the driver, by our broken-down office truck, I told them to leave it and have a lift with me. Luckily, Tommy turned up and put the office truck on tow. Later he muttered to me about the stupidity of abandoning it; I didn't say that I'd ordered it, but it was obvious he knew. I justified myself with the reflection that I was allowed one mistake seeing that, by emulating the Nelson touch, I had ensured that we had any trucks at all to escape on. We got out through the minefields and fled eastwards; the enemy, no doubt, was hurling everything at Tobruk to seize it before the garrison settled, and this is why the noose had not closed on us earlier. There must have been some adventures during our escape, but I cannot remember them – the War Diary records that we had losses; perhaps some trucks stuck in the minefields. Long-distance memories become highly personalised: one remembers one's own fate, and forgets about others.

We rattled on to the Egyptian frontier across the evil plateau at the top of the Sollum escarpment, where the surface is solid slabs of rock at varying angles, with sand in all the crevices. The truck jolts, the sand fills the air, and you sit there sweating, wearing goggles, with cloths tied round your mouth and nose and filling the gap at your shirt neck. Then down Halfaya Pass (always called Hellfire, of course). Here on the watch was the solitary Australian we had seen before as we came up, wearing the standard antipodean uniform of shorts, boots, identity tags on tarry string round his neck and adorning his bronzed and naked torso. His task was to blow up the pass if the enemy drew near. He had boasted when we last saw him of the mighty explosion that he would trigger off one day. Now he waved to us exultantly – his hour had come. 'Yer just made it,' he bellowed. On the flat below the escarpment and a couple of miles further on we ran off the road and leaguered up for the night. There was a mighty explosion on the escarpment, a multicoloured flash with long, rolling reverberations. The solitary dynamiter's destiny was fulfilled, his long vigil over. In the middle of the night there was a rumble of traffic on the road. I was alarmed; we must have been at the very end of the retreat seeing we had been stuck at El Adem for so long; could this be the enemy? I went over and found a file of three-tonners going past, ours. I asked a driver which way he had come, and he said 'Down the pass.' Yes, he agreed, they had found it rather bumpy.

We returned to the battalion on 20 June. Battalion HQ had been informed on 14 June that 8th Army was to withdraw, leaving the Indian Brigade and ourselves in the El Adem box; I think that by now they had almost given up hope of seeing us again. According to the War Diary, our transport was taken away to refit Z company, but on 24 June we were refitted with new trucks and informed that we were to go under command of 10 Indian Division 'to hold an outpost line West and Southwest of Matruh'. It seemed as if Tommy was now established as 8th Army rearguard expert.

So we went southwards into the vast minefield belt which made Mersa Matruh the last desert strong point before the Delta. Tommy went round to put each gun platoon in position, and I dug in the HQ. There was no sign of infantry or any other troops. Nothing happened that night, so the next morning I was sent off to Mersa Matruh to find out who was in charge and to ask for orders. There were criss-crossing tracks and minefields, so it took me some time to get through: the little white town was deserted, a ghost town, not a soul to be seen. I went to the NAAFI, the doors were open, the shelves packed with good things. I loaded up with a choice selection, tinned fruit, bacon and sausages, McConaghy's, chocolate. There was no sign of the grog; first things first, when they fled they had at least taken that with them. So off back to Tommy, who was thunderstruck at the news. He went off to see two of the platoons, and I went to see the other. Not difficult to find, since its guns were firing. By the time I got there, they were silent again. The position was hardly visible, everyone dug in deep and heads down. On the skyline, clouds of dust were swirling. The enemy was skirting the minefields and bypassing us at top speed. A vehicle hove momentarily into view, our guns blasted at it and it slipped down below the ridge line. I shouted to Bob, the platoon commander. 'I'm not coming out there,' he shouted back. 'You can come over if you like.'

I put some NAAFI tins in my pockets and crawled over. He took them, but wanted no more; he just wanted to be left alone lest his position was given away. Suddenly I realised that, as second-in-command, I was no longer a member of the confraternity of junior officers. Company commanders and their deputies did the recces, positioned the guns, kept contact with the overall strategic authority, went off making all sorts of arrangements. Doing all this they got their fair share of shot and shell, but it was interesting, creative warfare as it were, while the platoon commanders were limited to a straightforward task in the zone where it's kill or be killed.

Things were much the same with the other two platoons. There was no rearguarding to do: we were being bypassed. Nobody had stayed in Matruh with us. We either got out now or we stayed put and in due course the enemy would collect us at his leisure. Tommy decided, against his ingrained military training, but in accordance with common sense, we had to go. He told me to set off at once with the company HQ – my truck, the office truck with sergeant major, the MT corporal and his vehicle, the colour sergeant and his, and the water tanker – to go via Matruh onto the coastal road eastwards, and to race on in the hope of beating the closing of the trap around us. He himself would extricate the gun platoons during the night and find a way out to the south through the minefields. It would take a long time, so he might have to delay his breakout to the following night. With my little convoy I departed forthwith.

Going eastwards from Matruh the road was empty. Then, after ten miles or so, we found a platoon of infantry dug in facing the wrong way, the way we were going. The enemy had cut the road ahead. To the right, towards the foot of the escarpment, there were numerous vehicles and a sort of purposeless milling around. The odd shell was falling, but seemingly unaimed, so there was not much danger. I turned off to the left and drove the mile or so to the sea; nobody else had gone off this side of the road and all was peaceful. The trucks were spread out in case of air attack. Everyone chose to stay beside his vehicle. Nobody asked what I intended to do. I went to the beach and sat there alone, looking into the gently lapping waves, blue and translucent. This is the time when you are conscious that all your men are with you whole-heartedly; they know that you are no longer under orders from above, as it were, to force them into danger, but that you have the big decision to make and all their futures depend on it.

As twilight closed in I drove back across the road and southwards towards the escarpment, which runs from east to west. In the half light, other vehicles were moving. I picked out a battery of 25-pounders, in line astern, well organised, with a pickup van leading, so I tacked on behind them. They knew a good track up the escarpment running diagonally, and we were soon in open desert. By now I no longer had maps of the area; I had to go by compass and common sense. The artillery were going slowly, and in any case it was unfair to increase the size of their party, so I pushed off into the gloom on a south compass bearing. After five miles or so, the desert, empty so far, became populated. In the darkness, trucks galore were milling about, there was lots of shouting, total confusion. 'Minefield ahead,' someone yelled at me: sure enough there was the wire and the skull and crossbones sign. There was some shooting: it was not clear where it came from. A bullet struck a spark from a stone, but there was no ricochet – it must have been an isolated rifleman firing from a considerable distance at the noise. An officer in charge of a convoy of heavy lorries yelled at me: 'You're infantry, go out there and get the buggers.' I decided to drive along the wire looking for a gap, and I went westwards, following the logic that since eastwards was the way we were going, if there was a gap that side it would have been found by now. An engineer lieutenant in a pickup truck had the same idea, so we joined forces. He went under the wire two or three times and prodded around. 'I'll bet it's a dummy,' he said, 'I'm going to drive through. If you like, follow my tracks. If I am wrong, try to pull me out.' I told my driver to follow precisely in his wheel marks and with fierce concentration he obeyed. We had sandbags under our seats, but while, as the phrase went, this preserved 'our backsides and balls' from splinters, an explosion might well have taken a foot off. We got through: it must have been a dummy – or we had been astonishingly favoured by luck. Though we were seen going through by various other parties, no one followed us. I parted company with my engineer guide: 'See you in Alex.' He went roaring off, I went at a sedate pace to keep our convoy together.

By now there was moonlight, enough to see twenty or thirty yards ahead. At one point, I thought I heard noises and stopped. There was a slight rise ahead, coming to a point in a mound. Crawling up the mound I saw a procession of tanks and accompanying vehicles grinding eastwards. We waited quite a while after they had gone before venturing on, crossing their tracks at right angles as we kept on southwards. My truck was in the lead, and I stood up all the time, compass in hand, checking the general direction and peering into the moonlit night. The going was good, firm and level, but with scattered humps of camel-thorn around which sand had gathered, at most a foot high. The drivers weaved their way so that, as far as possible, the wheels evaded them. It must have been well towards morning, though still dark, when we ran into disaster. Suddenly we found that we were coasting in silence through an encampment of geometrically scattered German vehicles, leaguered up for the night. Sentries, steel-hatted, rifles slung on shoulder, were pacing up and down. Without moving an inch I whispered to Martin, 'Keep on, slowly.' We passed through unchallenged, it seemed unnoticed, accepted by the sentries as legitimate travellers of their own side. Just as we came to the far end of this huge encampment, shouting and firing began. Down went the accelerator and we were lurching over the camel-thorn sending up a spray of dust and shingle. I stopped after a mile. Only the water truck was with us. The noise had died away, no more shooting. We had to assume that the other trucks had been stopped and that the rest of company headquarters was 'in the bag'.

We kept on steadily and as dawn broke an armoured car came racing from the west after us. We had not seen it, but fortunately they fired too early and down went the accelerator again. There were no camel-thorn humps now, just smooth fast going, with little shells and tiny stones crackling under the wheels, good enough going for an attempt on the land speed record. The armoured car kept firing, but we soon shook it off. Without maps, it was now guesswork. We had several big jerrycans of spare petrol each, a whole stock of NAAFI supplies, and a water tanker full to the brim; we could go on for a long time. After the last foray I was not taking risks, so instead of turning eastwards I kept on south until we reached the edge of the Qatara Depression. You could see its cliff-like edges rosy in the sunset. We couldn't get right there, because there were peculiar sandhills in the way, individual humps about ten feet high with dry grey desert thorns growing on their sides. They were close together, but the ground between them was firm. We pulled into a gap and round the corner so we were hidden, then anchored each vehicle to a knoll-side with camouflage nets to avoid detection from the air. Then a meal from the NAAFI loot; surprisingly, we ate little, but there were endless cups of tea. There were four of us, Spuggy Martin, the two water-truck men and myself. 'No need for a sentry,' I said, and they rolled up in their blankets, boots off, totally worn out. I sat, back to the front wheel of the truck, reflecting. Martin came across. 'So you're keeping watch, then?' 'Not really,' I said, 'I'm too wound up to sleep.' 'I'll watch out if you like,' he said. I walked round the hillocks and looked into the darkness of the vast desert plain we had traversed. Then I came back. 'We'd better all sleep,' I said. Strangely, I cannot remember praying, or giving thanks to God.

We stayed there all the next day, taking shelter from the sun and often dozing off. The day after, I set off an hour before dawn, steering east along the fringes of the Qatara Depression, then about noon turned north-east: by now we must have outrun the German advance and had probably reached a point level with the strategic area where 8th Army would have to make its last stand. What if we ran into soft sand or rock outcrops? Which way did we go to outflank them? Getting stuck would mean a long, maybe impossible walk for us, with no means of escaping from a German armoured car or motor patrol. Out of nowhere a plane dived on us and we hurled ourselves out of the trucks onto the ground. The pilot didn't pull the trigger to strafe us. It was one of ours and we had the red, white and blue roundel painted on our bonnets. Even if he'd just incapacitated the vehicles, we'd have been stranded in the wilderness.

On the morning of the next day I could see something out of the ordinary on a solitary hillock on the skyline. Leaving the water truck behind I drove forward observing through binoculars. It was a truck, with a flag raised. Nearer still and it was a huge Union Jack. There was an officer there waiting to direct the lost. 'Northumberland Fusiliers: Major Hamilton of your lot passed here a couple of hours ago, you'll probably catch him' – and he gave me a compass bearing. So we did, finding Tommy and his driver sitting disconsolately at the side of their pickup truck having a lunch of bully and army biscuits. The NAAFI loot provided them with dessert and my party with both courses. Tommy's adventures had resembled mine, and like me he had got through because he had been going first – it is all or nothing when you are leading: either you get shot and those behind get the chance to flee, or you slip through and those behind are caught. I was full of euphoria at having escaped, but Tommy was haunted by the loss of the entire company, his first command. 'Where do you suppose we'll report?' he asked. 'Sidi Bishr,' I replied, 'it's where we always go after a defeat and where all the girl friends know where to find us.' We hit the coast road and went on to Alexandria. There was traffic both ways, battered, dusty travellers (though by now only a few) going back to what passed for civilisation, smart and grim-looking troops going west towards the last line of defence at Alamein. As we drove through the slums of Alex the hostility of the locals was evident, like an evil miasma in the air. There were some jeers, some thumbs down and something else they had learnt from us, the V sign of contempt, not V for victory but derision with upward jabbing motions. They were looking forward to looting our camps (considering their misery, could one blame them?) and to getting new profits from the advancing Germans. But no one dared to proceed to hostile acts. We were a downcast defeated lot, but armed and easily provoked.

8

Defence and Attack at El Alamein

We were among the last stragglers to return. We had a touching reception; suddenly one realised, if it had not been clear, that the battalion was a proud unity welded together by shared experiences of danger, and as such, it welcomed its own. More than half of us were missing, the worst hit company being ours, X Company, annihilated except for the six of us who had just driven into camp. This is what one would expect to happen to a rearguard in a rout. Battalion HQ was not in a much better state than we were. The War Diary records what had happened to it. On 27 June they were fleeing down the coastal road, having got a great deal further east than I could do later, when a display of green Very lights in the sky showed that the enemy had reached the sea and cut them off. On the 28th they found themselves amid 'a vast concourse of vehicles', and a common decision was taken to try to escape that night, going inland for fifteen miles south then turning east towards Fuka, site of an airfield and supply dumps. But only a mile from the top of the escarpment, they had run into a minefield, with firing coming in from the left, and on the right a deep ravine, impassable to vehicles. In the bright moonlight the convoy was an easy target, so they decided to abandon the trucks and walk out in small parties down the ravine, hoping to be picked up by fleeing British vehicles rather than advancing German ones. Among the few who made it were the commanding officer and the intelligence officer, Tubby Martin and Wilfred Hillman. Missing were the adjutant Hugh Holmes, Lieutenant Quartermaster Bell (who had succeeded Charles Dipper), and Sergeant O'Brien, the orderly room sergeant; as for his truck and the battalion files, they were lost for ever on the edge of the ravine in the desert. Our crack company, Z, had been the luckiest, and was still recognisable. Derek Lloyd, the regular major who commanded it, haggard, long-haired and frail-looking was a hero, winner of the Military Cross with another one to come; he had that indefinable gift of drawing his platoon officers into a band of fighting brothers, the sort of reckless, piratical soldier who wins wars but never rises far within the constraints of peace-time soldiering. Of his platoon commanders, Freddy Ward (Military Cross), the handsomest officer in the battalion, had got back, so too had Bill Sanderson, the youngest.

There was a lot of enquiring about missing friends, but no certain news except for a few undoubted deaths. Jack Watson was missing; what I found out about his probable fate was not reassuring, and I failed to write to Dorothy. In due course she wrote with a hint of justified reproach, and I devised a letter that contained some gleams of optimism. Much later we heard he was a prisoner, and later still that he had escaped from the POW camp in Italy and got to Switzerland. Though everyone was asking about the missing, few of us said a word about our own adventures in the retreat – I didn't even hear Tommy's story, and I certainly did not tell him mine. In my elder son's account of his campaign in the Falklands, we hear of precautions in the Commando mess to stifle the war bores: a sandbag and a hanging lantern, so there would be cries of 'Pull up the sandbag' and 'Set the lantern swinging' when references to the ships, the landings or the battles were made. But they had won against the odds. Not so desperately against the odds, we had lost.

The morning after our arrival, Tommy told me to take two days off before we got down to rebuilding the company. I think he proposed to start this himself right away; soldiers from the Cheshire Regiment had been sent to us, and we were to incorporate them. This included persuading them to change their cap badges (how could one possibly have persuaded Northumberland Fusiliers to do such a thing?). I went off and stayed at the Union Club. Returning, I went to lunch in the mess tent and Tommy joined me, having just had a session with Tubby Martin. 'I'm afraid we have to part, Mac, Tubby wants you to be his adjutant.' A great honour for an amateur in the regular 1st Battalion – but it was a wrench to leave Tommy and the company.

The custom of the battalion was that, provided both parties were willing, an officer took his batman with him when he moved up a peg, and a good batman was a treasure indeed. 'Spuggy' Martin was, I think, happy to move into the prestigious ambience of battalion HQ. True, he no longer had the knockabout confraternity of the fighting company, and he no longer had a chance to give me his blunt advice about where I was going wrong, but he was freer from constraints and in a position to be 'in the know' or, almost as good, to be supposed to be in the know. In Civvy Street he had worked for the biggest Newcastle haulage firm, and was well paid, being a driver and in charge of his unit's operations. Sometimes he would ferry immense loads (once a vast ship's propeller) the length of the country, at others he would be doing a domestic removal job. He had endless stories to tell of adventures on the road, with suspicious policemen checking if the van was overloaded, and suspicious-looking crooks hoping to lighten it. In domestic moves there was an art in rigging a broken article and tricking the owner into being the first to touch it; there was the routine of putting the tea-making things on the van last and thus first to come off: 'Here you are, lady, make yourself your first cuppa in the new place', (understood, 'for us too'). It was a black day, however, when you had to move a parson: always a piano, always a lot of books, and the tip minimal. Given his background of ingenious contrivance, Martin saw to my comfort with his own invented devices. Just as he had set up a water distillery in Tobruk, he now provided me with superior accommodation in the desert. He made two canvas tents, one on each side of the truck, rolled up high on the framework of the cover when moving. When we stopped, down they came – a sloping wall, a straight wall that turned under at the bottom to make a floor, and side flaps keeping out wind and sand and screening off light. After a day on the move, I could lie inside on my camp bed reading by the light of the vehicle's inspection lamp. I had John Donne's poems with me and – I suppose a very young man's choice – *Les Fleurs du Mal*.

Tubby Martin ('Tubby' so called by jocular opposites), slight, wiry, dried-up and wrinkled with not an ounce of weight to spare, was a formidable character, often in a state of suppressed rage and occasionally unsuppressed, and even when in genial mood, frightening. He had a nervous tic which put a tigerish similitude of a smile on his face, and woe betide the simple soul who smiled back. Whether in the field or in barracks he drank a good deal of whisky every night when the day's duties were over, which made his first couple of hours every morning one of his suppressed rage periods, but he would sit in judgement on the erring fusiliers marched before him with scrupulous fairness and, on occasion, with a gruff and almost grudging sympathy. The offender, puzzled by his light sentence, would be marched out, and Tubby would make some aside to me as I stood there alongside the regimental sergeant-major: 'Good man that', or 'We'll make something of him yet', or even, 'Ridiculous charge for the Military Police to bring'. When

Fusilier Gibson was up for stealing a horse-drawn cab (gharry) and driving himself back to the camp at Sidi Bishr, where it was found in the morning at the gates, the contented animal, freed from toil, browsing peaceably, Tubby could scarce contain his mirth. (For ever after in the battalion Gibson was 'Ghary Gibson'.) Non-regular officers would commiserate with me for having to put up with Tubby's bad temper; they were mistaken: it is easy to serve a man who is master of his job, whose demands are ruthless but who genuinely helps you to learn the ropes, and who draws a clear line between military duty and personal relationships. Once, after a day of banging the table and being, in his favourite phrase, 'pig sick' of everything, Tubby took me out to a lavish dinner at a swish hotel in Cairo, urged me to dance with any young women who were presentable, and told anecdotes about his home town in Ireland – and listened to mine about home in England. Then, the following morning, back to his usual bouts of anger. One thing you needed to understand was how to interpret his orders (carrying the can if he decided to note that he had not been obeyed to the letter – as Jack Watson had failed to interpret the scope of his 'hard arse' directive). 'I want you to summon Lieutenant T– and tell him he is not allowed to drink port and lemon in the mess: it's a drink for old tarts.' T– was well off, wore a number of rings on his fingers and we called him not Arthur but 'Arturo', a genial soul who in his way was as much out of place in the Army as I was. Naturally, I didn't summon him or declare him to be in the 'old tarts' league, but just got him to change his tipple without bringing the colonel's name into it.

Tubby – so far as I knew no one ever called him this to his face; I always said 'Colonel' – was a masterly planner and organiser. When a problem arose he had to be brought a clipboard with a pad of clean white paper and three newly sharpened pencils, and he would rapidly sketch out possible solutions. Early on he taught me a crucial point about the art of presenting a case in the military context. I suggested something to him and he immediately said, 'Right, we'll do it.' Then I pointed out some disadvantages and another possibility, not so good, but viable. 'No!' he said. 'You never let me come down in a decision if there are alternatives; I have to know from the start that they exist; you say that first of all.' Another time I wasn't sure he was being reasonable about some point of protocol, but I saw that I'd have to be careful about it. An order came in, I forget what, and as he was not around, I took action and informed all concerned about preparations. Returning, Tubby went straight to the mess tent before looking in at his office, and some brash character corrected him on some detail or other, using my information. When we met shortly afterwards, there was no explosion, but my boss was clearly unhappy. The rule for an adjutant is to ensure his battalion commander's authority, getting things done but taking care not to claim personal credit and making sure that his briefings are always up to date. In our battalion, the regular one, with the key posts of company commander held by regulars and the platoons under amateurs, the adjutant's role as intermediary was crucial. The ruthless hierarchical structure of command must be maintained, but a lot of quiet negotiation was needed, both in transmitting the CO's wishes to the regulars and to bring regulars and non-regulars into reasonably happy relationships, contributing to making the battalion into a harmonious whole.

Along with the regimental sergeant-major, the adjutant has a special responsibility for discipline, and this was not easy for me to handle. It was a question of acting the part. Early in my tenure an incident took place that showed me how to do it. I was in my office consisting of one half of a large marquee, with the second in command, Forbes Watson, in the other, when the phone rang. 'Sir, Sergeant-Major Foreman wants to know if it's OK for the company to go swimming this afternoon.' A surge of rage swept over me, 'Who's that?' I roared. 'Corporal …' whoever it was. 'How dare you ring me, get Sergeant-Major Foreman.' When Foreman, a regular, came to the phone, I pitched into him. Tubby could not have done it better. It had been a try-on, of course, a new non-regular adjutant could be treated cavalierly. Well, no more now. As I slanged the hapless sergeant-major, Forbes put his head round the canvas partition: 'Well done, Mac, you've got the idea now.' This is how the Army worked. The hierarchy was sacrosanct, and everybody had to realise exactly where they stood. That night, I took Betty to an open-air cinema and as we sat there, Sergeant-Major Foreman came in, a girl on his arm. He was wearing his hat and, as it happened, his eye caught mine across the width of the auditorium. His right hand flew up in a tremendous salute. Now I had arrived. The real self, diffident and reflective, had to be disguised. At last I had mastered the script.

There was one other occasion when I blew up in the way real adjutants do. We were leaguered up in the desert – it must have been in our three months at Timimi, refitting and retraining before we were launched into the final assault on the Mareth line on the way to Tunis. An army technical expert entirely new to me turned up, a lieutenant dentist, in a spacious caravan with rows of glittering instruments. We had instructions from Division: every man was to be sent for a dental inspection – there was no question of refinements like fillings, just extractions if necessary. After consulting the dentist about timings, I sent out my orders, and early in the morning when the first company was due to send its first platoon, I turned up in person. A corporal and half a dozen fusiliers were there; they were in and out in a quarter of an hour and the dentist was left with nothing to do for the next two hours. This was par for the course, he told me, nobody valued his services, and he was miserable because he never got a chance to do a proper day's work. Immediately, I instituted a reign of terror, ordering company sergeant-majors to be there on the spot until every man in their company had been seen, and I kept going back – if there was a hold-up I wanted to know why. For the first time, said the dentist, he had been enabled to do his job, and in gratitude he spent his evenings working on my teeth, giving me fillings that excited the admiration of every dentist I saw in Civvy Street for years afterwards. Every time I heard them praise the work of this desert practitioner plying his skills in the intervals of battle, my mind went back to the half-forgotten days when I psyched myself up to be a professional bastard.

There was another role I could play, an odd one for an adjutant perhaps, but a contribution to keeping up morale. Since we had been so far from home for so long, the domestic problems of individual fusiliers could become desperate. The battalion needed a welfare officer. Partly by a sort of pastoral inclination on my part, partly because company commanders realised that their men (especially the non-regular soldiers) would find it easier to confide in someone who was in authority but outside the direct command structure, and partly because there was an obvious advantage in having a single person building up a knowledge of the sources of help and guidance available back in the UK, I found the task falling to me. The drill was to compile a dossier on each case, and send it to that invaluable organisation, the SSAFA, the Soldiers', Sailors' and Airmen's Families Association; its local agents, voluntary workers of every kind, would investigate, and once the true situation was established, the association would join me in doing what seemed necessary – bringing in a particular charity or a church organisation, getting compassionate leave home for the fusilier in trouble (this with precautions against being hoodwinked by a tragedy collusively invented to get the man back – which could happen). Some cases concerned inadequacy or frivolity at home which good advice or a warning could put right: a fusilier is accepting the maximum deduction from his wage to obtain an enhanced allowance for his wife, then finds she cannot handle the money, confusion reigns at home and there are no savings; or, by contrast, the wife lives it up with the proceeds of his thrift, and if he cuts off supply the pair of them lose the subsidy which the government gives to married couples. One or two cases had an aura of comedy, in spite of the worry and exasperation. A big, handsome sergeant receives beautifully phrased letters from his wife – she is in love with someone else, though only platonically so; she had met her idol at an art-appreciation class and now they sit up to all hours reading poetry together, and they want this to continue all their lives. Compassionate leave for the sergeant, and the problem is solved once his virile presence turns up on the doorstep. If a dreamy aesthete turned up next morning at his reserved occupation with a black eye, that did not concern the adjutant of 1RNF. Another dossier revealed the darkest depths of human nature, a distillation of pure evil. A quiet, shy fusilier received letters from a fellow-soldier serving in an anti-aircraft battery back in England near his home – letters describing the hours spent in his wife's bedroom, detailing her doings and the décor of the room, leaving no leeway for doubt and nothing to the imagination. All the SSAFA could do was to make the legal arrangements for a divorce. I wanted to know the address of the tormentor's unit so I could write to his commanding officer, but I was not allowed to know – the SSAFA helped victims, but did not avenge them.

These mature and, one fears, complacent reflections after the event on my work as adjutant do not reflect how I felt on starting: gauche, clueless, groping for guidance and unsure of what tone to adopt in official relations – for example, with the regular officers who commanded the companies. There was no predecessor to consult, Hugh Holmes having vanished in the retreat (later, to the especial delight of his family and fiancée, the news came that he was a prisoner). There were no files to browse in: they were somewhere in the desert. True, there was a survivor from the past, Sergeant-Major Richardson, a former orderly room sergeant. However, he was available only at an Olympian distance, for the devastation of the battalion had left him as the senior warrant officer, entitled to expect to succeed the missing regimental sergeant-major. He insisted on his right, and he filled the key office of RSM with distinction, a fine façade and a brisk effectiveness. He made it clear that he no longer had any connection with the battalion office, but he did drop in occasionally to give his awestruck successor a word of advice and, more rarely, would stalk in to see me, hefty gold-topped stick clamped under his arm, to warn me of impending problems. As it happened, two of these visits came too late, when the damage had been done. One was to say that recommendations for decorations must be submitted with a duplicate recommendation for a mention in despatches if the major one fails. Tubby had given me his citations to have typed and sent off; he didn't say whether I could read them, and when I did so I had a bad conscience – though indeed I needed to check the typing. I knew then why he had made me give a detailed account of Tommy Hamilton's first day in battle (he got the MC) and, alas, I knew afterwards which of us had missed out because of my inexperience. The other visit of RSM Richardson which came too late concerned the promotion of an NCO. A solid regular company sergeant-major, under the influence of drink, yielded to an invitation of an Alexandrian lady of the night and on the VD form had to admit that to the question 'Was a sheath used, Yes, No?' that 'No' was the answer. He was away for treatment and automatically went down to sergeant. The time came when he got his seniority back, but in the confusion of the newly organised orderly room he was overlooked on our lists, and somebody else went up to the CSM rank that ought by rights have been his again. He did not complain, which made me feel still worse about it once RSM Richardson had pointed out the mistake. I hope he did not think of me as the puritanical adjutant who was punishing him further. Luckily, as it happened, he did not have long to wait.

The new battalion office was set up by Sergeant Pilkington; I think he had been the clerk of one of the companies. He was comfortable in build and his round face seemed made for merriment, yet was generally beset by a sort of lugubrious puzzlement. Like me, he had been pitched into a tricky new job. But he worked day and night and kept on going whether jolting on the move or amid the risks of battle, methodically mastering the office drills to cope with all the bureaucratic crises of army life. We also got a new lieutenant quartermaster. The custom of the regiment was that an officer would leave whatever he was doing to come back to the First Battalion when he was needed for a post of his rank, so Norman Rogers left his job in some office concerned with statistics and high-level administration to join us.

It was difficult to see how he had come to join the Army in the ranks, for he was so intelligent, and difficult to see why he stayed in because he had such a poor opinion of the whole system, including regular officers – he was a bolshy intellectual risen from the ranks. But when Tubby sent for him, back he came, leaving a sheltered job which he enjoyed for a dangerous one he disliked, but which he performed with sardonic efficiency. He and RSM Richardson were my chief unofficial advisers. Wilfred Hillman was still intelligence officer and he told me about the codes and ciphers. And Tubby himself gave me a tutorial in the art of framing charges against the delinquents who were paraded before him for summary justice. The charge has to be exactly tailored to the offence, and if carelessly drafted, the case falls. Specimens galore are all there in the book, and I prided myself in getting the exact formulation, and not feebly resorting to the insurance of adding Section 40 of the Army Act, 'conduct prejudicial to good order and discipline'. It was in this tutorial that Tubby passed on the aphorism: 'You can do anything you like provided it could not be brought up as a question in the House of Commons.'

It was a miracle that the battalion rose again from the ashes after the Great Retreat. We had lost so many of the old desert hands and technical experts, and we were saddled with a mass of new fusiliers who had to be taught machine-gun drill. More than this, we had entered into a new phase of warfare in which the dashing, highly mobile groups of machine-gunners were devalued by the exponents of the slogging set-piece battle, whose ideas were more relevant to the desperate defence of the Alamein front. As we had been constituted, we were not immediately very useful: our role would come to us once again when the army was racing forward over open desert. That we were reborn was largely owing to Tubby's genius for organisation and his indefatigable determination. Our heavy training programme notwithstanding, we were continually called on to do mundane guard duties and to dig defensive posts in various areas, generally abandoned before they were finished because of changes in the strategic plan drawn up at GHQ. We sent a company for a while to the Alam el Halfa position where it saw action with the Motor Brigade, though the platoons were used more often as riflemen, rather than machine-gunners. Under the ephemeral 'Delta Force' and, after 3 August, under 50 Division, we laid out and dug defence posts, and sent platoons to do guard duties at Rosetta (to counter raids from the sea), at the main wireless station and at other strategic points which might be targets for parachutists. The War Diary records that the adjutant and the intelligence officer, in the absence of the colonel, went to 12 Division HQ to protest against this proliferation of guard duties. I guess that all we dared to do was to call on the GII or someone about his level, and that we had gone because Tubby in going off to GHQ had ordered us to raise hell if a single extra duty was laid on us.

During this period battalion HQ was stationed for a time in a hutted camp at Amyria, where Tubby worked night and day drawing up a defence fire plan. While I have forgotten so much else, the discomforts of that hutted camp stay with me. There were mosquitoes everywhere. We now had a battalion doctor, Doc Devlin, an Irishman, an irreverent, tiny, cheerful sprite who ignored Army discipline. He asked me one day if I'd like a few days off: 'I've just certified Bill Sanderson as suffering from post-battle nervous tension, and needing a week in Alex; I thought I'd put you next on the list.' I can imagine the explosion if we'd try to sell this proposition to Tubby. There was, in fact, an explosion over the mosquitoes. 'It's the doctor who has to fix this,' roared Tubby after a buzz-filled sleepless night, 'Get hold of him and tell him.' Being Irish and a rebel, Doc Devlin argued that it was up to the battalion to get rid of its mosquitoes, while the doctor's duty was limited to treating the bites. (He had a net.) But I persuaded him that preventive medicine was included in his duties; his orderly was seen going round with two cans of oil to spread on the stagnant water under the huts, and we all slept again.

There were other vexations. After working twelve hours a day driving all over and plotting out areas of fire and fortification on maps, Tubby was abruptly informed by GHQ that there was in existence an old map of defence positions and that we were now to demarcate and dig in accordance with it. It turned out to be ridiculous and we gave up trying. Nevertheless, in spite of the distractions, Tubby managed to retrain and re-equip the battalion. It took a quantity of paper on the clipboard and a number of tense visits to GHQ to get this through. The trouble was that the battalion had developed its peculiar expertise and its entitlement of equipment and trucks during its three years' training in the desert before the war: its mobile role was the working out of an original concept of desert warfare. There was no officially sanctioned list of our entitlement – and properly printed schedules of kit are the Army's laws of the Medes and Persians: they can receive additions, but they cannot be cancelled. On 21 August Tubby came back from Cairo with an agreement to fit out three companies with trucks (hassle because GHQ had tried hard to decrease their number) and one company carrier-borne (something new). On 8 September a staff officer from GHQ visited us, and 'in confidence with the CO and the adjutant' was put in the picture about all our requirements. On the 15th the whole battalion was paraded and the machine-gun companies were reconstituted so far as possible to fit the new establishment. By the end of the month, two companies complete with trucks were available to go forward, a third was designated as a training cadre, and the fourth had begun learning how to handle carriers.

In the midst of all this frantic build-up, we were given an assignment which, if it had been carried out, would have meant the end of the battalion and of all of us. (This is a story that does not figure in the War Diary, and is only discreetly and obliquely referred to in the St George's Gazette.) Tubby was summoned to GHQ, and came back trembling with rage and apprehension. 'I won't do this, Mac, Forbes can take the battalion if he's willing but I simply won't do it' – I really do think that he meant to throw away his career rather than connive at folly. Some clever young staff officers had marked a point on the map where the coast road runs close to the sea half-way between Alex and Tobruk, well beyond Mersa Matruh. They had on their hands a 'Mountain battery' (27 Indian Mountain Battery) of light portable artillery pieces, designed to be carried on the backs of mules, and they proposed to unite it with our machine-guns and a company of infantry and land us astride the coastal road – as Forbes said, 'to knock hell out of the German l of c' (lines of communication). Unlike the staff officers, we had been there. The three or four hundred yards between sea and road was close-packed with sand bumps each about ten feet high; then on the inland side of the road there was flat hard desert for miles. Our little fortress would not hold up any vehicle after the first; we could be bypassed without loss of speed. there would be no chance of our ranging around for targets as we would not have our transport. We would sit there uselessly until the Germans decided to take the trouble to destroy us. The following day, Tubby, grimly calm, went off to see an ex-Northumberland Fusilier high in the councils of the mighty – General de Guingand. It took a few days to get off the hook, but the absurd orders were finally countermanded.

In these feverish weeks before the battle, our horizon of speculation was dominated by General Montgomery: for the first time, 8th Army had a brilliant self-publicist at its head. The officers' mess disliked him, and whatever the fusiliers thought they certainly had the dour northeast hatred of show-offs. To them, Monty's Australian hat and many badges were a pain in the posterior. I was with Tubby at the assembly of officers (lieutenant colonel and above) when Monty told us his battle plan and ordered us to inform all our men. I can't remember more than a phrase or two but he made it clear that the days of 'Jock columns' and hit-and-run raids were over. And that he was not going to use the standard turning movement round the flanks. We would fight a set-piece old-fashioned battle driving through the enemy line at the coast (here, the key unit against us was the Italian 'Young Fascists': 'Soon, they won't be feeling as young as they were before'). In fact, in the actual battle he tried to break through on a wider front and had to add new drives when the original ones were held up. At the time, mere captain though I was, I disliked the plan, since it ignored the fact that for the first time in the Desert War we enjoyed air superiority. Relays of planes from the Egyptian airfields had just smashed Rommel's turning move from the south against our semicircle of dug-in tanks at Alam Halfa – Forbes and I had seen the area afterwards, littered with the tail fins of the bombs and burnt-out vehicles. Had we gone round the south with our massive air cover, the enemy might have been broken more easily than by the 'soldiers' battle' that was launched, with its renewed onslaughts on different axes of attack and its heavy losses.

For the Alamein battle the battalion HQ was by the side of one of the tracks ('Hat', 'Boat', 'Bottle' and the like) marked out to direct the units moving to the front line. Not far from us was a battery of 25-pounders, and right next to us was a squadron of armoured cars, waiting until the enemy line was breached and they could race through to fan out in the rear. Our discipline of dispersion had to be abandoned and our vehicles were crowded in among others – a sign of the end of the danger from the air. The night of the offensive – 23 October – came and we sat there in the darkness and silence looking at our watches as the minutes ticked off towards zero. The order to fire was faintly heard from the nearby battery just as the heavens erupted in thunder and the night was turned to day by gun flashes. It was impossible not to exult, though no one cheered – as we had when we first saw British bombers hitting the enemy positions during the break out from Tobruk. The age of retreat and acceptance of defeat was over. Monty's psychological conditioning had worked. We really believed that the tide had turned.

The Battle of Alamein lasted from the opening barrage of the night of 23 October to 4 November, when Rommel finally gave the order to retreat. During this time, the routine business of the Army, churned out as easily on the battlefield as in barracks, went on. The best example I can remember is the signal giving details about putting boots in for repair on a battalion basis. But there were, of course, many operational signals useful to our companies, such as the location of newly discovered minefields, and these were circulated right away. Now, at last, this was easily done, for we had been given two wireless sets just before the attack went in. They were both mounted on a single large White scout car – a signaller on each set – so messages to battalion HQ could be relayed to the companies without delay. It was a system of only limited use to a unit like ours, since the companies were normally off on independent tasks, and their commanders would have preferred being on the net of the unit they worked with, tanks, armoured cars, infantry, etc. Still, the adjutant could let everyone know quickly how to get boots repaired.

During the battle, Forbes Watson, as a second in command, was a free agent, and when he was not fulfilling a specific role for Tubby, his choice was to go up to the platoons in the firing line, courting danger. Sometimes he would take me along to look after some problem or another. I recollect one occasion when we stood on the safe edge of a curtain of shellfire – a few yards on and you entered a grey haze with only ten or twenty yards visibility ahead, within it shrapnel and debris flying. Forbes told me to stay there and I sat in my truck and watched his little pick-up truck drive into the maelstrom. No doubt when he found the company he would dive into the trench with them, but the thought of his journey there and back made me suppose, for the hour or two he was gone, that I was hardly likely to see him again.

By both comparison and contrast, Tubby was always on the move, though he was going round the company commanders then upwards from them to higher headquarters, Division, anti-tank regiments,

Corps. The days 28, 29, 30 and 31 October in the War Diary are in my handwriting, and I give them here (with the abbreviations for the most part spelt out) as examples of his activities.

25 Oct. CO and Intelligence Officer visit 10 Corps HQ, Hammer Group and 1 Armoured Division.

Z Coy are near Alamein Station.

26 Oct. CO's further visits to these HQs.

Z Coy go to 7 Motor Brigade.

2 I/C (Major Forbes Watson) visits W, X and Z Coys forward on Moon track (where it crosses the 2nd German minefield).

28 Oct. CO, 2 I/C and Adjutant visit the Companies – meet CSM Z Coy looking for their 'B' echelon – also find Sergeant Hall bringing back the missing platoon of W Coy – it goes back to Hammer Group to refit. CO and Adjutant to Tac 10 Armoured Division. (see General Gatehouse) HQ 133 Infantry Brigade (with W under command). CO takes OC Z Coy to General Gatehouse, as Z are sitting alongside a 'Deacon' battery and being shelled to no purpose. Agreed [i.e., agreed that Z Coy can move].

29 Oct. CO sees Brigadier General Staff 10 Corps. (1) NF are Corps Troops. (2) Tac HQ may go under Hammer Force. (3) deal with Corps ref. transport, equipment, personnel.

Z Coy return; system of daily conferences at 0800 at Battalion HQ attended by coy reps, QM, MTO – rations etc. will continue via own formations. The LAD [vehicle repairs] come up to Hammer Force HQ to refit the platoon of W Coy (now back under Lt Ayton's command). Meanwhile there is a general search for X Coy!

30 Oct. Z are to cooperate with Hammer force in a scheme – 8 days rations and petrol for 200 miles. – Meanwhile instructions from CO (from BGS Corps) that Z go under 73 Anti-Tank Regiment. Liaison Officer from 73 Anti-Tank arrives. Adjutant to 10 Corps – GI agrees that nothing be done until situation clarified. 2030 hours Raymond (from Hammer Force) tells us Z are to 73 Anti-Tank after all.

Intelligence Officer, Signals Officer and 2 I/C are searching for X Coy – discovered today with 76 Anti-Tank Regiment (under 11 RHA, 2nd Armoured Brigade, 10 Armoured Division).

(CO has visited 8 Armoured Division – secret – drawing up a table for Medium Machine-guns in a landing.)

31 Oct.   We take 3, 4 Battalion Sergeants onto establishment. X come in, –.to reorganise on a 2 Platoon basis, Selby and cadre of NCOs to be LOB [left out of battle]

8 Armoured Division move back – decided Rear Battalion HQ come forward under Hammer Force. W Coy – news that Lt Cooper and 14 of his men are missing.

CO to 1 Armoured Division – agree ref employment of Z Coy. (1) employ as a company (2) not to go forward until position stabilised (3) work with Anti-Tank Guns.

This account of Tubby's wanderings on the battlefield over four days illustrates the role which can be played by the commanding officer of a peculiar battalion whose companies go off to do individual tasks under varying commands. He had found the stragglers of a platoon that had been overrun, organised them and sent them for a refit; had intervened with a divisional commander to get a company moved from a position of unnecessary danger; located a lost company that had taken a battering and got it pulled out to reorganise; come to an agreement with another divisional commander to ensure that one of our companies attached to his anti-tank regiment would be allowed to operate in its optimum fashion, making use of its mobility, firing at the longer ranges which are the medium machine-gun speciality, not being frittered away as supplementary infantry or extra Bren guns. He had intervened over a confusion in the orders issued to Z company – on the one hand Hammer Force was proposing a long-range raiding mission (8 days' rations, 200 miles petrol) and on the other Corps was sending the company to work with an anti-tank regiment. That was why Tubby sent me to persuade the GI at Corps to suspend everything until the situation was clarified – which it was when the raiding mission was cancelled. On the narrower battalion front, Tubby had fixed up a daily early morning meeting with company representatives over problems of supply and repairs, and, more sweepingly, made a concordat with Corps HQ establishing us as 'Corps troops', and thereby having easier access to transport and equipment, and more likely to be used in the more interesting tactical roles spanning the whole battlefield. This not settled in an office tent with clipboard and pad, but on the battlefield, with a lot of unpleasant stuff flying in the air.

9

On to Tunis

One morning we woke up to find the armoured cars gone, and we packed up to move. For a few days two of our companies, despite fatigue and the disruptive effect of battle upon their organisations, quickly reorganised to play a mobile role in the pursuit of the enemy, but by 10 November, the whole battalion was together again. The War Diary for that day records, 'Orderly room was held again' – a backlog of minor disciplinary offences was cleared off. On 13 November, in the early light of dawn, in line astern we ground our way up the pass at Sollum; two days after, Z Company was detached and went off to join the armoured cars far ahead, maintaining contact with the enemy. Rommel had abandoned his hapless Italian infantry in the centre and south of his line, leaving them stranded without transport, but he had extricated the crucial part of his forces, and in a long, slow movement westwards we followed. We had air superiority, so we moved forward in convoy head to tail, continually starting and stopping and confined to the road by the menace of mines in the verges. The journey was miserable; with mouth, eyes, nose and our clothing full of sand; only tea in quantity could alleviate the lot of the fusiliers on the back of the open gun trucks, and if they started a brew when the convoy halted, sure enough we'd be off again before the water boiled. So with our new signals officer, Ken Rosenvinge, I devised a drill to cope. As adjutant, I was in the leading vehicle of the battalion, and Ken in his jeep came immediately behind me. At each halt he would race ahead along the convoy to find the place of the hold-up, then drive back furiously to give me an estimate of time available. On these forays he was the object of imprecations from senior officers of other units, but he was just the man to brave them – very young, light-hearted and Nordic, with a fiery temper: an accountant, he had become a soldier 'for the duration' and was impatient with the regular Army and all its ways. I had issued each platoon with a green flag on a stick, 'the brew-up flag' and if Ken thought we'd be stationary for at least half an hour, I'd give the signal, the flags would go up along the column and the billy cans would come rattling out.

Another device for well-organised travelling (was it an innovation? we had no idea what regulars did before the war) concerned communications when we went off the road to disperse in the desert for the night. The new wireless communication with the companies was not reliable if a message was urgent, and whatever experts said, I knew that finding one's way around at night was difficult. So we had a signaller from each company armed with a drum of telephone wire travelling in the battalion signals truck, and when we stopped for the night Ken would send them off before it was dark laying a line to their own company headquarters.

10 Corps headquarters and the battalion with it came to a halt in the desert beyond Tobruk at Timimi (not a real place, just a map reference), an area less forbidding than most of the surrounding featureless wilderness, for here was a vast vista of irregular terrain diversified with clumps of dry, grey bushes. This was about 21 November, and at that date Corps put us under the command of 1st Armoured Division. Tubby lost no time in writing to General Briggs, the divisional commander, to inform him that we were desperately in need of training, and the General promised us a month – in fact, we were all at Timimi for three and a half months before the westward drive began again. Given training time, with the famous clipboard pad of paper, Tubby sketched out a ruthless programme. When the work was in full swing, Tubby took me with him on the long run to check on Z Company in the forward area with the armoured cars. We found them at Mersa Brega (El Agheila), the standard cut-off point for desert warfare, between the sea on one hand and dunes and marshes on the other, at the bend of Cyrenaica, barring the way equally to forces coming south down the road from Benghazi and those coming across the desert by the Mechili track. The Germans held this point, and we had deployed against them, one platoon on the beach, one astride the road and one mobile on the flank. Derek Lloyd had experimented by mounting the guns of the flank force on jeeps (then called 'bantams'), intending to rove around shooting up the Germans, and he was full of complaints that the armoured cars banned him from firing in case it interfered with their observation of the enemy. We got back on 4 December, and on the 20th news arrived that Tubby was to leave us to be commandant of the Middle East Staff

College with the rank of brigadier. Two days later, he was gone, and Forbes-Watson took over. I did not see Tubby again until, eight years later, he breezed unannounced into my room in Oxford, where I had two undergraduates for a tutorial. He was just over from Ireland, eyebrows as bushy as ever, facial grimace and brusque bustling manner still the same. 'These young chaps don't mind going off now, plenty of time for them later. Two old veterans going to talk over the Desert War, it was high adventure, high adventure.' They hastened out obediently, reacting instantly to the order, just as I did when he tore up my application to go off from fighting the war to writing the war history.

Forbes was the antithesis of Tubby in appearance, character and style of command. He was hefty, bald-headed, cheerful, cultured and well read, a witty conversationalist whose speciality was puns, a family man, who took no alcohol beyond a modest glass of whisky after dinner. Planning and admin were meat and drink to Tubby: Forbes regarded them as painful necessities, though he could be recklessly inventive in devising new ways to do things. He saw his role as leadership in battle, leading from the front, taking more risks than anyone else. At Alamein, while Tubby was covering the battalion interests by whizzing round headquarters of all kinds, Forbes was in his element going to see the machine-gun sections forward. When he came back to battalion HQ, his batman Fusilier Murray, still with his tin hat firmly clamped on his head, would prepare an evening meal, recounting all the while to Martin the story of all the four-letter hazards which they had so gratuitously incurred. Tubby was desiccated and difficult, but a superbly efficient battalion commander. It was a nerve-wracking pleasure to serve under a man who was totally master of his job. Forbes I served – so far as this is possible in the military context – as a friend, a commanding officer who inspired all who worked under him with affection and that peculiar kind of respect which one accords to extraordinary courage – as Dr Johnson said of Charles XII of Sweden, 'Mankind reverence those who have got over fear, which is so common a weakness.'

Early in Forbes's reign there was a sad incident, a problem he inherited. We had a platoon commander, not long with us, who was dour and difficult, and had fallen out with his company commander. On the morning of 24 December, Forbes told me that he had produced an 'Adverse confidential report: officers' and that 'D' (the officer concerned) had refused to initial it to certify he had seen it. It was the standard, routine procedure, but he would have none of it, even when ordered to do so. There was nothing for it but a court martial, that is, going back to the field court-martial centre at Tobruk. It was obviously unreasonable for the commanding officer to go back there, so I had to order D to sign and when he refused, arrest him and, acting as escort myself, drive off to Tobruk for an instant sitting of the court. So we finally set off across the desert and down the coast road, D and I chatting all the way, but he remaining adamant. We spent a bleak Christmas Eve in sleeping bags under the stars just outside the court martial tent, then early on Christmas morning presenting ourselves before a panel of three lawyers in uniform, one to be the prisoner's advocate. As the sole witness, I told my story.

'How long did you give Lieutenant D to consider his refusal?'

'Well, my colonel said ...'

'Ah, this is hearsay, not admissible as evidence.'

'In that case, I only gave him a couple of minutes.' I forbore to mention the four hours in the truck, since I felt I had talked to D as a friend, not as adjutant. The court imposed a reprimand, and we sped back to Timimi, getting back as darkness fell. An embarrassing return for all concerned, but at least our Christmas dinner had been saved for us and the bustard meat was full of flavour. D left us soon, was severely wounded and won the Military Cross with an infantry unit.

Four days after this grim Christmas, the corps commander visited us. We gave him a march past and did the form square drill so he could address us. He declared we 'had the best arms drill he had seen', and we 'were the steadiest on parade'. In peacetime these sort of affairs are arranged by the adjutant. I cannot remember doing anything at all towards this triumph: it must have been Regimental Sergeant-Major Richardson's doing.

The training schemes initiated by Tubby, with imaginative additions by Forbes, were strictly for warfare indeed, for the coming offensive against Rommel in which we'd be working under 1st Armoured Division. Our role had been established: together with the anti-tank guns we were to throw out protective 'screens', covering the flanks when our tanks attacked, and providing them with secure bases for regrouping and re-supply. Thus, in addition to machine-gun refresher courses and field firing, we had TEWTs and 'mutual admiration' sessions with 76

Anti-Tank Regiment, demonstrating our weapons and explaining our problems of supply and deployment, as well as refining the details of tactical cooperation. Two difficulties were identified. One was defence at night time; by day, we could fill the air with flying lead, but we were vulnerable in darkness to commando-style infantry infiltration. The other concerned reconnaissance: joint recce parties were too unwieldy and slow, and the answer seemed to be that one arm or the other would have to lay down the tasks and dispositions; normally, this would be the anti-tank gunners. A problem remained: with the best will in the world, the two sides could fall out.

Surprisingly, there were cultural additions to this severely practical programme. The Division offered 'a musical divertissement', recorded in the War Diary but not in my memory and, within the battalion, we had three debates, attended by officers and warrant officers; the subjects were 'That this house believes war can be abolished' (lost); '... believes in freedom of the press' (yes); and '... believes peace can only be achieved by force of arms' (yes). I have an idea that I had the good sense to keep quiet, there being a danger of finding oneself typecast as the battalion intellectual – fatal for an adjutant – and that the warrant officers did most of the talking and, in fact, showed sound reasoning and wit.

Division HQ joined in the training occasionally to keep us on our toes. Once it was a sudden order: an officer to report to some map reference deep inland and far away. Naturally Forbes decided to do the task himself, having already surveyed in various points and corrected the existing map for a pastime. He took me along for the ride. After five hours he suddenly said, 'Well, Mac, we are here now, exactly.' There was nothing in sight. We drove on for 200 yards and there, hidden in a deep hollow and undetectable except at close hand, was a divisional signals vehicle with its aerial down. We had a leisurely meal then steamed off triumphantly. Whether anyone else got there and how long it took them I have no idea.

In our earlier days at Timimi, when he was second in command, Forbes went out hunting bustards; they were small, stringy turkeys, running like the wind through the thorn bushes, with the occasional flutter that betrayed their presence. Forbes and his batman driver pursued them in a jeep; as his driver slewed to a stop, Forbes stood up in the vehicle and fired with a sub-machine-gun set at single shot. Rarely did he miss, and he added daily to the row of bustards hanging outside the mess tent, so that in the end there were enough to include all the officers of the battalion in a joint Christmas dinner. The Fusiliers were not too popular at Division HQ: the classic case of the unconventional old desert hands suspect to newcomers, and on one of his shooting forays Forbes was unlucky enough to exemplify our '*je m'en foutisme*' in an encounter with the divisional commander. His jeep skidded to a halt on top of a sandhill amid showers of dust, and he fired like lightning killing his bird, but with the shot flying just over the heads of the general and one of his staff who were poring over a map spread out on the bonnet of their vehicle.

During our long halt at Timimi a padre joined us, Captain S. T. James. We had had two church parades recently, taken by visiting chaplains; now someone in authority had woken up to the fact that we did not have one of our own. James had been forced upon us, Forbes taking the line laid down by Tubby; we worked in separate companies, so we could rarely come together for proper church parades. (The origin of this edict excluding chaplains dates from the siege of Tobruk. When the Australian Division was pulled out, Tubby had insisted that we stay – 'tails up' and all the standard gung-ho jargon. A padre in the garrison, Quinn, went to the highest authority to complain that Tubby was being unfair to his men, who wanted nothing better than to go.) Forbes greeted Padre James noncommittally, then gloomily consigned him to my care – 'He's in your line of country, you deal with him.' But James was so decent, unobtrusive and helpful that Forbes came to like him, calling him 'Sidi James' – this nickname derived from his initials 'ST', that is 'saint', and 'Sidi' is the Arabic for holy man. So, when our padre was wounded by a bomb, Forbes refused all replacements and agitated to get Sidi back as soon as he recovered.

All the while, our battle-hardened Z Company was with the armoured cars on outpost duty at Mersa Brega. Forbes took me up with him when he went to see them. Once there, of course, he spent all his time with the sections on the guns. But the time was past when the enemy might mount a counter-stroke, for Monty had built up his organisation and supplies and brought the Desert Air Force forward. We got back to the battalion at Timimi on 9 February, and at the beginning of March we were off in convoy again going west.

There was skirmishing on the way to Tripoli, the companies working

together with the anti-tank batteries, and Forbes was in his element
now, away from training programmes and administration – instead,
just fraternising with the fusiliers on the guns. Although he relished this
hectic moving around, he also enjoyed quiet reflection in lonely places,
gazing out on unusual landscapes. I remember coming back with him
from one of his forays to the companies when we were struck by a
prospect of the Tripolitanian countryside; the track ran along the edge
of a sown field with the green shoots showing, and behind there was a
grove of palm trees with the white tower of a tiny mosque; on the other
side of the track, the desert. It was an Omar Khayyám prospect, on the
margin 'between the desert and the sown' – the idea came to us simultaneously. So Forbes decided we'd sit for a while to savour it, while our
batmen brought mugs of tea. After a while, this gentle silence was
broken by a single sinister plop, manifestly a mortar bomb landing just
behind the date palms. 'Gosh!' said Forbes, taking a leisurely sip of his
tea, 'that was a narrow squeak.'

The Germans made their stand on the Mareth Line, the old French
defences of concrete pillboxes and minefields. On 18 March Forbes
went to an army commander's conference, and on the 20th called all
officers together to explain the plan of attack Monty had devised: there
was to be a 'left hook' sweeping far to the south before turning into the
rear of the enemy; 1st Armoured Division with ourselves in attendance
was to go with the New Zealanders on this outflanking movement. At
2200 hours on the night of 23 March we moved into position with the
New Zealand column. As we had hastily packed up for the left hook, I
had made an elementary error. I sent a signal to the companies to fill up
with petrol for a long journey, but failed to send a copy to the MT officer at battalion headquarters. Topper Brown, the MTO, another amateur soldier and a master of his job, was someone I saw every day; along
with Ken Rosenvinge, the signals officer, he was my daily contact and
advisor – only, as it happened, we had not run into each other that day.
Topper got us filled up from the divisional baggage train by confronting
a refusal with a demand to have it in writing. An angry major
declaimed about a 'young puppy' 'holding a pistol at my head', but surrendered the petrol all the same. Topper did not blame me, but only
himself for forgetting to fill up as was his normal practice. These are the
sort of friends to have.

Driving round in the left hook – 200 miles altogether – was a hectic, non-stop business, except when the traffic jammed. At one point the whole force had to grind down in single file into a steep-sided depression, then up the other side. At the bottom was the oasis of Bene Ulid; the inhabitants watched us rattling through in astonishment; in the gathering dusk they all seemed to have purple eyes, a result, one imagined, of the inbreeding of centuries. As we came out of the southern desert into the borderland of sparse vegetation, and fanned out to either side, orders came, phrased with an untoward emphasis, that all non-fighting men and vehicles were to be left behind; only a pared down fighting force would move into the attack. So all admin vehicles and the whole battalion HQ stayed put, while Forbes and his batman driver trundled off leading the companies and their gun trucks. On the following evening I was called to the signals scout car. It was Forbes, speaking from I know not what radio link. 'Mac, it's grim up here, I need company, can you get up to join me?' I set off in the darkness with 'Spuggy' Martin at the wheel; there was nothing scientific about our search, no map references, no compass bearings. Indispensable as these are when ranging over the desert, it is something of a myth that they are useful on the set-piece battlefield; you follow the tank and truck tracks in approximately the right direction and in due course ask somebody.

At first light we reached a line of tanks, well spaced out, facing north. There was desultory shelling, but it seemed directed to harassing targets already behind us. It was clearly the front line, and the tanks were closed down waiting for the order to go. A sergeant opened his lid and told me that I was roughly on the central axis of the advance. Obviously, Forbes would be off to one side or the other and not too far back. I made the correct guess, went off to the left and found him about half a mile back from the front, in the midst of a vast flat landscape diversified by the odd shell falling purposelessly. He and his driver (Martin's old friend Murray)were huddling in blankets, keeping warm, before they set out on their usual journey round the companies and platoons. There were still plenty of tins of delicacies on my truck, loot from the NAAFI at Matruh, and Martin thought the occasion called for a prestigious breakfast. From my truck two deck chairs and the folding table were produced, a white cloth was laid, three tins were opened, and soon Forbes and I were enjoying bacon, tomatoes and sausages. We were gentlemen at leisure, comfortable in our suede desert boots, long trousers and open-necked shirts; no hats (let along tin ones), no

'Spuggy' Martin preparing breakfast

weapons or binoculars (gun belts, pistols and binoculars reposed in the 'glove boxes' of our vehicles); we were eating off plates, admittedly tin but decorated with coloured patterns, and drinking tea from real china mugs. Then a jeep raced up and slewed to a halt. Out leapt the divisional commander and his ADC, tin-hatted, armed, map cases and binoculars slung about their persons. A difficult moment. Without a hat Forbes could not salute, but he hastened over and gave a similitude of heel clicking to attention so far as suede boots allowed. I didn't hear what was said. The general drove off in a cloud of dust. Forbes, like Drake on the Plymouth bowling green, insisted on remaining unruffled, finished breakfast, chatted for a quarter of an hour, then set off to inspect our companies in the anti-tank screen. Like the bustard-shooting adventure, this was a further nail in the coffin of Forbes's claim to the decoration he ought to have had ten times over. Nobody in high authority was ever there to see him risking his life in the thunder of every action any unit of the battalion got into, but he was inevitably caught with his adjutant and a forbidden non-fighting vehicle enjoying a nonchalant and civilised breakfast.

Thanks partly to the joint training at Timimi, the screens of machine-guns and anti-tank guns were remarkably effective in the battle to break through the flank protection the Germans put out to cover the Mareth position. A copybook case was on 27 March, the second day of our attack. At dawn, an enemy tank squadron attacked the rear of our column. The carriers of our Y Company and a battery of Deacons went back to counter it, the Deacons blasting at the tanks and the machine-guns cutting down the crews of the big 88 mm guns coming up behind – they were there to knock out our armour once it had been lured into a confrontation, a sort of mobile ambush driving towards us. This time, however, the ambush came from our side, Jimmy Heygate's machine-gun platoon doing the execution. Three days later, Forbes, wandering the front line as was his wont, spotted one of these 88 mms in its ambush position, and not having one of his machine-gun platoons available got onto someone's wireless link to give the divisional artillery the precise map reference, with deadly results. After these exploits, Y came back to base, and Tufton Beamish, MC, a hero of the early fighting of the war in France, and having had astonishing adventures in the Far East, arrived to take command of the company (Reggie Kent had been tragically killed in the minefields.) Two days later, on 4 April, Y

Company and battalion HQ had a joint Sunday service taken by our
padre. But the following Sunday, headquarters was attacked by a plane
showering anti-personnel bombs. Sidi James was severely wounded and
his truck, carrying the red and white paper roses for St George's Day,
was destroyed. Even amid the chaos of battle, desperate measures were
taken to deal with the roses crisis. A signal went back to the Delta com-
missioning the urgent manufacture and purchase of more, and Forbes
took on himself quasi-canonical authority to adjust the ecclesiastical
calendar, decreeing that we would observe St George's Day three weeks
later than the official 23 April.

Now we broke through into Tunisia, green hills and valleys and
enclosed country, with farmhouses, olive groves, fields and hedges.
Some of the European farmers had fled, and their houses had suffered
damage and break-ins (the usual draconian orders came round about
the death penalty for looting). Those who stayed did not welcome us as
we drove our trucks onto their holdings and dispersed under camouflage. I asked a middle-aged French lady how she had found the Germans – '*très correct*'. I suppose this was meant to stimulate us to rival
them in correctness. I got the impression they didn't care who won the
war so long as the troops kept out of their orchards and farmyards.
'Tuf' Beamish, however, made quite a difference. He gave little parties
for the locals, 'carrier picnics', and battalion HQ emulated him by
inviting the most important local landowner to lunch in the mess tent.

On 12 April the War Diary records that the CO and Adjutant went
to visit Z Company 'about 15 miles from Sfax, resting on their laurels
and sending expeditions into Sfax for kegs of fish and red wine'. On our
return we found the second in command, Major Kingsley Foster (who
had come up to join us once Tubby left), had been to a divisional commander's conference and received the news that we were to be sent off
on a minor left hook, to join 1st Army and the US II Corps, who were
due to start their drive on Tunis from the west on 22 April. Our orders
included a change in our appearance and life-style as we moved round
to the new front. We were to be smartly shaved, wear our tin hats, sit
upright in the trucks, in short, try to look like British troops fresh from
the UK, thus concealing from the enemy that the desert forces were
operating on a new axis. The quartermaster had been issued a lot of
black and green paint to change the colour of the trucks; the paint soon
ran short, and most of our vehicles were left piebald, half north

European and half desert camouflage. The first little place we drove through was decorated with rudimentary banners strung across the street by the locals: 'Welcum too 8 Army'.

I cannot remember what the companies did in our 1st Army phase of the war, and the Diary does not help. But I have a clear picture of our first meeting with the Americans, and finding them very civilised and not in the least brash and boastful as legend then had it. They insisted on telling us that they were new to warfare and had a lot to learn, and they pressed on our fusiliers shares in their splendid rations and their first-rate cigarettes (our cigarettes, with a galleon in full sail on the cheap blue packet were filthy, the sweepings of floors in the Egyptian factory that made them). We too had some learning to do, now we were in close country where the arts of desert warfare no longer applied. Safety, for us, had lain in dispersal. But on 25 April, with battalion HQ well spread out in a vast, flower-studded meadow near a lake, we were mercilessly shelled. (Bombers swoop over once, the gunners can keep going.) The orderly room clerk and a signaller were badly wounded, the orderly room truck had its radiator perforated, and a fusilier had the greatcoat he was wearing ruined by two huge shrapnel slashes. We moved hastily down to the lakeside to hide under thick vegetation in the beds of tributary streams. Later, on 2 May, dispersion was to blame when a German patrol infiltrated, took an anti-tank officer prisoner and shot three of our men in their beds. From now on, we close-leaguered at night, battalion HQ and the HQ of 76 Anti-Tank Regiment joining to make a little fortress. And as we ended our successful liaison with the anti-tank batteries I was conscious of the latent tensions that underlay our friendship. Forbes now was doing what was unnecessary, and something no other commander would do, he was going round in the night to see that the companies were safe. Not surprisingly, one night even he got lost and he wirelessed to me to put up a burst of tracer on the anti-aircraft Bren to give him a bearing. I did this, to the rage of the HQ of 76 Anti-Tank, leaguered up near us. The darkness was full of imprecations and cries that I was bringing down the enemy upon us. At the end of April, signals came awarding decorations: a bar to Derek Lloyd's MC and an MC for one of his officers, and the DSO to the colonel of the Anti-Tanks. There was nothing for Forbes.

At the end of the North African campaign, the battalion was together again as a unit, united in a fellowship of achievement and survival: the collective mental state was one of mingled weariness and euphoria. I recollect a few fragments of personal experience. One was a minor mystery to me. A lieutenant belonging to a great aristocratic family joined us at the end of May, fresh from the Staff College. Someone had spotted his talents for staff work before he had served in a fighting unit. A few days later he had gone. Some of the younger officers told me that he had declared to them he had been sent to take over as adjutant. Forbes said nothing to me and I did not ask. I remember going to Tunis and spending a night in the shabby splendours of the Del Mahares Hotel with its 'fornication bathrooms' (one between each two bedrooms with bolts on both sides of the two doors, one to keep your neighbour out of the bathroom and one to bar his way to your bedroom – with sinful variants). I went to look for the ruins of ancient Carthage and saw only what appeared to be the remains of a sewer conduit in the cliff face, quite probably Roman, but still no fun – those in the forward units of armies rarely get the opportunity to find themselves guidebooks to double war with tourism. The Cape Bon peninsula was littered with enemy tanks and vehicles, seemingly in pristine condition, and as I stood there one day I saw the sky black with relays of bombers – going where? There was a quiet feeling of satisfaction at seeing this lethal armada roaring off seawards; for so long in Tobruk we had suffered under the German monopoly of the air that we never got over the elation of seeing the tables turned. What I had been watching was the vast concerted raid on the little fortress island of Pantelleria, which brought its surrender within hours.

10

Tripoli, Damascus, Jerusalem

With Tunis captured and the next campaign still in the planning stage, 1st Armoured Division (and 1 RNF with it) was sent back to await orders at Tripoli. We expected we would go by sea to our next destination, and Tripoli was as good a place to embark as any. The battalion set off eastwards on 21 May and we arrived at our staging area at Suani Ben Adam, sixteen miles south of the town. It was an agreeable spot so far as scenery went, a vista of vines and olive groves. We had six boring weeks here; the weather was very hot, sometimes reaching 130F, and there was nothing to do, apart from perfunctory training, but to try to keep fit and to sleep as much as possible. Visiting Tripoli was not worth while – nowhere to eat well or to stay with comfort, and the souvenirs on sale were junk, though perhaps one ought to have acquired one of the scarves specially made for the Germans to buy, adorned with the swastika, but now made viable to our susceptibilities by the addition of a boot giving the Nazi symbol a kick.

There was one great day, doubly great for an adjutant, during our sojourn at Suani Ben Adam, the King's visit to Tripoli to pay tribute to his soldiers who had evicted Rommel from Africa. This was on 25 June 1943, with the whole 1st Armoured Division lining one side of the Suani–Aziza road while King George VI was driven slowly along, stopping to talk to each commanding officer. A disgruntled letter writer in the *Daily Telegraph* some years ago described how 'battle weary troops ordered to line the route for hours in the hot African sun' ignored the order to cheer and greeted the royal car 'with a deafening silence'. This may have been so with other units for all I know; if so, it just shows the superiority of the organisation of 1 RNF. The news of the royal visit reached us with a lot of bumph about timings, which Forbes dismissed with scepticism. We did our own thing. The day before I was at a meeting allocating the various stretches of road and, having noted our sector, I was on location long before dawn the next morning with the RSM and a task force. We pegged in the sand three parallel rows of string with knots at precise intervals, exactly calculated so that each man stood on his knot. Behind, among the palm trees, we marked out company rest areas, with tea-brewing stations and latrine points. Like every other unit we had to march into position hours beforehand, but once every man had been stationed on his knot, we fell out in the shade. A cloud of fragrant tobacco smoke floated agreeably among the palm fronds. We heard noise drawing nearer – at least some people were cheering – then Ken Rosenvinge who had been lurking in his jeep on a track parallel to the road, swept up: estimated time of arrival, fifteen minutes. Forbes waited judiciously, then nodded to the RSM. Without even a shouted order, the fusiliers glided into position like ghosts. I suppose we stood a whole ten minutes in that 'hot African sun'.

My recollection is precise, and I recount it here. It does not fit in with the War Diary, which puts Monty's visit to the battalion *before* the King's visit. But the Diary was often written up long afterwards, and in this case almost certainly after the return to the Delta and, I imagine, by someone who had not been present at the parade of 25 June. The *St George's Gazette*, of course, followed the Diary.

Forbes had read and mastered the 'state of the battalion' file the day before, so he knew exactly how many men we had, how many sick, how many on courses, all about our casualties, all about the decorations we had won. The King arrived with General Montgomery and the commander of 1st Armoured by him in the open car. George VI looked drawn and miserable; there was a hectic touch of sunburn against the grey pallor and one could deduce a touch of 'Gippy tummy'. Forbes gave immediate, accurate and rather amusingly turned replies to the hesitant royal questions. Finally, 'How long have you been abroad, Colonel?' the King stammered.

'Twelve years, sir,' said Forbes – an unprecedentedly long time.

The King turned to Monty. 'That seems too long,' he said.

'They were in India before the war, sir,' said the general.

'No, sir,' said Forbes, 'in Jamaica.'

It is not given to every lieutenant colonel to contradict his army commander to the King. Monty's lean, austere countenance was a mask of stifled rage: he looked like a Red Indian setting off on a scalping expedition. 'Total disaster,' muttered Forbes out of the side of his mouth as the royal cortège drove off, yet he retained sufficient presence of mind to lead us off through the sandhills and patches of weedy cultivation on a track he had reconnoitred the day before, getting us back to camp while most of the units on parade were stranded there for ages. 'Battalion on full alert, Mac,' he said in the mess that night, 'the sword of Damocles is hanging over us.'

So it was. I got a phone call from Monty's ADC the next morning: the general would visit the battalion 'informally' some time in the next few days, 'work to go on as usual, no preparations'. Forbes's interpretation of work as usual was brilliantly conceived. The battalion was organised into maximum, manifest and demonstrable efficiency, and kept there as long as it took. The hand-picked guard at the entrance stayed put, doing nothing but practising the 'present arms' at steady intervals. (Someone in the mess had said it was a pity we couldn't muster 'a fanfare of trumpets' to usher Monty in, but, given our commander's puritanical attitude to life, Forbes thought 'a funfair of strumpets' would never do.) An impressively medalled sergeant waited to direct the official car to the mess, where the CO and a little group of officers (all, as it happened, with the Military Cross) were waiting, fortified by an array of bottles of soft drinks, with no sign of the hard stuff. The general's car would pass a group of men being taught to strip the lock of a machine-gun – they all could do it blindfold already. Smart orderlies were walking from one company office tent to another across the official path, carrying a specially selected file and ready to give long-range salutes. For a whole day they walked, the lock was taken to bits and reassembled, the officers gloomily eyed the lemonade, the squad at the entrance perfected the 'present arms'.

The next day, the grand inquisitor arrived. All went like clockwork. I saluted Monty outside the mess tent, the RSM by me, conscious that we had put up an invulnerable show. Forbes emerged nonchalantly from the mess tent – after all, he had been caught by surprise relaxing with a few of his officers. A glimpse through the flap of the tent showed the blue and white ribbons on their shirts as they followed. Monty snapped out a few questions, then declared he must go. 'Won't you come and have a drink, sir?' asked Forbes, hastily adding 'a soft drink, of course'. 'Certainly not,' said Monty as he got into the car and banged the door, 'drive on, driver!' The clutch was let in with a jerk, and the back wheels sank deep into the sand. I hissed to the RSM to get shovels and sand channels. Scuttling orderlies did their blue-arsed fly impersonations. Shovels and sand channels could not be found. The officers emerged from the mess and pushed and sweated, and finally Monty lurched off in a cloud of sand. 'You win some and lose some,' said Forbes philosophically as the mess corporal changed around the bottles on display in the mess.

After Monty's visitation, we moved from Suani Ben Adam to a more agreeable spot by the sea, near to the Roman ruins of Leptis Magna with its romantic amphitheatre, where the blue waters formed a vast tranquil backdrop to the half-ruined arches. The mess tent was set up on smooth green turf running to the beach on one side and to the sandhills inland on the other. There was one absorbing topic of conversation: where next? The forces massed from east and west along the North African coast must be used to strike somewhere: Sicily, Sardinia, the Italian mainland or even Corsica or Greece were talked of. What part would we play? After all, our regimental motto was *Quo fata vocant*. Shortly after setting up camp near Leptis Magna, Forbes came back from Division: we were not scheduled to take part in the invasion, wherever it would be, but we were to go back to Egypt. He announced the news in the mess that night with a despondent air – 'The men will be disappointed. Just when they had their tails up and were raring to go.' Before turning in that night, Forbes and I took a stroll outside by the dark waters, with the sound of the rhythmic lapping of the waves. I plucked up courage to tell him I was glad we were out of the next battle, and that I was sure that the rest of the amateur soldiers in the battalion were of the same mind. He was surprised, but sympathetic, and assured me he was sincere; he had become a professional soldier knowing his duty was to fight when his country required it, and he was proud to do it; he was doing his duty and fulfilling his ambition. It was the simplest of statements. It explained his courage: he was not insensitively brave by nature, but steeled by pride and duty.

Our move back to the Delta was to be by sea, on two ships sailing from Tripoli on 25 and 26 July, to dock at Alex at the end of the month. An advance party was to go by road, and Forbes decided to go himself, taking with him Ken Rosenvinge the signals officer and me, each of us with our own vehicle and driver. On 20 July, the day before we set off, I was conspiratorially approached by Corporal Whelan, the mechanic in charge of the transport of Headquarters Company. He had been a regular soldier since his youth; the son of a clergyman, well educated, but without ambition, wanting to be anonymous in the ranks, not seeking promotion. He was a genius as a mechanic, and at the moment had three Italian vehicles annexed to his stud, including a tractor about ten feet high, with huge rear wheels, which could haul a Herculean load and pull a stranded vehicle out of the most voracious of quicksands. Whelan's problem was that in the years before the war he had gone into partnership with an Arab to establish a photographic business in Cairo (needless to say, he was a technical expert with cameras); but orders from on high had reached the battalion saying he was to be sent back to England immediately. His old father, from the depths of his rural vicarage, had summoned up the resolution to ask the War Office why his son had been such a prodigious length of time abroad without being sent home on leave. (The answer, at least in part, was probably because the eccentric corporal had chosen to linger in exotic surroundings). Anyway, now he was off. If he could get onto our advance party, there would be a few spare days before the battalion caught up with us, and he'd manage to get up to Cairo, wind up his affairs with his partner, and go home with a full wallet. Could I fix this without betraying his secret to the CO? In fact I did betray the secret and Forbes laughingly agreed. Early on the morning of 21 July, after saying sad goodbyes to his illegal fleet of vehicles, Whelan appeared to join our party, being helped along by friends with a formidable load of baggage packed in strangely adapted containers. As it turned out, it was fortunate we took him.

We drove at as high a speed as was safe, all day and most of the night, along the narrow strip of road, keeping off the irregular edges where land mines might have been laid in the fissures. We were making good time, when we ran into an obstacle. In rocky terrain without possibility of detour, the road was destroyed, whether by demolition or a landslide. On the left were boulders, on the right a jagged hillside cleft by wadis. The road had collapsed at the point where it ran across one of these wadis, and now the rains had come and there was a torrent of water surging down. The only way to get the vehicles over was to roll stones to make a bridge – even if the water stopped flowing, a causeway would still be needed. The bridge would also form a dam, so it had to be contrived to let the water through as well as support the trucks. This engineering problem was the subject of extended discussion. The batman drivers fatalistically brewed up tea; what were officers for if they did not settle these questions? Corporal Whelan brooded aloof; his sophisticated expertise would be profaned by being turned to rough and ready improvisations. The officers deliberated, and two plans emerged, the McManners work of art and the Rosenvinge direct slog: Forbes looked at the map, and seeing this was 'the Wadi Cam', he ruled that as I was an Oxford man the task must be given to Ken – whose plan was, in fact, the realistic one.

Not long after we had hazardously negotiated this obstacle, Forbes's truck broke down. By protocol, the driver had the right and duty of fixing it, though Whelan obviously had the role of senior consultant. The officers sat in a group drinking the inevitable mugs of tea; the batmen drivers and the corporal sat around the stricken vehicle, all drinking tea except the wretched man who was doing the repair while his allotted mug of tea went cold. I went over to check. Whelan took me aside. He alone could fix it, but a new part would have to be made, and to make it he would have to use precision tools he had collected from the enemy over the years of desert warfare, tools he was not entitled to keep. Could I persuade the colonel to walk away somewhere for an hour? I suggested to Forbes that for reasons best left unexplained, he and I might take a walk to the highest point on the hillside and look across at whatever there was to see; this is probably what he would have done anyway, as he was a connoisseur of desert scenery, savouring the quirks and beauties of savage, barren landscapes. Over the crest was worth seeing: we could have landed on the moon. When we came down, I went ahead to check on progress, arriving just in time to see Whelan's tools as he repacked them into various holdalls and display cases – drills, delicate tweezers, jeweller's eye-pieces, calipers, and gleaming chromium instruments that a surgeon would have coveted. I hope he got all this paraphernalia onto the plane for England, as well as his wad of currency from the Cairo business. What happened to him after his leave at the vicarage was over? He could never have found such an interesting niche in the battlefields as he had in the Desert War; had his old father got him home, perhaps, just in time to die in the D-Day landings?

Once the battalion was back in its old haunt at Sidi Bishr, Forbes was given leave to go and see his wife and small children in South Africa, and the second in command took over. This was Kingsley Foster, a big, heavy jovial figure who, with the rank of colonel, had been in a comfortable staff job in Cairo. But when the 1st Battalion called, he came back at once, coming down to the rank of major. He had enjoyed a life of ease away from the battlefields, but from the moment he joined us in Tunisia, like Tommy Hamilton coming back from the Staff College, he had acted like a seasoned campaigner, indifferent to hardship, imperturbable under fire. He knew administration inside out and was helpful and approachable, a boon for an adjutant who still had a lot to learn. He relished signing the comic letters I sometimes wrote to Area HQ on trivia of bureaucratic business: 'Kingsley loves an office joke,' said QM Norman Rogers. Tubby Martin would not have been amused, Forbes would have laughed but not sent them.

No sooner had Forbes departed, than disaster struck one of the platoon commanders of our heroic Z Company (Derek Lloyd's). The officer in question, Donald, was sent to collect the company pay in Alexandria, and lost half of it. He had the cash in two bags down at his feet in the front of the truck, when an Arab youth shouted at him, pointing to his front tyre. Like a fool he got out to look and an accomplice snatched one of the bags. He collared the first boy, but the one with the cash had vanished. The news of the theft got back to Sidi Bishr and at once Kingsley Foster came into my office. 'Mac, have you a girl friend in Alex? OK, ring her now and take her to lunch. I don't want you back until late tonight. I don't think you ought to be concerned with this.' While I was away, Kingsley got in touch with an old ally, the Egyptian chief of police in Alex, who ensured that the youth talked. Having found out where the boy came from, the next step was to muster a group of NCOs, all hardened regulars, and send them down in a three-tonner, armed with pick helves. They smashed up the street and recovered half the money, mostly hidden in mattresses. But a substantial sum was still missing, so Donald had to be court-martialled. Before the trial came up, the battalion was ordered to move to Palestine. Derek Lloyd, as company commander, obviously had the duty to stay in Alex to help his officer, and Kingsley left me there too, seeing that a few weeks before the theft I had circulated a warning from Area HQ to the effect that officers collecting cash from the Field Service Paymaster had to travel with an armed escort. We would not subvert the legal branch by taking my evidence out of their reach, but on the other hand none of us said a word about it: only if they asked specifically for my testimony would they get it. This was fair enough, but it was not obvious why Freddy Ward and Bill Sanderson, the other platoon commanders of Z

Company, had to stay in Alex, unless it was out of consideration for their girl friends. On Kingsley's advice, Donald hired an Egyptian barrister, who appeared in court in wig and gown with labyrinthine eloquence. The prosecution called only the obvious factual evidence, and I made myself scarce for two days before the trial so that they'd find it hard to run me down at the last minute. Donald got off lightly.

Derek Lloyd, of course, decided that there was no need to rush off to the battalion; if there had been a battle in progress, he'd have been back like a shot. So we had an idyllic extra week in Alex. I lived in the Union Club, read in the library all morning, ringing the bell half-way to get coffee and éclairs brought in – among other things, I read and re-read all the works of P. G. Wodehouse. In the afternoons, tennis at the French *lycée*, and sometimes at night take Betty to dinner. I had an ally in Area HQ, and I'd call on him on alternate days, 'just in passing', to see if trouble was brewing for us. The blow fell. 'Mac,' he said one day, 'your colonel has sent a signal to the Brigadier asking why five of his officers are being detained so long.' I went off to look for the others; they were still in bed in their hotel and I had to wake them. Alarm and confusion! While they got organised I went off to find our truck and driver and gave him a rendezvous on the Corniche for two o'clock that afternoon. We drove on all through the night; Derek was in the front with his driver and the rest of us piled in the back, getting covered in sand as we raced along the narrow road across the Sinai desert. 'A long trial, then,' said Kingsley as he joined me in the office. 'Not so much that, Colonel, as a succession of delays.'

From Palestine we moved on 18 September to a hutted camp at Qatana, not far from Damascus; apparently we were to be available if needed against a Vichy French military insurrection. Qatana was a dire posting, set in rolling hills of lush green grass with never a tree in sight, too far from Damascus to get there except exceptionally, and near nothing else at all. Damascus, largely unspoilt at that time, was an enjoyable day for a tourist itinerary – a couple of mosques and the niche on the wall where St Paul was let down in a basket – but it offered none of the pleasures unfurled before battle-hardened soldiers in sinful Alex. I went there once with Wilfred Hillman and we had a strange, agreeable experience. In a quiet street lined with white, windowless houses, we were called softly, almost in a whisper, to enter through a heavy, richly carved door, and found ourselves in a courtyard with a fountain playing. We were invited to sit on piles of white cushions in a colonnaded arcade, and take cooling drinks. There were a mother and father and two charming daughters, Christian Arabs, rich but lonely among their Moslem neighbours, and they wanted to talk to fellow Christians (it was in French), even just for a few moments. They did not say so, but it seemed as if they had chosen an opportunity to ask us in when there was no one else in the street, and that they seemed careful to let us out in the same cautious fashion. Another day, I went with Forbes. As we drove over the hills above the town, we saw clear and brilliantly sparkling streams rushing over the rocks. '"Are not Abana and Pharphar, the rivers of Damascus, better than all the waters of Israel?"' he said, stealing my biblical line.

A Damascus cameo stays in the mind. The big hall of the Orient Palace Hotel, the largest in the city; under its Arabian Nights-style arches an unenthusiastic dance band is playing. Here and there are a few people seated at little tables, and at three pushed together, six young officers entertaining a single girl, Anne-Marie, one of Mrs Barker's concert party, so nice and diffident that everyone loved her, more especially Topper Brown, our MTO. She had been sent to visit a relative and was surprised to find the Fusiliers here. The band strikes up 'Deep in the Heart of Texas', one of the concert party numbers. We all clap hands in time, as the song demands, and led by Anne-Marie we form file, holding each other from behind by the waist, and sway and circle round the empty dance floor. An older woman accompanied by a gigolo with oiled curly hair looks envious of youth. Two Levantine businessmen look on with uncomprehending contempt. We will fight our war and go, their property deal will stay.

There was a vast amount of office work to handle in this Damascus period, and a good deal of quasi-official social liaison bringing people to agreement; the details are forgotten. But for the first time I understood what army life is like in peace time, and I could see the force of the jest (by Andrew Bonham-Carter?), 'I wish this damned war was over so we could get down to some proper soldiering again.' There were a few agreeable days off, and these remain in the memory.

Once, it was a trip to Baalbek to see the ruins dating from the late Roman Empire. I went with Henry, the commander of our HQ company. We had our photographs taken by an Arab under the famous frieze and the lion's head – that is how I know my companion was

Henry on this trip, for his likeness is alongside mine in the picture, large, jovial, gap-toothed, a most efficient man and with that indefinable aura of efficiency around him. Then, there was a weekend in Beirut, dropped there at the Normandie hotel on the Saturday and picked up on the Sunday morning. Kingsley told me to be sure to be in the bar at midnight, and to dine at the Lucullus, 'avoiding the fish but looking behind the fish tank'. In the lounge before dinner I met a major who had some sedentary local job. Had I seen Beirut from the top of the hills looking down on it? he asked. Well, had I noticed how red the sand was. 'The city', he said, 'is like a harlot on her pillow, her long red hair spread about her, a city to which you always return.' At the Lucullus, one wall consisted of a glass-fronted fish tank: you chose your fish and from behind and above a hairy arm appeared wielding a seaside shrimp net, and the fish was whipped out. It certainly put you off the fish course. As instructed, I slipped round behind and saw there was another tank; no doubt the captured fish went there and lived to fight again; it certainly wasn't the one that appeared on your plate, even if you hadn't by now decided you preferred the meat course after all. It was hard to last out to midnight, so I read a book in the lounge and pushed into the crowded bar about 11.45. As midnight struck on the clock behind, there were cries for action, and the barmaid was hoisted up onto the counter by many willing hands, where she stood majestically displaying a vast amount behind and before as she sang '*Auprès de ma blonde*'... '*Les tours de Notre-Dame, les tours de mon pays*' – we had her word for it that she was a true Parisienne.

Forbes insisted that I go off to see the Krak des Chevaliers – it was his duty to ensure that a historian, passing this way, had an opportunity to go there. So he invented an excuse for me to get there – take a jeep with batman driver and orderly and go to the School of Mountain Warfare at Amyoun to inquire about the feasibility of producing a harness to carry a machine-gun tripod, leaving the hands free. This mission was performed – as it happened, usefully. I stayed overnight at the mess of the school, then set off to the real destination. Taking a cup of coffee at Tripoli, which at that time was focused round a cobbled square shaded by ancient gnarled trees, I met an old Teddy Hall man who constituted the local British presence. He was in civilian dress, and knowledgeable about all the affairs of the area. It seemed a pleasant job to have, though perhaps not. The Krak was visible from afar as we drove eastwards on an empty road through barren country. The track off to it was rudimentary, and half-way up the climb it seemed unreasonable to drive the jeep further. We brewed up and I walked around while Martin and his fellow fusilier were left to agree on what to do: one would have to stay with the vehicle, the other could come with me. They argued, and it took me a while to see what the problem was. Neither wanted to do the climb, both wanted to stay. The vast bleak fortress loomed above us, a reproach to their indifference to antiquity. I went up alone. The castle is not at the summit, but on a knife-edged ridge going out sideways, with a sheer drop on three sides; there was a single doorway pierced in the huge smooth wall on the accessible face, and the massive door was locked. As I despaired of getting in, an Arab materialised, near to me before I noticed him; he must have been reposing in the shade of the rocks. He bore a huge key. It was only then that I realised that I had left my belt and pistol as usual in the glove box of the jeep. I need not have worried. I gave him a good tip and was allowed to wander inside at will. The fortress was as its crusading builders created it, no subsequent changes for more comfortable living, no ornamentation, loopholes but no windows, no balustrades for the stairs – a place with vast storage areas for food and water, and everything else a platform to fight from. T. E. Lawrence had signed the visitors' book, and I signed too. I think of the krak and Lawrence's researches on the crusading castles of the Middle East every time I look at his portrait by Augustus John in our common room at All Souls.

Early in October we got orders to move south again, to Palestine, then after that to the Delta once more. Forbes and I in our respective vehicles went on in advance. As we got near to Jerusalem, evil weather set in, cold with wind and driving rain. My truck broke down and Forbes said he would press ahead beyond the city to find some quiet place to camp in – he loved to get away from streets and habitations and urban clutter, to sleep in lonely places and watch the sun rise as he had breakfast. I would have to decide whether to follow him or, if it got dark before we were repaired, to slip in somewhere else for the night. It took Martin some time to get us going, it was getting dark, and I saw an Army signpost to the something or other base hospital. It struck a chord. 'Turn off,' I told Martin, 'I foresee a good dinner with Jake.' Jack Shannon, 'Jake', Father's old curate, was now an Army chaplain. I remembered that in one of the letters from home I had been told that

'Jake was a chaplain in the big hospital in Jerusalem', so off we went there through the rain. What a time we had: Martin absorbed into the confraternity of nurses, male and female, while I was in the officers' mess – hot bath, superb dinner (the medical experts did themselves proud), agreeable conversation, news from home, and sitting up late by a roaring fire. We had to set off again early in the morning, but not without being fortified by eggs and bacon, and we caught up with Forbes and Murray drying out their blankets on a dank hillside. Martin and I were too sensible, and respectful of authority, to boast about our good fortune. A shame Forbes had not stayed back with us, for him and also for Jake, who would have enjoyed having the colonel of a famous fighting unit as a guest, as well as one of its captains.

While we staged for a few days in Palestine, encamped among the orange groves, oranges everywhere for none could be exported, I plucked up courage and overcame genuine reluctance to ask Forbes if he would try to get me a 'staff job', putting it crudely (which I wasn't doing), away from the firing line. Lots of people came and went in the battalion, and I was now one of the few old hands. Wilfred Hillman had laid down the codes and War Diary and had left the job of intelligence officer, going I knew not where, though it turned out to be a strange assignment. Lieutenant Norman Rogers had left being quartermaster and returned to England 'posted to home establishment'. I was starting to say – which was the sort of argument Forbes would have completely understood – that I knew I could not rise further in the battalion because a regular would always come back to be a major and command a company, but I hastily pulled myself together and told the truth, which was just the opposite. I was frightened by the prospect of having to command a company, even in a distant prospect: I did not feel that I could carry the responsibility. And more than that: up to now, I had thought of myself as invulnerable; even with the fragments of two bullets in me from Tobruk, I had never supposed that I would actually be killed. That strange certainty had gone. I knew the next time would be the last time for me. The spring had been stretched too far. If it had meant leaving Forbes without the sort of adjutant he liked, I would not have asked, but my eventual successor was already there ready to take over, for it was understood between Forbes, Kingsley and myself that this would be Matthew Lasseter, an admirable young regular officer who had joined us on the way to Tunisia.

Forbes did me proud. There was always someone high up in the Army who belonged to the Northumberland Fusiliers 'mafia' available to help, just as de Guignand had done when Tubby appealed to him about the proposal to send us to die in the cause of 'knocking hell out of the enemy's l. of c.' 'I'll get on to Godfrey' – Colonel Godfrey Hobbes, a full colonel, chief of staff of GHQ Allies. Godfrey, it turned out, wanted a GII, a major, as his right-hand man, and off I went to Cairo to meet him and his general. My interview with the general commanding GHQ Allies, on 6 November, turned out oddly. After about an hour he suddenly asked, 'Do you know modern Greek?' The answer, of course, was no. 'Right, you'll take over the Greek Mission. I am fed up with these Greek-speaking experts who are deep in their miserable politics. I want an honest man I can trust, for a change.' So I was given my promotion to field rank, major GSO II with staff pay, on the explicit ground that I was without any prior knowledge of the people I was to work with.

It was a sad parting with old friends in the battalion, but it was made easier by being necessarily perfunctory, since we were under orders to go back to Syria, starting off on the next day, 14 November – there was danger of trouble of some kind in the Southern Lebanon.

Only recently have I discovered that the battalion recorded a testimonial to me far beyond what I could possibly have deserved – this was published in the *St George's Gazette* in its number of April 1944. It described

the departure of Capt McManners to the Staff on promotion to Field Rank. 'Mac' had held the adjutancy for nearly two hectic years, and in that time rendered outstanding service to the Regiment. It is a far cry from the peaceful cloisters of a university college to the battlefields of the Middle East, and the life of an Oxford Don is very different from that of an Adjutant. Yet McManners filled the one role as successfully as we believe he must have filled the other. His scholastic brilliance, in itself of the greatest value to the Battalion, was matched only by his personal bravery. It is to be hoped that in time to come he will devote a part of his genius to the writing of the Regimental History, for should he do so we will indeed be fortunate. For the moment and until we can lay our hands on him again we wish him the good fortune he so richly deserves. His place has been taken by Capt Lasseter.

Belatedly, more than half a century later, I am trying to fulfil this invitation to write about the Fusiliers in the Desert War, but alas, all I can do now is to offer personal anecdotes and a tribute to a heroic battalion and the men that made it so – falling far short of the regimental history that it deserves.

11

The Greek Army in Exile: Ismailia

I began work with 210 BLU (the Greek Mission) with one immediate duty: to set up an Officers' Training Centre at Ismailia on the Suez Canal. I reported progress directly to Godfrey Hobbes, the GI of GHQ Allies, though a lieutenant colonel who seemed to have some role called on me in the early days at Ismailia; he was more interested in talking about romantic topics like Byron's fate at Missolonghi than about what was happening in the here and now, and after his one visit he vanished from the scene. While building up the Officers' Centre I came to have the responsibility for two Greek guard battalions and a company of Pioneers, stationed in the Delta, and was given the title of Officer Commanding 210 BLU, which I am not sure that I had when I started operating with the Mission. Thereafter, the responsibility fell to me for three new Greek battalions founded in Cyrenaica and Tripolitania; they were set up to occupy troops whose Left-wing inclinations and agitations rendered them unfit to be used in more serious fighting formations. There was also a collection of rebels and extremists kept in an old prisoner of war cage in the desert at Timimi. At first none of these units, in the Delta or along the African coast westwards, had liaison officers with them, but GHQ Allies gradually appointed them, first in the Canal Zone after the period of revolutionary activity there ended, then later in Cyrenaica and Tripolitania. This was my rag-tag empire as it developed, but I had nothing to do with the Greek Brigade, which by the end of 1943 was in its final stage of training before going off (it was fervently hoped) to win glory for Greek arms in Italy.

Ismailia, on Lake Timsah on the canal north of the Great Bitter Lake, was a pretty little town of white houses with small lush gardens set among palm trees. There was a fashionable *plage*, the Jardin des Enfants, the children not in evidence, but nubile young women of indeterminate race and lithe thrusting figures; there were also, in addition to the numerous Greek officers, groups of bronzed young men with muscular torsos. What did they do for a living? No doubt making money from the occupying British forces. The camp for the Training Centre, where I established my HQ, was on a sandy road running out of town; there was a forest of marquee-style tents with two brick enclosures, one a cookhouse, the other open-air latrines, with the usual rows of pierced, lidded seats over the usual deep drop. The amount of fertiliser deposited in these cavernous pits by the soldiery must have been prodigious; no doubt by now enterprising locals have reclaimed it to improve the crops of the Delta.

My task force to set up the Training Centre consisted of a lieutenant quartermaster, Jerry Herrick, a reprobate regular given to drink, but a loyal ally and a great favourite among the Greeks, his batman driver and mine, and two Greek lieutenants as interpreters. One of these was Evangelos Louisos, a Cypriot in his late thirties, substantially built and moustached, from a wealthy family of Famagusta. His father had been mayor, and the stationmaster would keep the train waiting for him when he made one of his forays into town. Jerry Herrick knew a man of substance when he saw one, and finding it difficult to pronounce Evangelos and to remember Louisos, especially in his cups, dubbed him 'Squire', a nickname which delighted Louisos and which was adopted in our little enclave. One of Squire's themes was women; I remember with what quiet satisfaction he pointed out an ATS girl whose favours he had enjoyed, stroking his moustache appreciatively. He had an anecdote concerning an adventure on a long-distance train in Turkey, a train which must have had plenty of vacant space, for on board he had enjoyed the company of a sixteen-year-old girl and they had gone further than the proprieties prescribed. He then went to find her father, who was travelling in splendour having booked a whole carriage for himself, to ask for the girl's hand in marriage.

'No, certainly not.'

'But unfortunately, it has happened.'

'Well?'

'I take it that you would welcome me fulfilling the obligation I consider myself to have undertaken.'

'Unfortunate, I agree, obligation maybe, but I won't have you as a son-in-law.'

'You have something against me, then?'

'No, I don't know you, the matter is closed.'

'Your daughter, then?'

'Leave her here.'

Do we believe this story? It would be a pity to doubt it.

My other liaison officer was George Leroudias, a Greek from Alexandria –the Egyptian Greeks were called up into the Greek Army in exile, willy-nilly, mostly nilly. He had been educated at the English college in Alex, and spoke perfect English with a superbly posh accent. He was of stocky, athletic build, and a soccer player of distinction, having played for Egypt. He could not possibly approve of Squire, partly because he was so rich, and partly because of his cheerful wickedness with women: George was a devotee of *Boys' Own Paper* chivalry, and women were doubly unapproachable to him because he was a platonic admirer of male beauty. (It would be unfair to adopt the modern fashion of 'outing' him as gay, which did not quite fit the case.) He was inclined to the royalist side in Greek politics, which made him particularly useful in discussions with the senior Greek officers, who were mainly on the far Right. Squire was a republican, and my man for talking to the younger officers; all those who were graduates or otherwise well-educated, had inclinations to the Left, though they were generally anti-Communist. But the key fact was that both liaison officers were on our side, the British side. The Egyptian Greeks resented their call-up and regarded many of the Greeks from Greece as boorish, while they had a strong personal interest in hoping that we would keep the Germans out of the Delta. The family of Louisos had been against us in Cyprus. (Squire and I once went to a lecture given to the troops by Sir Ronald Storr, the governor of Cyprus whose house was burned down in the troubles. After the talk, we approached our prestigious lecturer. 'Louisos,' ruminated Sir Ronald, 'I think I know that name.' 'Yes, sir, you put my father in prison,' said Squire.) But outside of Cyprus, it was different. Both he and George realised that we had risked all against Hitler, and had jeopardised our war effort in North Africa to help Greece to fight. They saw the wider picture and wanted to help us defeat Hitler, wherever the battlefield, for the benefit of the whole of Europe; they were free from the parochialism which made so many of the mainland Greeks reluctant to fight anywhere but in Greece itself, to rid their homeland of the Germans and by doing so to be in a position to dictate the nature of the future government.

Squire and George really understood what England was like. So many of their compatriots thought of us as a great power with huge

With Squire at Sabratah, Libya

resources, but they knew us as a small island fighting against well-nigh impossible odds, a Greece if you like which had not been brought to surrender. The British Council in Cairo, whom I viewed with ambiva-lence, used to send me propaganda for the Greeks, posters showing our soldiers triumphantly bearing down on tanks, or sailors on the bridge of a battleship scanning far horizons. I wrote to them protesting against these phoney manifestos: here I am telling Greeks that they can't have an extra truck or motor cycle, so don't give us an empire of unlimited resources, of reeking tube and iron shard and the boasting of the Gen-tiles – give us posters of green fields, country inns, church towers, the England we are fighting for. Thereafter, the Council sent us a few pic-ture books, half a dozen all told.

The senior officers of the Greek Army spoke French of a sort, as many had been to the French War School, so I could talk to them in confidence if I wished. The key man to work with was Colonel Tsacalotos, the commandant of the Officers' Training Centre – short and slight in stature, handsome in a rakish way with dark oiled hair going back in a bouffant sweep: 'A pity he looks like a head waiter, as he seems to be a real soldier,' was the graceless comment by someone in GHQ who ought to have known better. In fact Tsacalotos was a dashing, volatile romantic patriot, who was to prove himself by com-manding the Greek force that ultimately did well fighting in Italy at Rimini, and as chief of staff of the Army in the post-war battles against the Communist guerrillas on the Albanian frontier. He was, of course, an arch-intriguer and a politician up to his eyebrows (which of them wasn't?). I respected him, though the fact that he was devoid of a sense of humour and of the warmth of human sympathy meant that I could not enjoy his company. Ranking next to Tsacalotos was Colonel Assimocopulos, who spoke polished French and expressive English ('We shall have that one' was his all-purpose phrase of acceptance). Before the war he had been military attaché in Sofia: 'Mon ami, attaché militaire en temps de paix est assez difficile, en temps de guerre c'est terrible, mais avec les Bulgares, mon Dieu!' He was the intellectual sol-dier of the Training Centre who taught tactics and strategy; he was amusing to talk to, and we became allies. He was in demand as a guest among Greek families living in Egypt; I went with him on one of these nights out, and he was indeed good company. On one occasion, I fear, I gave him (and myself) embarrassment, but did him a good turn on another. He called me in to comment, as a machine-gun specialist, on his vast and carefully drawn diagram of the plans of lines of fire around the perimeter of a fortress. I was undiplomatic enough to tell him how the British Army is accustomed to post the guns in sections of two together, to facilitate expert fire control, and that the Vickers gun has a much longer range than he had supposed, because of the new streamlined ammunition. To my horror, he had the whole thing redrawn. A mistake on my part. When, out of courtesy, you are asked to give your views, suggest only minor amendments or, indeed, just ask a few questions and later on have a private word with your superior about relevant factors of which he may be unaware. The good turn came about when I discovered that he was a crack shot and yearned to learn to handle a sniper's rifle. So I got him a place on the field officer's (majors and above) sniper's course in Palestine – fine, until I discovered that a condition of having him was that I must accompany him in person, not as a liaison man, but as an actual member of the course. We had all the best shots in the Middle East and others flown back from the Italian front in attendance, and competitive marks for success on the targets were posted daily. 'Ah, we shall have that one,' said Assimocopulos on receiving the little tin shield awarded for coming third. Fortunately, wooden spoons were not presented.

The last member of the triumvirate of colonels at the top of the hierarchy of the Training Centre was Kitseos, a battered, weary-looking figure with a lined face, the most decorated officer in the Greek Army, the hero of the Albanian war against the Italians. He did not teach any particular subject, but was a figurehead, a standing reminder of the soldierly ideal. His politics were way out on the far Right, and a provocation to those younger republican officers who refused to be overawed by his towering reputation. Finally, there was an unromantic figure who continually figured on the agenda of the liaison team, Lieutenant Colonel Sirmas, the administrative man of the centre, jovial, bustling and asking for the earth. But he met his match in Jerry Herrick who, drunk or sober, was prepared to argue for ever. At one stage Sirmas was continually asking for wood for some building project, and thus, thanks to Herrick's gift for dubbing, became known to us as 'Woody'. Squire had to do the interpreting for the Woody-Herrick negotiations (which he did with relish, extracting the maximum amount of fun from them); George Leroudias, ever since Sirmas gave a lecture to the Greek community of Ismailia with a brand-new pair of leather gloves stuck in his belt ('boastfully bucolic'), could not stand him.

Though I could transact business in French with Tsacalotos and Assimocopulos, mostly I worked through interpreters. Experience as adjutant had shown me that it was best not to bypass the 'usual channels' – get everything clearly explained, with a witness to vouch for it. Besides, I stood to gain since both the interpreters were on my side. They would slip in a warning along with the literal translation, and I could get them to pretend that I misunderstood if I wanted to gain time to think before replying. Leroudias particularly enjoyed putting in deadpan asides on his own account. 'The colonel says, though for God's sake don't believe him, that he has no secrets from his British allies', or: 'This is the list of transport urgently necessary for the effective working of the Officers' Training Centre, and the colonel says he cannot do without it. But if you get him the staff car he wants to swank around in, he won't make much fuss about the others.' Both George and Squire, well-read and with a sense of style, appreciated my own stylistic devices, helping me to create a scenario of insuperable difficulties so that the negotiation would end with the meagre help I could offer looking almost generous. Messages by phone or telegram came to the Centre in English, and the commandant would have to have them translated, while his own messages went out by the reverse process. Usually, he would turn to Leroudias, the royalist. But whoever it was, if it concerned me I would be kept informed. Thus George told me of the signals that passed between Tsacalotos and the King of Greece, which settled the question of where his ultimate allegiance lay.

Giving speeches through an interpreter had its hazards – danger lurks in the ill-timed pause. Speaking at a banquet of officers, with George translating, I was praising, among others, Colonel Kitscos, the heroic royalist fanatic. 'Colonel Kitseos,' I said, 'gives me a lot of trouble –' pause. George panicked, stumbled and delayed, and a beginning of angry murmurs came from the men of the Right. 'British officers are always asking me to explain how a single soldier can win so many medals' – sighs of relief and much applause.

I did the obvious things to help with the training curriculum, like getting in visiting British speakers from various technical arms of the services. Occasionally, we had trips to British establishments, as to the Engineering School, with a demonstration of Bailey bridging, a ride in a landing craft on the lake and tea in the mess to round off the day. There were some perceptive questions from the Greeks, which helped to improve my relations with British hosts. For the most part, however, I was just around, to be consulted about some weapon or other and about standard tactics (see the Field Service pocket books), or to indent for some piece of equipment that was needed. Being in a base camp, we could be subjected to the visitations of the organisations for the improvement of the soldiery which provided cushy jobs in uniform for so many non-combatants. Mercifully, the Army Education Corps did not send emissaries to the forces of our allies, but we had a descent of three instructors of the Army physical training people, led by – was it a sergeant or, even, a lieutenant? – Hidenstam (I think this was the name, a convincing name for a body builder or a weight lifter). They were around bright and early in the morning wearing track suit bottoms with their oiled naked torsos on display, muscles rippling as they hurled medicine balls to each other, setting a good example to the odd bleary Greek officer shambling along breathing into his fag at this unaccustomed early hour. After two days, they left in despair.

To be an effective liaison officer it was essential to identify with the Greeks in all they did, and to avoid the temptation to find social life and pleasure outside their circle. The liaison team had its own mess, where we dined nightly, Squire and George with us, but I always lunched in the officers' mess of the Training Centre (Squire, George and Jerry were not there; they couldn't stand it). The food here was not appetising, and the kindness of my hosts made things even worse when we got to the period when my Lent was over while theirs still carried on; they insisted the cook prepare me special meat dishes, thus I could not possibly avoid eating them. I went to Greek weddings and came back clutching the traditional candy key given to guests, and stood with our senior officers for hours on the platform of Ismailia railway station waiting to salute the five Patriarchs of the Orthodox churches as they passed through on some special religious foray. At the social gatherings of the Greek community in Ismailia I could get along in French, but had George around to translate unobtrusively if there were speeches. At one, Tsacalotos gave an impassioned patriotic oration, concluding by saying that the bitterness of exile had been alleviated for him by the beautiful Mme Spanoudis, wife of the chief engineer of the Canal. 'My God, Mac, this is awful,' said George, *sotto voce*. And one got good fun going with the younger officers to the Jardin des Enfants. (One of our super swimmers was Cleo, who earned the scorn of George for doing 'saltimbango tricks' on the diving board. He also was the subject of a tirade by Jerry Herrick which Squire savoured enormously. Jerry, in the early morning, waiting with a truck to take Cleo off to collect some equipment, was enraged to be kept waiting – 'What the hell is Cleo doing,' he roared, 'sponging his cock?') Once, with a group of officers, I went to the local open-air cinema. The Greek proprietor rushed to greet us and insisted on putting a table in the aisle to serve us with drinks as we watched the Bing Crosby film. Half-way through, the sound failed. One by one then in twos and threes the audience went out, while courtesy compelled us to stay, watching a mute inglorious Bing for an hour.

The Greek club of Ismailia was not frequented by the young as its meals were expensive. Squire, however, discovered in their cellar a bottle of brandy there ever since the Canal was first cut. Being rich, he bought it, and one night the two of us drank it all along with a simple meal – it was liquid fire that did not burn us. I was glad that I was no longer a non-drinker, and I reflected that if one could drink like that, I could see some point in achieving riches.

A social occasion for the Training Centre I wish had never been forced upon us was the funeral of one of our young officers, who had been badly broken up in the crash of a truck. The British army doctor, just down the road from the Greek camp, sent him to the French hospital in Ismailia, where he was refused admission. Jolting in agony on the back of a truck his friends took him back to the British medical post; the doctor returned him to the French hospital with a note certifying that travelling any further would kill him and that the time was short. The news reached the camp and I went off to the French hospital shortly after the second rejection, where I found half a dozen officers standing round their dying colleague, who was still in the back of the truck. I rang the bell and hammered at the door and a couple of nurses appeared, cool and spiritual-looking in their nuns' habits appeared. They would not help and firmly closed the door on me. I hammered continually until they had to open again and I insisted that they informed the doctor in charge. Off they went and came back with another refusal. No doctor came. No one looked at the dying man. They were just shutting the door again when Squire shouted to me, 'It's no good now, he's gone.' 'Il est mort,' I said bitterly as the door closed finally. It was dark now, and must have been about time for the recitation of Compline. If there can be a sin for which there is no forgiveness, this was it.

Our camp had its own Greek doctor, who was not involved in this crisis and, indeed, I was unaware of his existence until orders came from Area HQ that we must all be inoculated against bubonic plague. Common sense told me to take a walk down the road to the British medical post, but since these sort of inconvenient orders are just the sort Greeks tend to ignore, I thought I must set a good example and be the first to report to the Greek doctor for the jab. Squire went ahead to exhort him to have all clean and ship-shape, new needle and so on, and I went to my fate, demonstrating to the eyes of the many assembled spectators, the *sang-froid* proud French aristos showed on the steps of the guillotine. The sight of a doctor who had not shaved for a couple of days made me feel that I was going to become a victim of my misplaced sense of duty. So it was: soon, my arm was hugely swollen and I was violently ill. Universally, my Greek friends, including the sophisticated ones, said I needed the *'ventouse'*. Back came the doctor (three days' whiskers – apparently he only shaved for the weekend) with his neat leather case of little glass cups, heated them on a spirit lamp, and clamped them on the swollen arm, raising a sweat and burning the skin. The remedy may have been worse than the affliction, but it worked.

It was only a month after I had started the Training Centre when Christmas arrived – Christmas 1943. I can't remember the celebrations, though at least it wasn't in the desert and we did not have a court martial. But I do recall how George Leroudias came to me in the afternoon of Christmas Eve to say that he had told the South African unit down the road that I was an Englishman alone among Greeks far from home, and that through him they invited me to their party at 8 p.m. I went along and had an enjoyable hour, until a drunken officer asked me what I was doing hanging around in an easy job instead of being in a fighting unit. I told him I'd served in the Western Desert in the Northumberland Fusiliers. 'Never heard of them.' 'Well, we were with the Australians in the siege of Tobruk.' An outcry arose. All unthinkingly, I had used the taboo word – the Australians had successfully resisted for seven months, the South African Division had held out in Tobruk only a few days on the second time round. The colonel came over to restore order. Having done this, he said 'And may I ask you how you come to be here, who invited you?' George Leroudias had been talking to an English unit next door and had got it wrong. 'Well, stay now you are here.' I stayed for five minutes then departed, wishing new friends and new foes a happy Christmas.

When it came to Easter Eve I attended the ceremonies in the Orthodox cathedral in Alex in the company of two Greek officers. I cannot recall their names, but both were graduates of the University of Athens, and one of them told me the story of the 'Minister's suitcase'. Shortly after the fall of Greece to the Germans, having escaped to Egypt, he was detailed to help a Cabinet minister, another refugee, with his voluminous baggage. There was a suitcase inordinately heavy for its size, and as he struggled along with it, the joints gave way and he had to gather up the contents and tie them back in with rope – gold bars.

The cathedral in Alex was packed and the two officers asked the people standing there if they would allow us to push forward, 'We want the British officer to see the ceremony.' As far as I knew, I was the only British soldier there and the words worked like a charm. We were pushed enthusiastically to the front, while candles were forced upon us so we could participate like the rest of the congregation. I found myself standing next to the King and Queen of Greece; he, with cropped hair, stiff bearing and in military uniform, looked Prussian, she looked icily beautiful. When the presiding prelate came out from behind the altar at midnight with his candle lighted (conventionally miraculous), he transferred the flame to the King's candle then on to the rest of us. I came a few places after the Queen. Within a minute, the whole church was ablaze with the resurrection light. At the end of the service, the congregation walked home through the deserted streets with their candles to transfer the flame to the lamp before the icon at home. The three of us did the same. 'Look, even the English have their candles lit.' To me, alas, it was just to the Union Club, which had a bar but no shrine.

While at Ismailia, my naval brother Tom came twice to see me. To the relief of all except himself he had not made it as a pilot in the Fleet Air Arm, and after some knockabout adventures on the ancient destroyer *Vortigern* on coastal patrol in the North Sea, he had been commissioned in the new radar branch of the Fleet. His first assignment was on a merchant ship that carried an expendable plane for submarine destruction – it was launched by his instructions then guided to its

The author's brother Tom

prey, then back again to be ditched in the water. Now, he was flight-direction officer to Admiral Troubridge on *Royalist*. The first visit he made was, literally out of the blue, for he got a lift on a plane from the ship. The pilot hit the wrong airfield, but I got a phone call while I stood by the runway elsewhere, and drove off like mad to meet him, and we had a couple of hours' chat in one of the wooden huts belonging to the Air Force. Since I had left England, Father had changed parishes, to Ferryhill, the village where he had been a miner, then a curate. The ancient, tottering, eccentric and holy clergyman – he was also a millionaire – who had been vicar there for a generation, refused to retire unless Father was named as his successor. So if I got back to England I'd be among the friends of school days and a multitude of people I had known well all my early life. Before the move from West Pelton, however, Tom had got engaged to Joan, the colliery engineer's daughter, my old girl friend. Mother had written to me anxiously about this. These items of family news and the saga of life in the Navy gave us a lot to talk about in a very short time. One of his stories struck a

chord, being the naval equivalent of what an amateur has to find out
when he joins a regular battalion. When he was appointed to the admiral's staff, Tom had been given a massive non-stop indoctrination
course in bridge playing, and quickly became a maestro. In his first
game, he doubled the admiral, who was three down. After the rubber
he was led aside and told the convention that admirals are never so far
out in their bidding that they can be doubled. He had been taught every
system from the forcing two to weird American devices of bluff, but no
one had thought to inculcate the diplomatic protocol of the game
afloat. All very much like Jack Watson's literal interpretation of 'hard
arse'.

On our second meeting, *Royalist* had anchored in Alexandria harbour. Tom came ashore and had lunch, then I went back with him to
the ship for a party and to spend the night there. During the night *Royalist* got unexpected orders to sail at once, and it looked as though I'd
have to sail with her, with heaven knows what consequences. But an
appeal to the admiral in person – with, no doubt, a rocket for Tom and
others – and a boat was found to whizz me ashore as the anchor was
weighed.

12

Conspiracies

The history of the Greek government in exile and of the Left-wing manoeuvres to coerce and dominate it is well documented. As a result, I can now look back and see the hidden springs of motive and machination that lay behind the crises I had to face in the army units in the Delta and Cyrenaica. The party of the extreme Left in Greece, EAM, had a Communist core with Russian contacts and it had its own guerrilla movement, ELAS; this fighting group waged war against the Germans, but also strove to extirpate rival groups of freedom fighters – to monopolise the glory of resistance and the arms and supplies brought in by the Allies. From 1941, EAM/ELAS had their 'anti-fascist' organisation among the Greeks in Egypt (under Zerbinis) and in the Army (ASO), Navy (AON) and Airforce (AOA). The Army group distributed four duplicated magazines, *Andifasista*, *Eleftheria*, *Asteras* and *Eleftheros*. Through these organs, the doings of ELAS (in so far as they concerned war against the Germans) were publicised among the Greek troops in exile. The tactical plan of EAM/ELAS followed the well-established pattern of modern revolutionary activity: there was the respectable political party, and for it a place in the government was demanded; there were the guerrilla fighters who, whatever negotiations took place, would never surrender their arms; there were the groups and cells working to undermine the organised military or police forces of the established régime.

Early in April 1944 EAM decided that the time was ripe to demand a place in the government, and Major Kladakis, the secretary of the ASO, with twelve other officers of the Army called on Tsouderos, the premier of the government in exile in Cairo, demanding it surrender power to a 'government of national unity'. Tsouderos had them arrested. There was an agitation led by the Greek Seamen's Union in Alex and on 7 April a mutiny among the crews of the Greek warships in harbour. The Brigade, ready to go to fight in Italy, revolted, and declared its camp on the coastal road to the west of the city a no-go area for the government.

After a week it looked as if EAM was winning, for the king of Greece dismissed Tsouderos, replacing him with Venizelos, the archetypical republican intriguer, a master of the manipulation of public opinion, and secretly in touch with EAM, as was fitting for a believer in the doctrine of no enemies on the Left. But the outright and overt revolt of the Brigade had been a fatal mistake, ruining the long-term strategy of EAM. Here had been a unit highly trained and well-armed, all set to depart for the battle-line in Italy, now disrupted and useless and, what was worse, a liability requiring a diversion of British forces to contain it.

There was no hope now that British policy would tolerate a compromise that took EAM into partnership. Venezelos was forced out of office and on 24 April Papandreou became premier, an anti-Communist. Three days later British troops forced the Brigade to surrender (one of our officers was killed by the rebels, an unforgivable crime against an ally, one which was hushed up at the time – neither from the English side nor the Greek side did I hear a word of it). In May, Papandreou held talks in the Lebanon with representatives of EAM and came to a meaningless agreement: the Army to be non-political, all guerrilla forces to cooperate, the constitution of Greece not to be settled until after the liberation. On 18 October, now that the Germans had retreated, the Papandreou government returned to Athens, under the protection of the British Army, and in December the ELAS guerrillas swept in to seize power by force of arms. They did not know that Stalin had abandoned them, leaving Greece to be a British sphere of influence; they were routed and withdrew to carry on guerrilla warfare in their mountain fortresses near the Albanian border – a war this time against the liberators of their country.

This was what was happening on the wider scale in 1944, so little of it known to me. I received no political briefings from GHQ Allies, nor did I ask for any. I was a soldier doing a soldier's work and that was good enough for me. In what follows, I describe what happened, so far as I can limiting myself to what I knew at the time. Apart from the revolt of the Brigade, which has been written up in detail, there seems to be no account of what happened among the other, routine Greek units of the army in exile, so with no documentation to go on, I fear that what I say must lack precise dates, and be a collection of anecdotes rather than coherent history.

My essential qualification to be appointed to command 210 BLU
had been ignorance – ignorance of the Greek language and Greek politics. Inevitably, one learnt something of both, but it was important not
to become fascinated by the endless vista of intrigues and, as knowledge
accumulated, drift into considering oneself an insider, and posing as an
expert. Some things were obvious: the linkage between geographical
areas and political allegiance (e.g. men from Chios tended to be republicans), the gap, already familiar, between the regular officers and the
amateurs, the importance of knowing how the older people had lined
up during the dictatorship years. But where all was double-speak and
all information slanted, it was best not to make too many assessments
from incidental happenings, but to talk to the younger officers of my
own kind, university graduates and those hoping for professional
careers after the war; they were as likely as anybody to give me an
honest picture. And of course, there were Louisos and Leroudias; they
held sharply differing political opinions, but the one as a Cypriot and
the other as an Alexandrian viewed current Greek affairs with a certain
detachment and critical disillusionment.

The rank and file of the Greek Army talked endlessly about politics,
deriving enormous enjoyment from their disputes and speculations.
There was a republican majority, but it had no coherence. What leadership there was came from the supporters of the EAM/ELAS guerrillas in
the resistance in Greece; their songs and doings were well known
among the troops in Egypt. Within the grouping devoted to the romantic doings of ELAS, there was a hard core of committed Communists,
regarding themselves as members of a European-wide Russian directed
revolutionary agency. When all was said and nothing done, however,
the soldiers, like soldiers everywhere, wanted to be out of the Army and
home. This nostalgic inertia was a counterweight to the EAM/ELAS
political leadership. A few, no doubt, went with it because being
untrustworthy to the British meant exemption from having to fight, but
most were just followers of a vague political instinct to have no enemies
on the Left. Having said this, however, for the rank and file here was
something more important than the political complexion of a liberated
Greece – just getting home.

The junior officers were mostly republican, some inclining to
EAM/ELAS because they feared the advent of another General
Metaxas, but generally against Communism and realising the dangers

of mixing politics with soldiering. They were admirers of Britain and had a touching enthusiasm for all things British. The high point of their national history was when they won independence from the Turks, and we had helped them – their 'shirtless patriots' would have got nowhere without the British Navy patrolling their coasts and islands. (One of their favourite stories was of Kolokotrones finding his band of guerrillas smartening themselves up as they had been invited to a party on a British man-of-war. 'You are not going,' he said, 'they think we are heroes, but once they clap eyes on us they'll be disillusioned.') The Greek War of Independence of 1821–9, which I had hardly ever thought about, was as fresh in its details in the minds of the Greek officers of 1944 as if it had happened yesterday. And we were admired in the present because of our lonely stand against Hitler. Only among the few genuine Communists were we hated. The regular officers who had achieved any sort of rank called themselves 'nationalists', in the context meaning royalists. No doubt GHQ Allies received political briefings concerning Churchill's design for the future of Greece. I knew nothing of this and I realised that it was probably better that way. But it was obvious that the aim would be to exclude Russia. The majority of Greeks, I am sure, hated the idea of Russian domination, but with a sort of 'Irishness' they did not want to make any adjustment of their own views to stop it; they would not diverge from their opportunist republicanism of the Venizelos tradition to make assurance doubly sure by working with the Right. We made assurance doubly sure by taking the royalist side. It worked and Russian and Communist rule were excluded, but in the long run the rule of the Colonels, the fall of the monarchy and the partition of Cyprus was the result. For me at the time it was all much simpler. My actions were directed to helping the Greek Army to become an efficient fighting force to join in toppling Hitler. At least, this was true of the task of building up the Greek Officers' Training Centre. But in handling the troubled affairs of the other units in the Delta and Cyrenaica, there was, realistically speaking, another motive. It was impossible to conceal from oneself that with so much dissension and disaffection, these were not troops who could be trusted in battle. They could do guard duties away from the front, not much more. One was keeping them marking time, hoping to prevent them from becoming a liability. So in the last resort, there had to be a political dimension in the soldiering – I insisted to myself that it must be kept subordinate.

It may have been unjust to the staff officers in Cairo, but I had the impression that they were not half as interested in my reports on Greek training and morale as in my offerings of political intelligence. There were, indeed, plenty of characters at the Officers' Training Centre who wanted to give me political briefings or, to be more accurate, denunciations of political opponents. I had a marquee to myself, divided by a partition into an office and sleeping quarters, and on occasion after dark a conspirator would put his head round the corner of the entrance, make a slight sound to draw attention, and leave a note for me. Depending on circumstance or who it was from (if I knew) I would get George or Squire to translate, though I was reluctant to involve them, or I might do the best I could myself. Mostly, the notes were denunciations of covert Communists and EAM/ELAS supporters, but some were identifying 'fascists'. I did not send these notes to GHQ, nor did I mention their existence; I passed on information which I considered would warn of possible dangers and was likely to help Anglo-Greek relations. Godfrey Hobbes never asked for more: he was well aware that there is a point of honour among soldiers involved in these murky affairs.

Not so with Security Intelligence Middle East: they wanted names for their dossiers and card indexes. One hot afternoon when I was having a snooze in my spacious tent, a visitor arrived, a corporal who introduced himself as from field security in Ismailia. He wanted an hour or two of my time to enable him to compile a list of Left-wing Greek officers. I was furious, with a rage for which Sergeant-Major Foreman's blowing up in my adjutant days was but a mere rehearsal. I ordered him out and as he left he had the gall to say that I would be noted down as 'uncooperative'. I complained about this unsolicited visit to GHQ Allies but not a word was said in reply. Not long after, when I was in Cairo, I called on Captain Burn, Security Intelligence, British Troops in Egypt. There was an ordinary block of flats with civilian residents of the usual mixed races all around, a number on the door but no name. When I rang the bell, a soft-footed Arab in flowing white opened the door. The lattices were closed, keeping out the sun. In the twilight, Burn sat, bald-headed and solemn behind his desk. In due course I saw him again, for it was he who came down to the Canal Zone with his dossiers of undesirables when the show-down between Right and Left took place in the two Greek guard battalions stationed there.

In addition to the newly-set up Officers' Training Centre, there were these two Greek units encamped somewhere around the Great Bitter Lake, presumably engaged in desultory training or guard duties – I can no longer remember. I would visit them and drink coffee and, with Squire or George translating, have long conversations. You were asked how you took your coffee by the commanding officer's coffee-maker, an old, wrinkled, heavily moustached soldier in his braces, who sat outside with his little brass pots on long handles, brewing up; and pretty well doing this all day. There were three kinds according to the amount of sugar – *skettos*, *metrios*, and *variglicos*; I always asked for the sweetest, *variglicos*. It was important to be able to recognise your cup when the tray was presented, the liaison officer coming first: the clue was the way the cup handles were facing. The shadow of political tensions hung over these meetings. Sometimes you were aware that there were individuals present who had a different agenda from that followed by the commanding officer, and at other times it was possible to sense the constraint preventing him expressing his real opinion. But our conversations were always light-hearted, even about politics. I had a few Greek phrases handy as conversation openers; the one getting the best laugh was '*Possas sinomosia echomen sirmira* (how many conspiracies have we here today)?' Far from giving offence or causing embarrassment, the question gave pleasure: the Greeks not only loved intrigue but enjoyed being described as intriguers; caught out in an attempt to deceive they would regard it as a splendid joke, evidence that they were the descendants of the wily Ulysses.

I went to a concert one night given by one of the battalions, with Squire alongside translating. Unlike concerts put on by British troops, there were few comic turns by individuals, and what jokes there were concerned politics, rather than sex or race. On the other hand, there was a vast amount of hearty community singing, and the songs they sang were of EAM/ELAS. The Greek national anthem would be included, incidentally as it were, with emphasis on the central theme of 'Liberty', a peculiar emphasis with a sinister force. One of the turns was the arrival on stage of the battalion poet-laureate, the Homer of instant versification. Long-haired, solemn, stooping and bespectacled, writing pad and pencil in hand, he would ask for pairs of rhyming words; everyone would shout their favourites, and when he had a sufficient list, he would vanish. Later in the evening he would reappear and read out the poem he had devised, structured on these verse endings. I dare say that in the tumult he had conveniently heard the rhymes he fancied, and they were incorporated in any order, not in the order in which he had noted them. Even so, one should not detract from his achievement, for a passable poem resulted, greeted with prolonged applause. Inevitably, the subject was political, in this case an exhortation not to be pushed around by the British, but to solve Greek problems in the 'people's way', ending with the punch line, 'And leave the bully beef to Zervas' (Zervas, the Right-wing guerrilla leader hated by ELAS more than they hated the Germans). A scruffy corporal asked me, through Squire, what I thought of this witticism. I replied that I hadn't noticed any unwillingness to eat British rations; Squire, no doubt judiciously, did not translate this.

Though for reasons of pride the majors commanding these two battalions tried to conceal the fact, truth was that they had been reduced to figureheads; the orders were being given by the Communist committee. It was fairly evident that compulsion was being used to subdue soldiers who disagreed with the official ELAS line. From Right-wingers I heard accusations of torture, including forcible infection with venereal disease; I was not sure what to make of this; without doubt there were threats, and the air was heavy with menace. I cannot remember how the reality of Communist control and its mechanism finally became clear; in one unit, it was the adjutant who told me. And Squire was an essential help; he was a comfortable, unsoldierly figure, but he was courageous when so many were keeping quiet and avoiding compromising themselves. No doubt GHQ Allies had their own sources of information. What with the Greek General Staff and Security Intelligence Middle East they probably had a fair picture of what was happening, though probably a too lurid one and, certainly, one that was in sharp black and white devoid of the nuances of reality.

In the end, I had to talk to the Area commander, Brigadier Green, about how to bring these units back under the control of their officers and how to separate troops willing to fight in the British version of the war from those who would fight only for an EAM/ELAS takeover in Greece. The brigadier ('Taxiarchos' to the Greeks), was large, corpulent, tough and jovial, a good Christian who always read the lessons at the chaplain's services at his HQ. He was a tolerant, understanding man, not taking the line which comes so naturally to regular soldiers, especially those in sheltered staff jobs, of demanding ruthless enforcement of discipline, whatever severities have to be used. To him, there were no good Greeks and bad Greeks, and no scandalous breakdown of discipline calling for punishment – but just a difficult situation to be righted with a minimum of trouble and ill-feeling. We put together a plan. Each soldier would be interviewed alone and allowed to state which side he was on. This would be done with the Greek battalion commander there, and a representative of British Security Intelligence Middle East to guard against men of the extreme Left insinuating themselves among the moderates who would constitute the new battalion. Brigadier Green insisted that he himself would be present all the time to see fair play (and I provided him with George to interpret). I was allowed a free hand to organise the Greek side of the operation. The danger was, of course, that the battalion would refuse to comply and defy us, leading to violence and chaos – another revolt of the Greek Brigade in miniature. We had to be ready for this, so British troops had to be there in the background. All the brigadier had to draw from were the non-fighting units, drivers and technicians and the like, so they would have to turn out with unaccustomed rifles slung on their shoulders with orders to look fierce. I got him to requisition a tank from the Ordnance Depot, taking the view that its grim silhouette would make it easier to surrender with honour, talking defiance without doing anything. Our little force would assemble near the battalion camp during the night, then at first light I'd drive in to talk the Greeks into cooperating with the plan to divide them into Right and Left. Taxiarchos was not happy with this part of the scheme – what if they took me as a hostage, or worse? I assured him, with more confidence than I actually felt, that they would consider they had an obligation to respect the well-known figure of their liaison officer, who had received their hospitality and enjoyed their company. This turned out to be exactly so. The Greeks were deceitful, even treacherous, but chivalrous. There never was any danger.

Astonishingly, everything went according to plan. Half a mile from the camp a big tent was erected as the brigadier's HQ for the night, and our soldiers – there can't have been more than fifty or sixty of them – moved into position in the darkness. So did our tank, with very satisfactory rumblings that must have been heard in the battalion lines. I had a sleep in the tent. Then just before first light my driver trundled me down to the camp. The Greeks, as always, knew when something was afoot and were buzzing with questions. I had not taken Leroudias or Louisos, they were back with the brigadier; there were English speakers among the officers who could translate. The major, who had been informed by the Greek General Staff what would be required of him, was apprehensive, and I fancy one or two of the characters around him were his 'minders'. I asked to see 'the committee'. The universal cry was, of course, that there was no such thing, but in the end they were forthcoming – an alarming sight, unshaven and fanatical, no officers, but corporals and ordinary soldiers, perhaps ten of them. We had a long debate. The atmosphere was tense, but we drank coffee, and amid lurid threats, there was continual laughter. They would, they said, fight to the death. I exhorted them to help against the Germans as priority. They harangued me on the evils of the dictatorship of Metaxas and the absence of true freedom in Greece before the war. They had a point there and there was no mileage for my case in trying to argue with them. One had to keep to the present, to our joint war for survival. But there was one decisive card I had to play, making the threat tangentially, without ostentation, so that the surface of argument about conflicting political ideals would not too evidently be broken by crude material considerations. What about the *exartimita*, the *pramata*, the kit, the possessions, the baggage? Every man had accumulated – by purchase, theft or devious means between the two – a mass of things to take home to Greece, where their families were miserable and starving; from tinned food to typewriters, pullovers, dresses and, above all, boots and shoes, they had possessions galore. If it came to a fight, all this would be lost, whereas, if they came forward to be sorted out, I would guarantee that all their *pramata* went with them. Finally we slipped into a discussion on just how this would be organised, and seeing that I would be staying with them all the time, not going off back to the British side, it was obvious that I would have to keep my word. So, lateish in the morning it was settled, and I sent my driver back to Brigadier Green's HQ to tell him to set the operation going. A few hundred yards from the camp a table and chairs were put down. At the table sat the brigadier, Captain Burn of Security, whose office I had visited in Cairo, the major commanding the battalion, and George Leroudias to interpret. The adjutant of the battalion joined them, which was courageous – a young university man, inclined to the republican side but accepting the risk of being identified with the royalists and the British. His presence impressed the soldiers as they came forward. A few British soldiers, rifles slung on shoulder, stood by; the rest of them and our token tank stayed away.

I sat on a blanket at the edge of the camp with Squire and a few Greek officers for company. The soldiers came as far as us in groups of two or three, one to go forward further in his turn, the others helping him with his piles of baggage. They staged with us, then with the baggage handlers assisting went on to the table of judgement. Half-way there a couple of British soldiers would take over the load and hang on to it until the decision was made, then help to move it to the right or to the left as the case might be. All this took place just too far from the camp for watchers without binoculars to be clear what the decision had been, and lorries drove off one by one with their loads as soon as full, bearing the two separated parties to separate staging places.

Not long afterwards, the other battalion was sorted, easy this time, for the news had spread about the first operation. Everyone knew it had been fairly done and that the fate of Left-wingers was nothing to worry about, just officially imposed idleness with a veneer of duties. I think that in each case the division was pretty well half and half, and the Left were sent off to be formed into new units in Cyrenaica and Tripolitania.

After these forays, it was agreeable to get back to my well-organised HQ at Ismailia in the revolution-free Officers' Training Centre. But an interruption came, a day of high drama. I find it hard to believe, but no one seems to have written the story of the Communist seizure of the Greek General Staff building in Cairo. As it is, I can only guess what really happened on that dramatic day, and all I can recount is its repercussions at Ismailia. Scarcely had I breakfasted than George Leroudias arrived, sounding the alarm. Communist troops from somewhere or another had gone up to Cairo and seized the offices of the Greek General Staff. Colonel Granitsas (commonly called 'Colonel Rockbottom' by the junior staff at GHQ Allies), a solemn heavy man with a creased brown face and a big greying moustache, had managed to escape, but the offices were occupied and the files were being ransacked. Tsacalotos was even now holding a conference with his senior officers. The heroic Kitseos, with all the glamour of his manifold decorations, was demanding decisive action. I rang up GHQ Cairo: they knew nothing about it. Just as well, for all that would have happened would have been the receipt of orders to do something unrealistic. In half an hour, Tsacalotos sent for me. It was Leroudias the royalist, of course, not Squire the republican who came over with the urgent invitation, but George did not come with me into the commandant's office. The meeting of officers had dispersed, and the room was hazy with the fragrant smoke of Turkish cigarettes. The usual pose of asking for advice was dropped. Tsacalotos laid down the law in the most emphatic French he could muster. There was a recital of terrible deeds in Cairo; he and the 'nationalist' officers were going to go there and throw out the Communists. They wanted me to get them more transport, and some weapons more effective than mere pistols. They proposed to be off at noon. He seemed to think that I could muster a few trucks and machine pistols, on the assumption that the British, being anti-Communist, would be glad to get volunteers to do the repressive work needed. I could see that it would be useless to get into an argument about first principles, to tell him he could not take the law into his own hands. He and the others were geared up for a gesture of heroism, and the essence of it would be to defy all the niceties. To say he had no right to take action would have provoked him to set off with what trucks and pistols he already had, and to go at once. I was satisfied that he was serious: had I been sent for when all the officers were there, I might have thought that I was being used to give the wiser heads my backing to restrain Kitseos and the hotheads, but as it was, with Tsacalotos alone interviewing me, the case seemed to me to be desperate. So I played for time by looking at the practical difficulties. I needed firm information from the British side before I could act; to get vehicles, let alone machine-guns and ammunition, meant getting certification down a whole bureaucratic chain. And what if the military police on the road blocks to Cairo decided to search the avenging convoy? (Actually, they never did search anybody, but I was saying to myself that in the last resort I'd warn them to intervene). The departure time must be postponed say, to 3 p.m. In the meantime, I'd call on the Area commander.

So it was settled. I arranged an urgent meeting with Brigadier Green and drove off to his HQ. He was at his desk, comfortably ensconced behind a pile of files – no doubt about vital matters like courts-martial for drunks, missing equipment, tents that had caught fire and pilfering natives – a large mug of coffee newly deposited at his elbow. He uttered a theatrical groan when I entered, but he was genial. The Greeks were a nuisance, but since the affair of winkling out Communists from the two battalions had gone so smoothly, he was disposed to think well of my ability to steer him through the murky confusion of Greek affairs. But my news alarmed him, all the more when he rang up Cairo and found that the Greek General Staff HQ really was occupied and nothing had been organised to deal with the situation. However, reassured to know that I was holding up the departure of the war party from Ismailia to 3 p.m. (I was flattered that he thought I could pull this off, I wouldn't have bet on it), he decided to summon Tsacalotos for precisely that time, without saying why. If the officers of the Training Centre took this to be an audience to wish them God-speed and happy Communist bashing, so much the better. But when the commandant came, if nothing else would suffice he'd give him a direct order to stand down. And in the meantime he'd have a road block set up not far from town to bar the way to Cairo, just in case.

There was an anxious wait to three o'clock. I took lunch at the Greek officers' mess as usual; Tsacalotos and the top brass were absent. Squire and George brought me constant news of the to-ing and fro-ing in the camp. The summons to Area HQ had come through on the phone to Tsacalotos, who asked George if he knew what it meant, then sent for me to make suspicious inquiries. I had told Brigadier Green the situation I said, but I could not say what his intentions were. Quite rightly, this was taken to mean that I was not allowed to say, not that I did not know. In due course, having asked GHQ Allies for news and getting none, I went on ahead to Area HQ. The brigadier's latest information from Cairo was that the Communists were still in undisputed possession. I reported to him that the leading royalist officers were gathered together somewhere in camp; the fact that they had missed lunch showing how serious things had become. So Taxiarchos prepared to pull rank and give orders. Tsacalotos was ushered in with George alongside him to interpret. Brigadier Green could have had an alternative career as an actor. He shed his geniality like a mask, his cheerful rubicund face set in stern lines, looking as if flushed by anger, his powerful bulk now acquiring an aura of menace.

The exchanges that followed remain fresh in my mind, give or take a phrase or two.

Brigadier to George: 'Ask Colonel Tsacalotos if he has heard about trouble at the Greek HQ in Cairo.'

George explains this to the commandant, then replies, 'The Colonel says he is aware of something of the kind and is naturally concerned, and though it is not directly his affair he would be glad to be informed about it.'

Brigadier: 'Tell the Colonel that I am worried about rumours that have come to my ears about activities in his unit in some way connected with affairs in Cairo.'

George: 'Colonel Tsacalotos assures the Brigadier that all is well in the Greek Officers' Training Centre, but if anything is wrong he will be glad to investigate any matter drawn to his attention.'

Brigadier: 'Tell him I have heard about the possibility of certain officers' proposing to act beyond their legal powers and intervene in Cairo.'

George: 'The Colonel assures the Brigadier that he would never countenance any such thing, and that the Brigadier can rely on him to obey implicitly all orders given by our allies and protectors the British.'

Brigadier: 'So I have unnecessarily concerned myself about affairs in the Greek Officers' Training Centre?'

George: 'The Colonel regrets indeed that you have been troubled, and he thanks you for giving him this audience and the opportunity to renew his assurances of loyalty and obedience.'

Brigadier Green and I exchanged looks as I went out with my party. Mine was one of shoulder-shrugging despair at the mystery of Greek affairs, his half-accusing me of panicking too easily and half-accusing Tsacalotos of some deep-pondered duplicity. The commandant swept off in his staff car, and George came back with me. 'The rogue,' he said, 'just as he was leaving he got a phone call that cheered him immensely – it must have been to say that the Communist takeover was finished.' So it was. British troops had cleared out the occupying group and the news had come to the Training Centre through the civilian telephone network, while Green and I had been left in ignorance by our respective headquarters.

13

Cyrenaica: The Last Conspiracy

The time for running Greek liaison from the Officers' Training Centre at Ismailia seemed to me to be over. The centre of gravity of the Greek problem had moved to Cyrenaica – at least, there were more Greek soldiers there than anywhere else, most of them taken from units in the Delta where they had been involved in Left-wing troubles. At Benghazi there was a guard battalion under Major Vassilopoulos, at Battisti another huge battalion doing desultory training under Major Vardis, and yet another guard battalion at Tripoli, easily the most comfortable place to be, with a live town and a local Greek community. There was also a prison camp with the revolutionary remnants of the once proud fighting Brigade; this was in the desert at Timimi, not far west of Tobruk, that area of sand and rolling scrub where Forbes had shot bustards for our Christmas dinner. Meanwhile, what units there were in Egypt were coasting along happily. The Officers' Training Centre was giving efficient instruction and laying the foundations of the battalion-size Brigade which finally went to fight in Italy under Tsacalotos. The other Greek units in Egypt, purged from revolutionary committees, now had their own British liaison officers – captains – in residence. There was Helier de Mourant, a civilised and cultivated lawyer from the Channel Islands, who as an exile himself sympathised with the exiled Greeks, and 'Berks' (I won't give his real name or nickname because of later events); there was also David Hunter, the former political journalist for the *News Chronicle* – '*poniros*' the Greeks called him, the cunning one. His unit was the Pioneer battalion, tired old men who pottered around doing non-specialist labouring tasks at the slowest possible pace. They caused no trouble, either administrative or political, and David could go off elsewhere to help if needed. And there was someone else, whose name I have forgotten. The logic of going up to the less well organised units in Cyrenaica was manifest. Only later did we get a liaison officer at Tripoli. Even so, there was astonishment in GHQ when I declared it my duty to go off westwards through the desert. Leaving the fleshpots of Egypt was no mean decision.

Jerry Herrick clearly had to come for questions of supply and transport; so did our two batmen drivers, and one of the interpreters – the other would have to stay behind in the Delta. Both wanted to go. But there was only one possible choice. Squire was republican and could cope with the men of the Left in Cyrenaica. George was royalist, an aesthete, with an educated disdain of anything boorish, and furthermore openly disapproving of Jerry Herrick and his toping. He would lose me allies all around. And Squire had a sense of humour, a quality we were both to need in the months ahead.

I travelled alone with my batman driver. Going back through the landscape of the Desert War was a nostalgic experience, but being confined to the road sanitised everything, for apart from a few stretches where I remembered being shelled and the occasional old notices of mines, it was the scenery with the war edited out. In the way that armies do in peacetime, everything had been neatly signposted, and the NAAFI had set up little transit pubs: the one at Derna, the oasis by the sea on the edge of the green hill country, was a particularly agreeable place and I was determined to make an overnight stop there. It was called the Red Lion; I remembered that Forbes had said, 'If they are going to give their pubs animal names, they should forsake the traditional English ones for at least two of them, in memory of the Aussies, The Pig's Arse and The Fair Cow.'

We stopped for a swim a couple of times, once in the shadow of the escarpment at Sollum. Mines were the worry when we pulled off the road; I had followed the war drill of having sandbags under the seats, but even so we went around gingerly inspecting and prodding before venturing the car wheels. At Tobruk we turned south onto the road to El Adem to look for my old gun positions on the Blue Line; although they had been just off to the left of the road, there was not a sign of them. The sand had obliterated every landmark. The vast minefield we had been covering in enfilade was not in evidence – the wire and the skull and crossbone markers had gone. Impossible to see anything, and out of the question to explore. On the whole, going back up the North African coast had been a disappointment. The only fun would have been another journey into the trackless south, where the desert terrain has an added interest from the effort to navigate, where every rise, outcrop, knoll and cliff has to be carefully observed. There was, how-ever, one delightful discovery about the coastal belt which I made during my five or six months' foray into Cyrenaica. After slight rain, so many of the barren rocky wadis were ablaze with masses of flowers of every hue, thin-stemmed and delicate, and lasting only for three or four days. The whole featureless plain just south of Benghazi was lit with ephemeral gold, and the magic was gone as unpredictably as it came. During the military campaigns, so far as I know, this never happened, as if the disturbance and dust caused by tanks and traffic had inhibited the seeds from growing.

When I called at HQ British troops in Cyrenaica, whom should I find but my old ally 'Taxiarchos', Brigadier Green, promoted here from the Canal Zone. Having escaped from the Greeks and their incomprehen-sible agitations, he now found that the Left-wingers and troublemak-ers who had been thrown out of Egypt had been dumped in his new diocese. It gave him a chance to make remarks of comic gloom, but he welcomed me with friendship. It was odd that some of my compatriots, angered by the Greeks, imputed a sort of guilt by association to me, but Green was delighted to have someone who would take most minor Hel-lenic troubles off his hands and offer advice on more difficult ones. He gave me the run of his mess and headquarters, and whenever I stayed there I had a splendid time – Squire too was made welcome. We had some hilarious evenings, some serious conversations, and sometimes, in the afternoon, we'd have a game of badminton on the tessellated marble floor of a spacious abandoned bank. Area HQ Benghazi was an island in the cold sea of military institutions and routines, colonised by a group of friends – much the result of Green's influence, an efficient and genial ruler of a contented empire.

Since the Italians had fled, the agreeable white buildings of Benghazi were occupied by British military units, the acronyms on the neatly painted directional signs showing that every sort of supply, repair and maintenance was provided for. The trouble for us was, every building had been taken over; there was no niche or corner into which a late-comer could be fitted. Jerry Herrick looked everywhere, but everything that was not dangerous or impossibly filthy had been taken. Our eye fell on a simple but delicately decorated pagoda in a grove of palm trees just outside town, but it was kept boarded-up and empty for the ulti-mate use of some Sennusi ruler, if ever one was to be restored. So I went off to Battisti, among the green hills of the Jebel, a white village built for Italian settlers – a church and municipal buildings on three sides of a square and about twenty white houses around. The church was out of bounds, the houses were smashed up, dirty and dangerous. The Greeks were all around in rows of tiny bivouacs; Major Vardis and his officers, to their credit, being in the same sort of tiny tents as their men. They had no mess, and only rudimentary cooking and washing facilities. However, there were the municipal buildings, intact and empty: there was a ban on their use but I overrode it and allotted rooms to Jerry, Squire, the two drivers and myself. It was a Spartan existence there, as winter came on. We had a paraffin stove in our communal eating room, and as bread came up to us from Benghazi we would toast slices on the stove, better than the bread as it was, but with a smoky oily flavour. As evening closed in, the Greeks had football on the square, with a goal rigged up and those who cared to join coming along as individuals – no teams. It was shooting, dribbling or passing as you felt inclined. Once again, I found football helpful – carefully avoiding getting into the mêlée, taking the ball when it came my way, doing a juggle and then, generally, passing rather than shooting. They were good at doing dashing things like heading and liked me to float in centres from the wings. But it was surprising how few of the vast number in the camp joined in. Courageous soldiers in their own mountains, boastful and reckless, they spurned keeping fit and enjoyed sheer idleness.

So long as we had fine weather, life at Battisti could be agreeable enough (though it was only my base and I was often on the move). There was swimming at the coast with some of the officers – the form of sport at which they excelled and the only form of exercise they all enjoyed. The first time I went with them was alarming. They used to go to a huge jetty of concrete pillars and girders running out far into deep water; the place had been an Italian submarine refuelling point, though there were no longer any traces of shore installations, and the jetty had been blown up at strategic points – to get to the far end needed a balancing act on a single girder at various places. Well out from the shore, the sea, wonderfully clear and blue, was moving up and down in huge smooth swells. At one moment the water would be two or three feet below, then at the next, fifteen to twenty feet. One had to dive in at the high and strike out away from the pillars of the structure. Out there it was fascinating, rising and falling smoothly with the rhythmic sweep of the ocean, with the translucent deep below. Once in, however, a problem arose – at least for an indifferent swimmer like me – how to get out again? It took good timing to get into position so the next rise gave a lift to the point where there was a projection, the end of a cable or something of the kind as an aid to clamber out. I once had a visit from two staff majors from GHQ 'to see how Mac was getting on', that is, to have a jaunt. I took them to see the sad and beautiful broken columns of the little temple of Cyrene in a wooded cleft, but not as they would have wished, for a swim. I wouldn't risk going off that jetty unless I had a party of the crack Greek swimmers around to pull me out if necessary.

As fate would have it, we were still in Cyrenaica when Christmas came round again. It would have been sensible to ensure that my affairs took me near the congenial Area HQ mess at Benghazi, but that would have meant abandoning the rest of my little headquarters, so I spent the festive season at Battisti. It was bleak and we huddled over paraffin stoves and had an indifferent, though jovial meal – none of the Timimi bustards Colonel Forbes-Watson had shot for us two years before. Once dinner and a certain amount of good cheer was over, we all sank into melancholy. Jerry Herrick, of course, drank too much, I got unreasonably vexed with him and he shed a maudlin tear. Even Squire began to look as if he wished he had stayed with Tsacalotos and spent Christmas in Alex or Cairo.

One of Brigadier Green's problems, and mine, was the camp in the desert at Timimi, where the extremists of the Left had been dumped after the Brigade had revolted on the eve of going to Italy. It was a prison camp all right, surrounded by high barbed wire fences. But the British guards, such as they were, had no patrolling to do, since there was nowhere to go outside but rolling desert. In charge was Major Kerr, a big sombre man with rimless glasses, stern, as he had to be, and disliking the Greeks and all their works, as was perhaps inevitable. I would visit the camp, go round and drink coffee, and talk over the news of the war. It was important to argue against the view that the defeat of Hitler was now inevitable, for this proposition was their instinctive justification for refusing to fight outside Greece for 'imperialist' Britain. They were sure that Russia would dominate the Balkans and Greece, if not all Europe, and that the future of their country lay with EAM/ELAS. I was told on more than one occasion, without malice though hardly convincing as the friendly warning it purported to be, that my name had been sent to Moscow to be dealt with when the Communist triumph came. Long afterwards, when I was on a Roumanian plane flying from Frankfurt to Bucharest for a meeting of the Union Académique Internationale, this ancient threat came to mind and I wondered how effective the card index of the Kremlin might be.

At the Timimi camp I always met Papa Heretis, or rather he always rushed up to greet me; he was a Greek Orthodox priest from Crete, portly, broad-shouldered, long-bearded, scruffy in an ancient threadbare cassock, with the reputation of having killed two or three Germans with his bare hands before escaping to Egypt. Now he was here behind the barbed wire, having been deeply involved in the conspiracy that wrecked the Greek Brigade. When we met we talked of religion (he knew my father's profession and my problems about ordination); also, he invariably recounted to me the agonies he suffered from arthritis, for which the only remedy would be to go back to Cairo for soothing baths and massage. Not surprisingly, Major Kerr would hear nothing of it. I grew to like Papa Heretis, and finally rescued him. On a visit westwards to Tripoli to see our battalion there, I found the local Greek community lamenting their lack of a priest, so I negotiated the release of Heretis into my charge and took him to Tripoli, where I installed him in the presbytery next to the little white church. This was a good work in which Taxiarchos Green willingly cooperated; 'Splendid,' he said, 'we'll get him out of Professor Kerr's academy.' The Greek community made their new pastor welcome and saw to his comfort. When we visited Tripoli, Squire and I would always dine (at midday) with Heretis. He would go out early to the market to get the best pieces of meat and offal to make a kebab, and we would sit back round the brazier watching the flames leaping from the glowing charcoal as the drips of fat fell. This meal would be supported by huge chunks of bread and washed down with a fearsome brandy, drunk as a table wine. After dinner we would sit on his balcony shaded by the overhang of the roof; on the white wall behind us the sunlight threw the grotesque shadows of the various items hanging from the eaves to dry – bunches of onions and herbs, and sometimes an octopus. On the Sundays, I would attend the church with the Greek officers of the battalion. Heretis insisted that I sat in a place of honour – after trying unsuccessfully to persuade me to sit on a chair behind the iconostasis to see the consecration. I didn't mind too much sitting on the chair where the Patriarch would be elevated if ever he came on a visit, but going behind the altar screen seemed a vaguely heretical infringement of the liturgical decencies. I hope Heretis got back safely to his parish in Crete to bask in the approval of his adventures in the Resistance, his entanglement with EAM/ELAS in the years of his exile forgotten.

Though the Greeks in Cyrenaica and Tripolitania were all Left-wing, or supposedly so, there were grades of political allegiance, ranging from a few who were glad to be regarded as too untrustworthy to be sent to fight, many who were traditional republicans and were unwilling to go along with the royalists, others whose family memories of the Metaxas regime had come to dominate their minds, others who thought EAM/ELAS was the winning side for the future, and finally, among them, the hard-core fanatical Communists. There was no guarantee that any particular unit would be stable. If there was trouble, it was bound to arise in the now traditional way; a Communist committee would force the battalion commander to become their puppet. So it happened with the guard battalion in Benghazi, up to now a smart (well, smartish) outfit and a model to the others. Its commander was Major Vassilopoulos, himself a man of the Left and out of favour with the Greek HQ in Cairo. He had a dark brown piratical countenance, a hook nose and a huge, bristling black moustache; he was going bald with the jet black tonsure all around plastered down, and there was a perpetual smile showing his large, brilliantly white teeth. He was continually jesting, and was given to dramatic gestures. I was going to play football for his unit against a British team, so he issued an order of the day to his men. 'Soldiers, our liaison officer, Major McManners is playing football for us today. On the left wing. We must extend all our endeavours to enable him to boast of us to our beloved British allies.' Mercifully, the match was cancelled.

The crisis came when the Communist committee called on Vassilopoulos, presented a petition with many signatures, and demanded to control the battalion in the name of the people. He drew his revolver, put it on the table and declared them all under arrest. His adjutant called in the loyal officers, and the committee and all the signatories of the petition were put under guard. Vassilopoulos then sent to Brigadier Green to inform him that he had a couple of hundred rebels, including nine officers, under arrest, and insisted that they be removed from his

battalion forthwith. Total astonishment at the somnolent HQ of Benghazi Area, except for the brigadier himself who was now seeing history
repeat itself. The standard marquee-type tents were rushed out of storage, and lorries ferried the rebels fifty or more miles down the road
southwards; a camp was set up a mile or so from the road, and a truck
went down every day with rations and water. Without means of transport the outcasts could not go anywhere else, and they were left to
make their own arrangements as to who was in charge and what they
did with their time – which was, of course, nothing.

During this crisis I had been at Battisti. Now I arrived with Squire to
assess the troubled situation. Vassilopoulos gave us a hilarious account
of the attempted revolution and the day of dupes that ensued. I don't
think he had been trying to reinstate himself with the royalist high command; it was simply that he was a tough character who refused to allow
himself to be pushed around. So far, the commanders of units had given
in to the Communists and tried to save face by concealing the fact: he
was too proud to follow these examples. Brigadier Green, his hands full
of the administrative problems of his vast diocese, might have been
tempted to wish that he had. I went to see the revolutionaries in their
desert exile; living in their big tents they were comfortable enough and
lay around chatting, smoking and waiting for the rations to arrive. Of
the officers, two were graduates of the University of Athens, whose
company I had enjoyed from time to time, generally in talking about
literature, especially modern poetry. Their hero was T. S. Eliot, whose
influence on their generation in Greece was profound. When I called on
the brigadier, he was cheerfully resigned – he had trod this path before
and it no longer held terrors for him – until, this time, GHQ Cairo
intervened. It would have been reasonable, in the short term anyway,
to leave the revolutionary committee and its supporters and any that
Vassilopoulos had lumped in with them, to stew in their own juice. It
was also reasonable – and fairer – to repeat the old manoeuvre of Canal
Zone days and sort out the hard-line Communists from the others,
giving those who might wish to get back into the British fold the chance
to apply to do so. Leave it to distant staff officers, however, to find the
most dangerous and self-defeating method possible.

Maybe it was not their own idea, it could be the Greek Army HQ
was pressing for it. Green was ordered to begin by separating six named
officers from the rest and putting them under arrest. After that, he was

to start the well-understood screening process. I was thunderstruck. We might meet resistance to the arrests and, once the six had been taken away, all the rest, officers and men, would feel they had to join them as a matter of honour and solidarity. Brigadier Green agreed with me when I rehearsed my misgivings but, he said, having stated his objections and having been overruled, there was nothing for it but to obey. Orders were orders. 'Deception is needed,' he declared, 'it will be on my conscience, not yours.' He would send a truck down to the camp with the driver bearing his written orders for the named officers to get on board and return to Benghazi to report to him. When they arrived, he would interrogate them about their loyalty, and taking whatever they said as unsatisfactory, he would put them under arrest. Then, the following day, the separation of Right and Left would take place – not that there would be many Right. I must handle my side of it as best I could. I was just going when a thought alarmed him – 'What if they smell a rat when my order reaches them and they send the wrong people?' I told him I'd meet the truck on the way back and identify the proscribed half dozen. (Squire would have to help me, of course, and it is a measure of his loyalty to the war effort and his courage that he was willing to do it.) So it was done. Quite early the next morning, Squire and I were driving down – ostensibly to the rebel camp – when we met the area HQ truck on the road coming in to Benghazi, and we stopped for a chat. I agreed that Taxiarchos was going to question them about their allegiance and conduct, but did not add that he meant to arrest them anyway. Then we turned round and went back with them. Speeding ahead, I reported to the brigadier that they would soon arrive and that they were, indeed, the men on the GHQ list. His office was on the second floor and from the window we looked down into a back courtyard; here, two covered trucks were waiting with five military policemen in attendance – red-topped hats, white blancoed pistol belts and shoulder straps, black boots darkly gleaming. 'Ah, McManners,' said Green as we looked down on this strangely comic sight, 'the tumbrils are waiting.'

Then for the tricky bit. With Squire and my driver, I went down to the camp, now buzzing like a hive of wasps disturbed with a stick. We had a sizeable tent on board, and our driver put it up while Squire and I went to confer with the three or four remaining officers over coffees. Two were my young graduates of Athens. No Communist committee came forward; perhaps, seeing the whole outfit had been defined as a Left-wing bloc by the purge of Vassilopoulos, they now settled all things in common or perhaps the officers had been allowed to lead. We explained that on the following morning Taxiarchos would be coming down to go through the drill of separating Left from Right, now so well understood. A couple of officers went off to tell the angry rank and file and to get their decision – there had been nothing for it but tell them that the arrested six would not be returning. Squire and I withdrew to our tent, had our evening meal, then returned to the Greek officers, who were now drinking coffee after theirs. The two emissaries were back: the decision had been made to delay the decision until the next morning. I knew this meant there'd be no trouble – an opportunity for revolutionary posturing had been prolonged; honour demanded delay – that was all. We then sat there talking far into the night, no longer about politics, revolution and the war, but about England and Greece, literature and art.

After breakfast, there was a universal packing up of the voluminous possessions, ready for the arrival of the brigadier. Vassilopoulos was with him and his adjutant and perhaps another officer – I cannot remember if a representative of British Security was there. There were few British troops. I was flattered to feel that I was trusted to succeed; given the way GHQ had stacked the odds against us, I couldn't have guaranteed it. I sat with the officers as one by one the soldiers and their baggage were escorted forwards. I tried to persuade my two graduates to join the British fold. They laughed and joked and made no commitment. As they went forward last of all they saluted me smartly and cheerfully and went off to join the vast majority, the Eritrean tourists. As darkness was falling I went to call on them all, now in a compound surrounded by barbed wire somewhere in Benghazi. Brigadier Green had laid on cooks and provisions and they had been given a hot dinner; their own fare under their own revolutionary régime had been Spartan indeed, and there was a mood of repletion and hilarity. There were lots of their ELAS songs and choruses, and a great deal of jesting, mainly political, of course. They were looking forward to their trip into a more distant exile. It would provide them with their credentials for respect in the new order which would arise in Europe in the wake of the Red Army.

14
Chairborne in Cairo

Shortly after the bleak Christmas at Battisti, I moved with my party, Squire, Jerry and drivers, back to the Delta. GHQ Allies wanted me back. We now had a first-rate young liaison officer at Tripoli and (I think) also at Benghazi.

When setting off on the return drive I called at the army transport depot at Benghazi to get a jerrycan to carry spare petrol. Needless to say, I had to sign for it. As second in command of X Company I had donated to the British Army a vast collection of jerrycans, having fitted out every vehicle with a number of these strong, self-locking containers – marked in different colours to show which carried petrol and which water, but to get one now I had to sign in triplicate with the undertaking to return it. Once in GHQ Allies, a series of letters arrived from Benghazi demanding the can or the money for it. I replied that it had been invaluable on the long journey and when I next came to Cyrenaica I'd return it. No! Similarly with my next somewhat disingenuous epistle saying that an unforeseen crisis in Greek affairs was preventing me from fulfilling my promise and earnest wish. Finally, to the delight of Sergeant Bakerman, my secretary in GHQ Allies, I produced the masterly letter that won the day. It began, 'I do not deny that I have the obligation to carry the can', and I offered to hand it in at a depot in Egypt and forward the receipt to Benghazi for their files. Reluctant agreement as a special concession. It took my driver the value of the jerrycan in expenditure on petrol to find the appropriate place to leave it.

Now at last I became a member of the great 'chairborne division' in the Egyptian capital, with a huge office high up in one of the commandeered hotels in the complex constituting GHQ Middle East. There was no officers' mess or common facilities: we lived where we liked in our own accommodation in town and dined at night in a restaurant of our choice, fortified by staff pay and living allowances. Thanks to Edgar Newton, another major in Allies, I got a comfortable bed-sitter in the apartment where he himself lived; our landlady was Mrs Betz, a Syrian housewife who looked after us with the solicitude of my last landlady in Oxford, in those naïve golden days which now seemed in another world and a distant era. She had a son, a shy, slight young man of twenty or so, whose ambition was to become an archaeologist. To reciprocate her care, I talked in an encouraging way to him about his subject, and rather against my will, yielded to his invitation to go to see an archaeological dig on the outer rim between town and desert. This was very boring, though here I learnt of the 'percussion bulge' in flint knapping, the only technicality of pre-history I have ever known. On another afternoon, however, he offered me a marvellously interesting tour of the Coptic churches of Cairo, picturesque in gloom and strangely sad with the shadow of persecution hanging over them, as it had for so many centuries. It was all far from the tourist circuit, especially as we had to go on trams, where more passengers were on the roof and hanging to the sides than rode within.

GHQ worked a long morning session, then again from 5 p.m. to 8 p.m. So that meant dining rather late. Sometimes I'd go with Squire, more especially to a restaurant called L'Ermitage, our favourite. Indeed, when he got back to Famagusta he set up his own Ermitage as one of his capital ventures, and installed his English mistress there as manageress. Or I would go to the Greek Club, a bigger establishment than the one for Canal employees at Ismailia, with Squire, or George or perhaps others – though all young and junior. Here, any evening might suddenly turn into a festive affair; a bout of singing would erupt spontaneously among junior officers, someone jumping up, or being pushed up, to sing a solo and everyone else joining in the chorus, not without banging on tables as accompaniment for appropriate ditties. But there were none of the revolutionary ballads of EAM/ELAS; we now had roistering drinking songs or sentimental laments, a shepherd yearning for his lost love, maybe. In the afternoons I almost invariably went to the Gezira Sporting Club, leaving GHQ in a taxi or on the one tram in Cairo on which you would normally find a British officer or two. I soon learnt how to make the journey free of charge: when the conductor pushed through to you, say 'King Farouk he pay' and there would be laughter all round. At Gezira, after a snack, I would meet with a naval officer who worked elsewhere in GHQ, to play tennis. We hired two of the Egyptian professionals who would bring the racquets and balls and summon a couple of ball-boys. The professionals always played together against us and, no doubt, they organised the run of the game to ensure we enjoyed it. Their skill was prodigious but they lacked physical strength, so we sometimes battered through their barrage of mastery by heavy serving and volleying. It was strange, employing four barefooted people just for the pleasure of the two of us, and for such a modest fee, an illustration of the injustice of the social order if you wish, but they manifestly enjoyed themselves just as we did. Thereafter, tea on the terrace and a swim. If Squire came there he would have had a snooze in the earlier part of the afternoon before tea and his swim. There were plenty of good-looking girls at the pool and even more sexy-looking ones; would one could slip for a moment or two into the ladies' changing rooms, said Squire, 'that would rejuvenate our jaded spirits'.

While lounging at the pool a couple of almost identical incidents occurred which would have delighted a connoisseur of absurdities had it not been for the element of personal tragedy involved. One day, coming out of the water, I lighted upon Captain 'Berks', one of our liaison officers in 210 BLU, sitting expansively at ease in a wicker chair and enjoying a long and manifestly extremely alcoholic drink. For a couple of months now he had been posted as absent without leave, and there was much speculation as to where he was hiding out. What to do? Wearing swimming trunks seemed to me to be a disqualification by protocol for authoritarian action on my part, so I had a chat with him; pointing out that it was to his advantage to give himself up rather than to wait until he was caught. He expressed remorse: 'Mac, I'll be at your office first thing tomorrow morning.' There was no sign of him the next day or any other day for a fortnight. Then, a repeat performance at the Gezira pool and a repetition of paternal admonition on my part and contrite promises on his. The case was hopeless, however, and finally, late one night, the military police caught him in Shepheard's Hotel after a chase through bars and lounges and corridors, upstairs and down. At the court martial, 'Berks' asked me to be a witness for character and I did what I could – tricky job with the Greeks, isolated life among foreign allies, difficult decisions in tense circumstances. The defence having produced a character witness, the prosecution was entitled to offer a rebuttal. I was presented with Berks's record of service: disciplinary offences galore. Did I know of these when he was appointed? No, I did not have the power of appointment; liaison officers were taken on and sent to units by higher authority in GHQ Allies. Would I have accepted him had I known of his record? And so on. I looked foolish, Berks was bowler-hatted and vanished. Strange were the labyrinthine workings of GHQ Allies. My liaison job, both *vis-à-vis* the Greeks and with regard to my own side, was a case of responsibility without power.

The complexity of Greek affairs, together with the steady pressure of Parkinson's Law that work has the capacity of expanding to occupy everyone available to do it, ensured that my desk at GHQ was never clear, and there was endless talking things over with people in various branches of the liaison business. As is the nature of human affairs, such big issues as I then dealt with are now forgotten; it is social relationships and unusual picturesque incidents that stay in the memory. My concept of the liaison officer's duty – at any rate for one of my comparatively junior rank – was to become steeped in the social life of the ally he assisted. This was a comfortable obligation now it could be fulfilled over morning coffee in Groppi's or dinner in the Greek Club.

One morning Squire and a couple of young officers took me to see the great literary figure of the exile, Seferis, who received us in his book-lined apartment in Cairo, arrayed in his dressing gown and smoking cigarettes in a long amber holder. The young officers showed him the verse translation into English Squire and I had made of a poem by some modern author ('Around your heart I set three sentries' – being the sun, the north wind and the eagle). He looked over it gravely, without saying anything – I hoped it was silent approval. Occasionally he would pull a handsome volume from his shelves and read a passage to illustrate his point; and of course there was much to say about T. S. Eliot. Seeing I had lost my copy long ago in the desert, Squire had found another one for me in Cairo, and inscribed it with the poet's own words, 'when we were measuring our lives with coffee spoons'.

Though Vassilopoulos had nipped revolution in the bud in Cyrenaica, the affairs of these distant Greeks were still of concern to GHQ Allies, and I made a journey there by plane. I was accompanied by Captain Psaros, of the Greek Paymaster's Branch, very mild and solemn and quiet. We had a lift in an old Anson plane to get us to Benghazi; there were the pilot and his assistant, and the two of us in the seats behind, that was all. Before we got far, it became obvious all was not well – oil was pouring down the wing and smoke came up from the floor between the pilot and co-pilot in front of us. Imperturbably, and with only a muttered word or two exchanged between them, the assistant squirted a fire extinguisher down onto the source of the smoke. Not a word was said to us and I was damned if I would ask. Psaros pulled a photograph out of his wallet, showed it silently to me, then sat there with his eyes fixed on it – his wife and three small children. We drew near to Mersa Matruh and the plane touched down. The pilot and his assistant got out: still not a word had passed their lips. We stayed where we were. Ten minutes later a mechanic on the ground-staff came to us. 'Better get out, this one can go no further.'

We got to Benghazi, and after that I went on to Tripoli – without Psaros this time – to be heartened by our liaison officer's remarkable work in building up a first-class and proud guard battalion. But the journey back from Tripoli to Benghazi, like the flight in the silent Anson, had its moments. I was ferried along to the American airfield for my lift. It was a relief to be told that the flight was off, it was too dangerous – dark skies, fierce winds and foul weather. However, I was enthusiastically invited to stay. Stranded as a guest of the Americans was no hardship – bacon, eggs, tomato, hot waffles overrunning with syrup and excellent coffee. Then, in the afternoon, as I snoozed in a deep armchair, up came a staff sergeant. 'There's one off to Benghazi; pilot says he'll be OK. Don't say I didn't warn you. Get on if you like, there's one born every minute.' Nothing for it but to set off across the windswept runway. The weather cleared up somewhat during the flight, but as the only passenger I wasn't much reassured when one of the crew came round to enlist my support: 'Say, reckon you've fought all over this goddam desert; keep an eye out and see if you recognise anything, the pilot's lost.' Very sensibly, the crew navigated westwards until they hit the coast and followed it. We got into Benghazi as darkness was closing in, wave-hopping very low to dodge under the worst of the storm.

I had assumed that the revolutionaries arrested by Major Vassilopoulos and verified to be so by Brigadier Green had been sent off to Eritrea; but not so. When I arrived back in Cairo they were still locked up along with other, earlier rebels in a prisoner-of-war cage in the Canal Zone, awaiting transport to their final exile. I was not aware of their presence until the military authorities had managed to ensure a major crisis by dictatorial handling of a very simple problem. Among the internees were fifty or so trachomatics, sufferers from a disease of the eyes which could be infectious and certainly needed treatment. Orders came from on high that they would be taken from the cage and sent to Kabrit, the camp for civilian refugees, for a medical cure. The imprisoned Greeks refused to let them go. They were united by their revolutionary faith in a pact of comradeship; the crafty British must not be allowed to separate them and so be free to instil their capitalist propaganda into the ears of the weak and susceptible. When the reiterated orders were again refused, the authorities decided to coerce them by cutting off their rations. They still refused to obey, saying they were going on hunger strike anyway as a protest.

It was at this point that someone decided to tell GHQ Allies about the crisis – or, more probably, Allies above me already knew and, egged on by the Greek General Staff, had agreed to the tough policy. I went round every day to see the revolutionaries, drank coffee (seemingly in good supply and not part of the strike) and argued. I had some difficulty in getting in, not from the Greeks, but from the British outside, who feared I'd be kidnapped and used for purposes of blackmail (I think that at one time I was actually forbidden to go inside). The hungry inmates of the camp made a dramatic performance out of their plight – histrionic, but I thought it rather touching. They were getting weaker they said, soon some of the feeble would collapse, but so long as they had coffee I would always be welcome to share it with them. The 'let-them-starve' pundits in GHQ would of course forget what they had said once a death occurred, and the intransigent Greek General Staff would have faded out and left it to the British ally. It took ten days to a fortnight for honour to be satisfied. I guaranteed that the trachomatics would be returned to them when they had received their course of treatment, and once they had been given this promise, out of their tents they rushed post-haste with a hungry show of triumph, and along came the rations right away to reward them. I took the blame at GHQ for this 'shameful surrender', something I ought never to have done on my own account and so on. The chairborne soldiers had preserved their self-image of authoritarian superiority – they did not make such cowardly compromises. Before I finally went home I sent David Hunter to Eritrea to take a look at the men of the Communist Left in what they called 'the British concentration camp'. As a former journalist of Left-wing opinions, David could be relied on not to connive at injustice. He reported them as spending their days on sunny beaches or in other sorts of idleness.

As a change from the crises of the Left, we had one from the Right –
one fitting in with the view that history repeats itself, first as tragedy,
then as farce. I had arrived early for the second session of the day's
work at 5 p.m., when a phone call came from an old ally at Alexandria
Area HQ – the mole who had given me the warning that the court-martial contingent from Z Company had better rush back to Palestine
because Kingsley Foster was on the warpath. After we had transacted
the business in hand, he complained about his tribulations with the
Greek Sacred Squadron. They were commandos, all officers, all
extreme royalists, and spent their time raiding the Greek islands. They
were normally based somewhere along the Syrian–Palestine coast, but a
small ship that was ferrying them on such a foray had blown its boiler,
and the British naval lieutenant commanding it had steered it into
Alexandria harbour for repairs. The stranded Sacred Squadron officers
were becoming a nuisance in town. He ended by saying, 'We are fed up
with them so we are sending them up to Cairo, where you can look
after them for a change.' While he was talking, Godfrey Hobbes's staff
major, his GII, had dropped in for a word and heard my side of the conversation. He guessed what it was about and I admitted it without a
second thought. I had got beyond panicking about Greek affairs by
now, there were wheels within wheels and what was given as certain
today would be contradicted tomorrow. Usually, I only passed on information when I knew that it was certain and when I expected something
useful could be done about it; otherwise, all sorts of ukases and ordi-
nances would be issued to make matters worse.

Towards 8 p.m., closing time for the bureaucracy of GHQ, Godfrey
Hobbes rang me up. His staff major had passed on the news that the
Sacred Squadron was being sent to Cairo. The Left-wingers and republicans in the other Greek units regarded them as a bunch of Fascists:
there would be fighting in the streets. So he had asked for a high-level
conference under a brigadier chief of staff (was this of Middle East
Command or of Allies GHQ?), a representative of the Navy, and one
of British troops in Egypt, while he would attend with me as his advisor
on Greek affairs. This would take place first thing tomorrow morning.
I inwardly cursed the staff major who had made himself important by
appearing so well-informed on the arcane ins and outs of Greek affairs
and got me into this interdepartmental fracas. I rang Alex and was just
in time to catch my ally: I now needed full and circumstantial details.

His final words about sending the Sacred Squadron to Cairo had just been a joke, a frivolous *boutade* to sign off with. 'I though you knew,' he laughed. 'You'll remember that I said they would by preference be sent up on Nile barges.' True, but I had taken that to be the jest tacked onto a genuine statement of intent, and not a prolongation of a fantasy scenario. What to do? Everyone had gone off to dine, while the bureaucratic and military machine was grinding on to a Brigadier General Staff's interdepartmental conference. It was a miserable night, but I decided to do exactly nothing, just go to the meeting and let events take their course. Godfrey was going to look ridiculous if he desperately started ringing round to revoke his initiative, so we'd have the showdown, and when the worst came to the worst I'd have to express my naïve astonishment and look ridiculous myself.

There we were early in the morning, when the vast headquarters had hardly got stirring, our hats in front of us on the table, each in its braid and badges reflecting the majesty of the arm of the service we represented. The whole gathering tore a strip off the naval chap: the Navy had camouflaged and disguised the vessel as one of the ordinary shabby coastal boats around the islands and had guaranteed that it would work – and it had failed at the very start. Godfrey testified to the menace of having the royalist commandos at large in Cairo. The colonel from British troops in Egypt, praise be, had not been properly briefed and had not had the wit to ring up Alexandria Area himself to find out. He was apologetic and said they had not been aware of such explosive consequences in organising temporary accommodation for these Greek desperadoes who were still just a name to him. As junior, I testified last. I said I had worked on the phone overnight and all concerned in Alexandria Area had agreed there should be no move. 'Well done,' said the Brigadier, 'you settled it all on your level, we are grateful.' 'Absolutely,' said Godfrey, beaming at his clever staff officer and annexing a vicarious share of his glory. As we walked back together, he for his pink gin and I for my coffee, he said, 'Ah well, one always has to be careful about rumours in Greek affairs.'

During my comfortable months as an honorary member of the chairborne division in Cairo, a signal came inviting me to rejoin the battalion. I cannot remember just when it arrived, very early in 1945 probably, possibly later – I hope later, nearer to the German surrender. 'Company now available. Do you wish to return?' When I received this,

I was accompanying Colonel Granitsas, chief of the Greek General Staff, on a visit to some Greek unit or other, with George Leroudias as my interpreter. We were staying in a most agreeable little officers' club and conversing in the bar. I remember the scene clearly and what happened. It was flattering to be regarded as one of the inner ring who would always come back to take a company command in the First, the regular battalion – as Tommy Hamilton had done, leaving the Staff College, and Kingsley Foster, coming down a rank and abandoning some high administrative job in the Delta. There was also a feeling of pride in being regarded as capable of commanding a company. But inwardly I knew the humiliating truth of it – it was a prestigious load that I could not carry. I had left the battalion knowing that I would find it hard to screw up the determination to face the battlefield again. A company commander goes round instructing his platoon commanders where to position their guns, and soldiers will pay with their lives for any foolish decision. All I knew was desert warfare; mountain warfare and operating in close country would be a trade that had to be learnt quickly. The job with the Greeks was fascinating, and I was looking forward to organising the return to Greece itself. My affection and admiration for the battalion was great, but the mind contradicted the heart and I allowed my reply to show it: 'If needed will come, but am happy here.' That was as far towards acceptance as I could bring myself to go. But I didn't play fair; I didn't leave my fate in the hands of my old commanding officer. I told George Leroudias, knowing full well he would pass it on to Granitsas. So it happened, right away. Granitsas went off to the phone to set the machinery in motion to prevent me being moved. It was not a particular compliment to their liaison officer, but a common-sense thing to do; my knowledge of Greek personalities and problems had taken time to accumulate; it was a pity to lose it just when the wind-down of the Greek army presence in the Middle East had to be organised. Soon, a signal came back from the battalion: 'Many thanks. We can manage fine. Good luck.'

Subsequently, I met two officers of the battalion of my days, one in happy circumstances, one tragic. When the Italians left the war and changed sides, Hugh Holmes, my predecessor as adjutant, was released from prison camp and came back to Alex to his family, and to marry his fiancée. This was the second marriage of an RNF officer to a girl of the famous Concert Party, Bill Sanderson having married Vivian, the star singer, earlier. I went to the splendid Holmes wedding; there was a strange feeling in the air that the war was really over, whatever news of fighting kept coming in.

The tragic meeting was with Wilfred Hillman in Cairo base hospital. Before I left the battalion, he had moved to a staff job, again by the good offices of Godfrey Hobbes, who recommended him to GHQ Allies. The liaison task he was given was with the Greek Sacred Squadron. This was outside my sphere of activity – 210 BLU did not work with units engaged in active operations – so I knew nothing of it. The Sacred Squadron, it will be remembered, was a small unit composed entirely of officers, commandos who from air or sea conducted raids on German outposts on the islands of the Aegean. It was astonishing that Wilfred, slight, frail and bespectacled, highly intelligent but not made for the rough and tumble of soldiering, should have been sent to work with this band of heroic desperadoes. Clearly, it was assumed that his role was not concerned with operations, but with the provision of equipment and accommodation and relations with British units living near their base. However, the whole squadron was sent on a major raid, and Wilfred felt that honour demanded he should go with them. In an odd fashion, this act of gratuitous heroism mirrored a bizarre earlier incident concerning an unqualified soldier who refused to stay behind. The commander of the Sacred Squadron was Colonel Tsigantes, fat, heavy and sybaritic, who spent his time in good cheer and social life, leaving his officers to organise and train as best they could. In his absence, they had all trained as parachutists, and a group of them were waiting at the airfield to lift off for their first airborne raid, when the portly figure of Tsigantes arrived. The airfield staff tried to prevent his going, but he pulled rank. It was not their business that he had never jumped before, he was the commanding officer and he was going – so he did.

Wilfred was lying in bed, weak and pale, having endured terrible privations, living without food and with very little water, and picked up only when he had reached the point of no return. He told me of his adventures on this disastrous raid, where he had finished up alone on an uninhabited rocky islet, though he concentrated on the comic incidents, not on the grim. One concerned his relations, early in the raid, with a journalist who had accompanied the foray; it was his duty to censor the copy sent out for the press, and he refused to allow 'Homer's wine-dark sea' on the ground it was a cliché. Should censorship extend to points of literary style? Thereafter he and the journalist were not on speaking terms. On a later visit to the hospital, I found Wilfred weaker still. There was no hope. He had fallen in love with the nurse who looked after him and had become a Roman Catholic in the hope of marrying her. We said goodbye when I went away: we both knew it was our last meeting.

Just before this I had paid a visit to the Jardin des Enfants at Ismailia, and passed a couple of hours on the beach with three Greek officers. A ship passed through the Canal, the rails lined with troops bound for the Far East. Their war was beginning, ours was drawing to an end. As we stood up in the water to wave to them, great shouts came from the crowded decks, 'You lucky people!' The envious shout had a more general application. This was the phrase to describe those of us who got through the war, 'you lucky people'. On Armistice Day we recite 'They shall not grow old, as we that are left grow old, age shall not weary them or the years condemn' – but those who were killed wanted to grow old, they did not fear the weariness or the condemnation of the years, they wanted no more than to live with their wives and lovers, see their children grow up and grow themselves in experience and affection. Remembering them is all we can do, but it is a poor thing; we are living our lives out, we are the 'lucky people'. Wilfred was dying, I was going on.

When news of the German surrender came, I was in Alexandria talking to the port authorities and drawing up a plan to repatriate the Greeks as soon as the sea lanes were safe. As ever, I stayed at the Union Club. There was no one to talk to, since few officers travelling or on leave chose to stay in these solemn Victorian splendours; amid the fat leather sofas, deep carpets and soft-footed waiters an uproarious laugh or upraised voice would have echoed embarrassingly, while there were plenty of cheap beds in hotels more conveniently situated for pleasure. There was no one around in town that I knew and Greek liaison officers were not required for business that was purely from the British side. As usual, I read in the library when the day's work was over and my driver had gone off to the transit camp at Sidi Bishr; then I dined in the near-empty dining room. After that, I supposed, more reading – but it seemed a pity to let this historic night go without celebrating or, at least, watching others celebrate, so I finally went out to the most respectable night club I knew, the one where we had celebrated Bill Sanderson's marriage to Vivian. The usual set-up: many little tables around a dance floor, a spacious arena but now crowded with officers of Army and Navy (I saw no Airforce), some in masculine groups, some with feminine company, respectable and not so respectable. I had a table to myself. From time to time the chorus girls came on to dance; if it wasn't to the tango (to a tune that haunts me but still remains anonymous to me) it was the can-can by Offenbach, with exiguous bikinis for the first and the regulation frilly skirts with displays of cellulite and suspenders for the second. As ever, one saw the sweat rolling down staining the edges of the bikinis, and the dead eyes in the pale faces above the fixed smiles clamped on to the bright red mouths. Of what nationalities were they, and what did the British victory mean to them? They would have gone on dancing just the same if German officers were sitting at the tables, and the incidents of the long night would have been much the same, just with different uniform jackets hanging on the back of the chair beside the bed. I sat alone drinking the most expensive soft drink in Egyptian history since Cleopatra dissolved pearls in the wine, the price of my blameless admission. Immense quantities of variegated alcohol were going down and the noise was deafening, but nothing more outrageous was overtly going on than a competition to balance pints of beer on heads until gravity intervened with a splash and a splintering. A decorous party of senior naval officers with lady guests, mostly from the armed services, was performing waltzes and quicksteps when the repertoire of the Levantine band and the absences of the chorus girls left the dance floor available. A dashing matron – someone I had met before in Alexandrian social life – swept past on the arm of one of the naval group and in the course of two circlings of the room urged me to come over and join their party. I declined the invitation and just sat there, watching and brooding and registering the sight. I realised then, if I had not done before, that I am by nature a historian, recording and recounting in detachment, not committed to the event, whether for good or evil, an interested and sympathetic non-participant. It was all sad and disillusioning. These years of devastation and dying, so many vanished, so many broken, so many left alone and this was all we could do to mark the end of the cruelty, the end of a Satanic era. We were not worthy of our own desperate and proud endeavours. Had I still been with the old battalion, wherever they were (probably in

the south of France and driving northwards now) I could have celebrated, reminiscing of adventures past and looking forward to the new
world before us as the guns fell silent.

I went back through the almost empty streets – half lit, for the street
lights had their glass painted blue with only a crescent left clear to
create the half-blackout that had prevailed in Alex. I reflected that
when this bizarre Islamic twilight went back to pre-war illumination,
the whole place would look even more sleazy in a pattern of too-reveal-
ing brightness and accentuated shadows. A little group of soldiers, tipsy
but subdued in their singing, passed by; the locals were not interested in
our victory, save one who hissed 'Hi, captain, all very good now, come
see my sister.' (In their limited vocabulary of commercial English, all
soldiers were 'George' and all officers 'captains'.) In the silent club I
sank into a chair; it was late, and the bar shutters were closed. I rang for
my lemonade and the white-robed Egyptian waiter who brought it put
the glass down unobtrusively, but with a certain indefinable empathy
as if he guessed what I was feeling.

Would I had kept a copy of my movement order for the repatriation
of the Greeks! With full leisure now to devote entirely to this single
task, and with everyone everywhere – GHQ Allies, the port authorities,
the area commands in Egypt and Cyrenaica – anxious to help (getting
rid of the Greeks and their impossible politics was a wonderful prospect
for them), and the Greeks themselves desperate to get home, one could
plan confidently for this final operation. Two ships were laid on, and
we were to divide each battalion into groups according to the port
where they would be put ashore. As the military units converged on
Alex these geographical groups would be conflated and finally each
would be packed into a certain space on board. There were the battalions in Egypt and those in Cyrenaica – I think we now had one liaison
officer in Tripoli, one in Benghazi and two in the Delta, and the order
detailing the arrangements went to each of them. And at the docks at
Alex I had made a crucial discovery: trains coming in from the west
made a complete turn about before they were shunted in to the quay, so
at the point of departure the groups had to be put on the train in the
reverse order to the one which one imagined would be convenient at the
quayside.

With, as I thought, the well-oiled machine turning smoothly, I went
out from Alex to meet the long train coming in from the west at the

railway halt at Amorea, where they were scheduled to stay for half an hour before going on. Here, to my chagrin, I found that the RTO (Rail Transport Officer) at the far end had deliberately refused to accept my information about what happened in the port and had overridden the liaison officers and packed the groups in the wrong order. It was probably the only significant job he had had to do since the end of the Desert War and he had obstinately got it wrong. I insisted on getting everyone out of their carriages and repacking them in the right order. There were groans and curses and threats of defiance – they had sat there so long that they had almost atrophied on their benches – while the officers' hold on authority was tenuous. However, in the end it was done. A couple of soldiers made a break for it and ran towards the distant village. I chased them in my truck and brought them back, then found they were Egyptian Greeks so I told them they could go. Belatedly realising that getting home from this desert rail halt was going to be more difficult than from Alex, they insisted on staying. The laughter helped to smooth over the bad-feeling simmering all around. Down at the docks all went well, and there was agreement that if they had stayed in their original places they would have been worn out by relays of baggage carrying. I dined that night with a sense of euphoria. In due course GHQ Allies received a report of how the repatriation had gone. As the ships sailed into harbour after harbour, the troops sang their hearty EAM/ELAS songs and found their reception was frosty, even hostile: there was a strange blend of families receiving their returning sons with joy and the universal disillusionment at their espousal of the now-hated guerrillas who had fought against the British liberators and smashed up Athens. As for the sea journey, the report of one of the ship's captains began, 'I was once proud of my beautiful clean ship …'

Now, to repatriate myself. Not long after returning to Cairo from Cyrenaica, Godfrey Hobbes had invited me to join him in Greece after the liberation, with promotion to lieutenant colonel and continuing liaison work with the Greek Army; Granitsas, Tsacalotos and the rest of the senior officers wanted me. It was attractive – this is what always happened to those who tangled in the affairs of the Greeks; they were friendly, witty and reckless and it was possible to become fascinated even by their feuds and treacheries. Though there had been fighting with ELAS in Athens after the German withdrawal, I had accepted Godfrey's offer and signed a paper promising to stay in the Army for another three years to see the business through. I don't know that I thought at all of ordination then; perhaps I was subconsciously trying to postpone a decision, perhaps never have to make one. Had I kept to this obligation, no doubt my whole life would have turned out differently. But for a combination of reasons, obscurely pressing on the mind and never logically formulated, I asked if I could withdraw my signature. Having been in the Army since the beginning of the war and abroad for most of the time, I was due for early release and, more interestingly still, for rapid repatriation. I still had not faced the issue of ordination squarely, and could only think straight about it at home. The yearning to see England and family again became insistent. My Greek friends urged me not to go to their country. There would be more fighting to come and no war is more cruel than a civil war. In this I would be decisively identified with the Right-wing cause; there would be no more light-hearted joking with the other side. Savage measures might be taken and I would be an accomplice. Did I trust Tsacalotos, Kitseos, Asimicopoulos, Sirmas and the rest of them enough to be their committed helper? Once this question was put, the answer had to be 'no'. They would be back in their own country and no longer in the last resort be obliged to yield to British insistence on moderation and tolerance. I had done my duty as a soldier and obeyed orders to help in the defeat of Germany, a cause I passionately believed in; was I willing to enlist again, as it were, and swear a new loyalty to a policy about which I had less than total conviction? I was just in time to withdraw. Godfrey Hobbes was angry to have his plans disrupted, but let me go.

This decision had been taken a while ago, some time before the Greek repatriation ships had sailed, so now I was due to go to England in the first wave of returning soldiers. Everything happened quickly. A movement order came out of the blue giving me barely twenty-four hours' notice. Fortunately, I had heard a few days beforehand that there would be hardly any warning, so I had said the goodbyes to Betty and the others who really mattered. I spent the morning in GHQ, writing a few letters to the British liaison officers and packing my effects. At the bottom of a steel filing cabinet was a huge Italian automatic pistol – had I inherited it with the furniture? What could I do about it? I just left it. I rushed off to inform my sorrowing Syrian landlady that I was leaving early the following morning, then went off to meet a few friends who were giving me a send-off at the Mena House Hotel. There were

George, Squire, David Hunter and someone else from Allies. In my years in and out of Egypt I had not climbed the Great Pyramid or gone inside, so it had been decided that I would be escorted to the Pyramid to complete my education as a tourist. We had a swim in the pool, of course, then a hearty lunch, a reflective coffee in the lounge, then out we ventured into the blazing sunshine. The Sphinx was a miserable sight, the back end falling down and propped up with odd lumps of rock. Someone recited the dubious army ditty (then new to me) which ends with 'which accounts for the hump of the camel, and the Sphinx's inscrutable smile'. We agreed that we could see no smile on the Sphinx, let alone an inscrutable one. As we approached the pyramid we could see British soldier tourists climbing up the huge step-like stones, being hauled by Arab guides. The soldiers were fresh from England, their faces pink and white and even pinker from the arduous climb. As we reached the foot of the stone mass, just above us a party emerged from the tunnel, blinking in the sunlight and sweating as a guide harangued them. We looked at each other with a single thought. 'Not for me,' I said, and we hastened back to Mena House for long cold drinks.

Home Again

Early the next morning I was at Cairo main railway station alone, with my various bags, army valise and a tin trunk. Everyone who had ever stored clothes at the Citadel had such a trunk, proof against moths, insects and (whatever it was) 'woolly bear'. The train to ferry returning warriors to Alex docks was at the platform being loaded. The RTO, a captain with a clipboard, saluted and asked if all was OK. I answered in surprise with his name – he was an undergraduate contemporary of mine at Oxford, though not in my circle, as he spent his time socialising and giving private lunches attended by fashionable people from London in formal dress. Glacially, he gave me no recognition. To meet a once familiar face in wartime had always led to reminiscences and a moment of hearty friendship even where none had existed before. Not in this case.

It would be fine if I could describe standing on deck as we sailed out of Alex and watched the lights of Africa fading, my five years there suddenly ended, but in fact we were all busy finding our baggage, cabins and places for dinner, and attending boat drill. A strange week in limbo followed: no employment, rank but no status, one world vanished and our old world, half-forgotten, drawing closer. There was a remarkable contrast between the voyage home and the grim voyage out on the *Pentland*, battened down and blacked out, with grey and freezing weather on deck and mephitic sweltering smog within, and the ever-present menace of submarine attack (since then, a torpedo had sent the *Pentland* to the bottom of the sea). Now it was Mediterranean sunshine all the way and the ship's lights bright at night; there were no second lieutenants wondering what war could be like, but older men of higher rank who knew all too well. The only resemblance between the two voyages was that both ships were crowded. There was no one aboard that I knew; there may have been among the other ranks (indeed, as I found later, there was at least one), but officers and other ranks were segregated. There was not much life in the conversation. Apart from a few garrulous and boastful bores, and more agreeable men temporarily demoted into that category by drink, no one wanted to boast about war experiences. We were looking forward to the future, but it was a private future for each of us, and it would have been wearisome to try to explain and introduce the characters on which it depended, those who were waiting for us. The search for the company of the limited number of women aboard, the dominant occupation of some and the envious object of observation by many on the voyage out, was not evident now. No doubt there had been many a sexual adventure during the years abroad, but these were to be forgotten now behind a chaste front for the renewal of the old legitimate ties and commitments in England. No one tried to keep fit, although there was a passion for sunbathing, to acquire or improve an exotic tan to impress the stay-at-homes. Insistently throughout the day, loudspeakers announced the amnesty offered to holders of guns and ammunition: hand them in at the purser's office with no questions asked. At first hardly any were produced, then a few more, rising finally to a great rush on the last day. In fact, when we arrived at Liverpool docks the customs men paid no attention to our baggage; we went straight to sorting units where we were furnished with instructions, travel warrants and ration coupons. All was efficiently done; I was coming back to an Army very different from the shambling institution I had joined at the beginning of the war.

My orders were to go to the Northumberland Fusiliers' training centre and depot, no longer at Fenham Barracks, but in Cheshire nearby, and from there I would be sent home on leave. It was a melancholy, purposeless place. Training was going on, but no heart in it. There were a few old dug-outs in the mess, who were nice to the returning warriors; there was no one like that snobbish old poseur who had been the PMC at Fenham. There were also a few officers staging en route to other jobs, especially in occupied Germany.

Walking across to the mess from my quarters I was conscious out of the corner of the eye of a sergeant-major according me a salute: not the rigid, quivering, stiff-handed variety of the old soldier putting on the 'bull', not the technically correct but slack and grudging salute of the brand of regular NCO who regrets having to acknowledge the existence of so many jumped-up amateur officers, but the perfect salute of a company sergeant-major at ease with himself and his rank, as well he might be, for he was wearing the Military Medal on his battledress blouse. It was Fram, still red-faced and bucolic, but no longer the clumsy recruit of Fenham days, a hero of the war and one who had been promoted to authority. It was wonderful meeting him; he had been with Derek Lloyd in the much-decorated Z Company. Like me, he was going home. And the next morning, another figure from long ago – Sergeant Redhead, still a sergeant. He had spent the whole war training recruits on the Vickers medium machine-gun, out of the firing line, but also out of the line for promotion. Amid his crudities, he had always declared how much he loved his wife; he had stayed with her and the children so that the war had not touched them by its tragedy, and this had left him a nobody in his career. Bitterly, he declared that he was getting out of the Army as soon as possible. His encounters with Sergeant-Major Fram in the sergeants' mess had not done anything to cheer him. I had thought that if ever I met Redhead again I'd be brusque to him, but this was impossible. He was so unhappy that I could only show sympathy. He had taught so many recruits the technicalities of machine-gunning, a real contribution to the war, though an unheroic one. I can still rectify the stoppages of the Vickers gun with all the appropriate jargon: 'ease, pull, tap', 'new lock two', and I could never fail to realign my sights before firing again.

Only very recently have I found out that Redhead did not carry out his embittered vow to leave the Army – he stayed on, fought in the 1st Battalion in Korea, was promoted and decorated for bravery. He was a soldier through and through, and devoted to the Royal Northumberland Fusiliers. Historians grow to admire the characters who served with zeal a worthy cause and helped it to prevail, yet in real life the very qualities which made them so efficient would turn us against them. So it was with Sergeant Redhead. I suppose it must be too late now, but I wish I could shake his hand and congratulate him, bastard as he was to us in those far distant recruit days. Perhaps I ought to have given his real name so I could now pay my tribute to him. Anyway, if any of the old recruits at Fenham Barracks read this they will recognise him and know how things turned out for him in the final test of war.

And now for home: at the vicarage, Ferryhill – the family had moved here while I had been in the Middle East. Ferryhill was the place where I had been born, grown up and went to school, much more familiar to me than West Pelton had been. My father had been a miner there and, later on, a curate. I remember Ferryhill vividly as it was in those early days and, with some changes, as it was just after the war. There was the old village green and duck pond, enclosed by three pubs and the 'Miners' Welfare' (the biggest pub of them all), the town hall with its clock and weather vane, the fish and chip shop and Foster's, the store that sold everything if you had time to wait until they found it, and the manor house just up the road where the doctor lived, with its walled garden and sundial, and the village church school opposite. On the west side lay the subsidiary annexe of Dean Bank, a multitude of bleak streets of back-to-back miners' cottages, each with its slate on the wall to inscribe messages to guide the 'knocker-up' for the night shift. Here was a different world from the old village, and those whose early years were spent in the idyllic church infants' school had to face the grim moment when they were transferred to the vast council-school complex of Dean Bank, a harsh and savage milieu. On the south, Darlington Road ran down from the village green to join up with the A1 north-south highway, which bypassed the houses by way of a deep excavation, 'the Cut'. Half way down Darlington Road was the sweets and sports equipment shop kept by my aunt and blind uncle, and further down still where the fields began, Ferryhill Athletic Football Ground, the scene of fights and raucous demonstrations on Saturday afternoons in winter, a place to which referees came with trepidation and might have to flee with ignominy. The road was the social centre for youth on Saturday and Sunday evenings, when the young people who had left school and started work demonstrated their adult status by strolling up and down in segregated sexual groups, which in time split up as male and female paired. Best suits were the order of the day, and a real 'masher' would branch out into plus fours or a sports jacket, the envy of all the rest who gazed long and hopelessly on the Montagu Burton catalogues. On the east of the old village, the 'Wood Lane' ran down from the higher ground where the manor house was situated through fields and on to 'Doggy Wood', a place of danger to schoolboys, for here gangs from another mining village, Cornforth, claimed territorial sovereignty, and woe betide any Ferryhiller who was caught – he would be pushed into the narrow cave in the hillside and blocked in with prickly branches torn from thorn bushes. Running south from the old centre, to the east of Darlington Road and parallel to it, the hill, here very steep, ran down to the railway station; on the left near the top was Milford Terrace; here, in number 15 I was born – three up and three down, a yard at the back and a huge bucket latrine in an outhouse, to be patronised by candlelight even by day, emptied once a week by the council men who slopped disinfectant over the road as they rolled in the new receptacles with metallic clanging sounds. Their lorry cut deep ruts in the unmade road at the back, which were generally filled with black water.

The most magnificent house in the old village, surpassing even the doctor's manor house, was the vicarage, set among trees just a short street away from the village green; it was built in the late nineteenth century from the limestone hacked out to form the 'cut', and being limestone was perpetually damp. But in all appearance here was a mansion for a gentleman cleric, with fine bay windows looking out southwards onto a lawn and a border of trees with open country beyond (soon to be occupied with council houses). Here had lived T. L. Lomax, the vicar, rich, eccentric, naive and deeply spiritual, with his three servants, chauffeur for his two cars, and two secretaries. For these latter he had built on a wooden extension of four rooms, and they spent their time typing his letters to all sorts of people whose names figured in the newspapers, urging them to repent, and his various pamphlets, like *Make Me a Clean Heart, O God* and *Bible Readings for Lent*.

This was the vicarage into which the family had moved while I had been overseas, and it was the new vantage point from which I was to observe the mining village where my childhood had been spent, all the while in awe of the lofty social rank of the dwellers in the vicarage.

When the slow train stopped at Ferryhill station, Mother and Father and the curate were on the platform ready to whisk me and my manifold baggage up the hill in the curate's large and ancient car. There will be no attempt to describe the emotions of that day, using the renewed excuse of Chateaubriand's dictum about the impossibility of exciting interest in the doings of the perfectly happy. Given wartime austerity and family poverty, the vicarage presented a different spectacle from the days of its glory in the years of T. L. Lomax. The lawn was dug over for potatoes, the kitchen garden doubled in size – local citizens were allowed to hold plots as allotments, with the family entitled to levy a feudal tribute of vegetables as required. The vicarage car was in a humble outhouse, and the big shed that had housed the Lomaxian Daimler was now occupied by an enormous pig – the result of heeding patriotic appeals to help the war effort; a pig exhorter from the government had come round to draw attention to vacant potential porcine accommodation (he did not say he had done the same job in the First War and no household that had yielded to his eloquence then was willing to try again). There was no lack of expert advice, for local pig fanciers would come and gaze over the half-door and proffer words of wisdom, including the wit who said, 'Feed 'em on alternate days, vicar, to keep the bacon streaky.'

Luckily it was summer when I came home, so we could live at ease in spacious surroundings; when winter closed in, we all crammed into one large room with the coal fire at one end and a paraffin stove at the other. Here there was always the question of whose turn it was to venture out down the long corridor to the huge and glacial kitchen to make the tea or the late-night Horlicks. And in winter time I was to learn something more of how parishes worked. The whole family would be sitting round when parishioners came in for discussions, unless they were very confidential ones, when they had to keep their overcoats on and talk to father in the drawing-room in front of an electric fire. I remember a gem of politically incorrect repartee from my father one night in the communal room. Jim Wood, who grew potatoes on the former lawn, said: 'Vicar, I never go to church but I know that when I die I'll go to heaven.' – 'Jim, if you're there it'll be a funny thing to me.'

A strange phenomenon of being back home was that sometimes a feeling of the insubstantiality of the walls and structure of the big house stole into the mind. As I had remembered it when in the Middle East, the vicarage at West Pelton was four-square and indestructible, but now, having seen so many shattered and gutted buildings in reality or in newsreels, and having been away so long that one had to reassess the whole milieu that was home, the fragility of the environment within which we build our happiness was apparent. In the whole vast complex of European civilisation there were multitudes of families without a roof over their heads; do not be too confident that what you have will last, seemed to be the moral of the times.

I had been mistaken in assuming that I would find myself surrounded by the old friends of grammar school days. The years at Oxford and in the Middle East had broken the continuity, while so many younger people had been taken away to serve in the armed forces or in factories. It was the older churchgoing people that I knew. During my time with the Greeks I had taken up smoking, something never indulged in before

– it was a question of endless, sometimes conspiratorial, conversations, in which they circulated magnificently scented cigarettes and in which one was obliged to reciprocate. But here in England cigarettes were all 'under the counter', kept for the regular customers, the only way to get them was to go to Durham and find a place in a shopping street without a hinterland of local residents – wearing uniform, of course: a mere civilian intruder would have aroused no sympathy. At weekends my youngest brother Joe came home: he was reading medicine at the Newcastle half of Durham University. Like all medical students in those days, he had taken up smoking, so from his secret supplier on Tyneside he could make sure that I could at least indulge in a cigarette after dinner on Sundays. We would play tennis together, and by general demand the best of my war anecdotes had to be repeated for his benefit. And on the Sunday mornings we would both accompany Mother, to sit in the vicarage pew; an occasion which I observed by putting on my regimental smartness – this always happened when returning warriors attended the parish service, for proud parents insisted on it. And there would be long, cheerful conversations outside in the porch and in the churchyard afterwards, chiefly with the men, for their wives had to rush off home to put on the potatoes and put the Yorkshire puddings in the oven.

Early in my leave I took a train up to Oxford for a few days of nostalgic recollection. This was a summer of sunshine, just as the summer at the Aldershot Machine-Gun OCTU had been, and the familiar college buildings were alive with the magic effects of light and shadow. My old digs were available, and my ever-caring landlady welcomed me, with everything just as it had been six years ago when I was taking the Finals Examination. I now had no bike, so I walked in down the Iffley Road, as I did so remembering that last week of nervous early-morning rides to the Examination Schools, leaving a lot of time lest a puncture or other accident prevented me from being the first to rush up the stairs to the South School to start the papers. St Edmund Hall quadrangle had its old bijou charm, on one side the late-seventeenth century chapel, its panelled interior a cool dark retreat for quiet reflection, at the angle to it the wall of the Junior Common Room with its magnolia and wisteria, and opposite the tall robinia tree leaning perilously over the lawn at an angle which foreshadowed its inevitable fall. (This was to happen one night six years later, and I saw the débris on my way to morning chapel.

Emden the Principal was there, brooding: 'I knew this must happen,' he said, 'but I am sad to be here to see it.' In the end he cheered up and had ashtrays made of the wood as souvenirs for old Aularians.)

I went to the University Parks. There was an empty stretch of grass where the tennis courts had been. Norman Morris, the groundsman, was nowhere to be found; he had brought slices of lemon at half-time in soccer matches and poured pint shandies in the pavilion afterwards, and brought in ladies who served tea and cakes at first-team tennis matches (amenities long since abandoned). Groundsmen, like librarians, tend to disapprove of those who use their facilities, disrupting their routines and symmetries, but Norman had been interested to see us win our matches and might turn up on the line to cheer. There was no cricket to watch. When I finished Finals (at lunchtime on a Saturday) I had gone to the Parks, and having observed the traditional ritual of sitting up all night swotting for the last paper (the Special Subject 'gobbets' paper) I had fallen asleep watching the cricket and awoke when everyone else had gone home. Naturally I had to go to the Bodleian Library, meaning to look at the books in the new-publications tray and leaf through recent numbers of history journals, but for the moment past events seemed of no interest after my years of adventure. So off across Radcliffe Square to the Camera, where there were few readers, all very young. I stood in the Gallery where, just after Finals, I had fulfilled a long-pondered reckless gesture. There was a pretty girl wearing a scholar's gown and, not knowing her name or college, I got the library boy who was fetching her books to deliver a note inviting her to tea. She came, but the end of term was near and, after it, the war. Then to the Codrington, library of All Souls College. Each undergraduate college was allowed to send one of its students to read there, and I had enjoyed the privilege, working in untroubled silence away from the clatter and crowding of the Radcliffe Camera, and looking with awe on the odd Fellow of the College wielding his private key and taking books out of the cases as he pleased. I don't suppose that when I totter in now with my key I inspire anything like the reverence I felt for Sir Charles Oman, with his heavy walking stick, his strange shock of hair and the majesty of one who knew many languages and had written many books.

A. B. Emden ('the Abe' to the undergraduates he ruled over at Teddy Hall) had been an ordinary seaman in the First World War, and on the strength of this had been given a high naval rank to run the cadets of the naval division, a task I am told he fulfilled portentously. Alas, he was not about on my brief visit; I owed much to him and would have relished giving him a cracking salute. But John Kelly, the Vice Principal, was around – still very young, but already Oxford's leading theologian. He took me to dinner in Hall, very different from the old days, for the college was full of army cadets, to all appearances schoolboys, who sat sheepishly without animation or joking during dinner, and who regarded me with gratifying awe. John filled me in with the news. He had summarised the Greek newspapers for the Foreign Office, then had monitored the South American press, learning Spanish in a single day to do it. George Ramsay, my old tutor, who had no interests in life beyond learned research, playing the piano and attending concerts, could have stayed out of the war being an Irishman, but he had volunteered and was now an administrative officer in the RAF in the Far East. The college had promised to put mothballs in his wardrobe, and it had just been discovered this had been forgotten, so he would return one day to a row of suits reduced to lacework. (Later, I was to enjoy telling credulous undergraduates that George had spent his spare time in the RAF playing the piano in the NAAFI for free beers.) One old friend, a rugger blue, had been killed in the raid on Saint-Nazaire. Another, a pacifist, had spent most of the war in jail, his health undermined. He was sincere, but had not had the foresight to register with some pacifist organisation or organise a witness or two to impress the exemption tribunal. Another, the only man of his year who had taken a degree in Russian, was allowed to become a pilot and was killed in the Battle of Britain – later, they were running fifteen-hours-a-day crash courses from scratch to produce Russian speakers for the Forces. Just a few people had written to the college from their service postings; the vast majority, like me, had not had the heart to maintain contact, initially because we were subconsciously acquiescing in a future of defeat or endless war, with the old privileged glorious days gone for ever.

Adventuring round the world has its satisfactions, even long term, for one has memories and, perhaps to the exasperation of friends, anecdotes. But I am sure that complete happiness is found only in the quiet oases of life, the little worlds of friendship and concern where you are understood, and understand. Life in the vicarage, with the parish comings and goings giving it purpose and flavour, was such a refuge, and one hoped, in turn, to build another family unit to the exclusion of the harshness of the too-busy world, and to exorcise the contrary curse of loneliness. And now, for me, there was Oxford, more and more during the years becoming my social and spiritual home. After six years I was visiting it again with a new, overriding certainty that this was not only the milieu which had moulded me and transformed me, but also the place above all others where happiness was to be found. I was to rejoin it and then to venture away again deliberately, for what can they know of Oxford who only Oxford know? But God has brought me here again. It is good to have done one's best work here, and it is good, when work is over, to look forward to dying here.

Meanwhile, while I was on leave the war in the Far East ground to its terrible end – important to our family, as Tom would come home. When news of the Japanese surrender came, there were celebrations that night on the village green (now no longer 'green' as it had been sur-faced with tarmac by the Council so more spaces could be rented out for stalls on market day – a sad act of vandalism). There were coloured lights, an amateur dance band and a lot of people milling around, though few trying to dance. I put on uniform to join in, but like VE Day in Alex, I was alone. It would have been more fun out of uniform: a major was a rare sight in the village and was deferentially left on his own.

It was a delight to idle away the days of this long, long leave in com-fortable, ancient civilian dress, reading and walking a great deal, in both occupations having the company of Patch, the vicarage fox terrier. This was a pious dog, who accompanied Father to the early morning service every day, and would lie with head sunk on paws to check that the liturgy was duly performed, then lead the way triumphantly back home across the churchyard; but not on Sunday, when he remained in his basket, knowing the churchwardens would not allow intrusions. But when, as often happened, the cry of 'Rat!' would be made from the sheds and stables at the back, he was off like a rocket, piety forgotten, a picture of ferocious zeal. Every now and then it was the pig, rather than the dog, which encouraged me to take exercise, for those ingenious ani-mals spend all their time devising methods of escape. On one Sunday morning, between the early communion service and the half-past nine 'Family Eucharist', such citizens of Ferryhill as were about were treated to the sight of a large and corpulent clergyman in dog collar and cassock and an Army major in Sam Browne belt and Johnson hat chasing the pig back home with cudgels. Another time, the animal was missing for four hours, and Bob Chat, the village policeman, told us darkly that he fancied he knew who had got It, and would have a look in his 'cree' (shed). It was found hoofing it down the steep bank from the village square towards the Great North Road, and was driven back in our direction by a posse of drinkers who tumbled out of the Post Boy Inn to head it off.

Not long after Japan surrendered, my vegetative bliss was interrupted by a rather unwelcome letter – I was delighted to hear from the writer, but had reservations about the message. John Brewis wrote from his theological college, St Chad's College, Durham. I had asked to be reminded, when the war was over, that I meant to be ordained, and he reminded me and offered a place in his college. My resolution had collapsed; my heart was no longer convinced. The decision had been taken at the first sight of sudden, savage death, of the cruelty of man to man. I had seen many more dead men now. Working with the Greeks had shown how fascinating administration and negotiation can be. My sense of dedication had soured into resentment against the compulsive sense of duty I would so gladly have shaken off. John Brewis proposed a gamble: take the government education grant available to returning soldiers and use it to study theology at Durham for the two years necessary for the diploma. This would be an acknowledgement of the original inspiration; then, if I still did not wish to be ordained, regard this as a sacrifice of two years to the cause of religion. This sounds stark and heroic, but was far from it, for there would be social life and intellectual stimulus in the university and time to forget the war and its bitterness. So it was agreed, with the term starting in October.

My leave came to an end, and before I could be sent off to Germany, orders for my release came through, signed by one Michael Brock, who had been an Oxford contemporary (later to be Warden of Nuffield College). So it was back to the RNF depot in Cheshire for documentation, and they ferried me out to a 'demob' centre to be given a permanent ration book, clothing coupons and the standard demob outfit of a suit with all the accessories, shoes and a pork-pie hat. On my way in the train from home I had talked to an old boy who was a tailor from one of the best Savile Row firms, and he told me how to identify their products, even though the mass of clothing on offer was supposedly anonymous. Thanks to his advice, I found a grey suit with a chalk pin stripe from their cutting room. So it was the end of the battledress and the barathea, the Sam Browne belt and the indestructible Herbert Johnson hat, consigned to moth balls and only taken out for children's dressing up games. Now one walked the streets a nobody, with never a salute to gratify the ego. In short a release into the old, sane world that had ended six years ago.

A few weeks before I became a civilian, Tom came back from naval duties, never to return to sea. His engagement to Joan was a thing of the past – she had chosen someone else – he was a single man ready to resume his degree studies at Durham. Thanks to wardroom life he was now a heavy smoker and thus, once his supply of naval cigarettes had run out, a continual victim of the parochially minded tobacconists, who had little regard for returning heroes. On his return, we had a rare family drink from a bottle of sherry he had brought back long ago, but hoarded at the vicarage 'until both the boys come home'. Tom drained his glass, put it down on the table and called out 'Freeman!' the name of the wardroom steward, horrifying Mother with a vision of chain drinking with calls for instant refills. She was even more alarmed by his account of calling on the Bishop of Durham at Auckland Castle. The scholarly bishop had met Tom on an earlier leave and pressed on him the loan of a book to read on his travels, and he had brought it back from the Far East with the back bent and discoloured, with foxed pages and loosened binding. Various versions were given of how he explained the damage to the bishop – orgies and drinking bouts on board, left ashore in louche bars and opium dens; the final version he conceded to be the true one was not entirely reassuring, 'Dropped it in the drink, my lord, fished it out the oggin.' Having spent so many hours at sea playing bridge with the admiral, Tom had become an enthusiast, so to carry on his hobby he had to teach us all at home the elements of the game, reducing the conventions of bidding to the bare minimum. So we played round the fire on the dark winter nights (provided no parish business intervened), Mother so nervous that she was delighted to get a bad hand so she did not have to bid, and volunteering to transfer to dummy if she by ill-luck had the contract, Father so ebullient that given seven of a suit he would bid up to a slam, in defiance of the obvious arithmetic of the situation.

In October, Tom and I began term at Durham; I was reading for the

diploma in theology, and he was continuing the degree course in history
he had begun before the war. He too was at St Chad's, Brewis having
shanghaied him, secular student though he was, with the odd result that
this haunt of ordinands had in its midst the captain of university soccer
and tennis, something unique in its annals. The student body at
Durham was a strange amalgam of fresh-faced young men coming
directly from school and battered old warriors. None of the service men
talked about their wartime adventures, but in the changing rooms after
a game you would see some livid scar or deep gash bearing testimony to
a narrow escape. The old soldiers were serious about work but too well
organised to swot, with money to spend but not given to frivolity, treating the dons with respect but as equals, which did not please all of
them. Unlike Oxford where those who could not afford to dine out, go
up to London or attend commem balls were very much outsiders in the
social round, Durham was a continual scene of social engagements;
there was a ball every term in the castle hall, flannel dances in summer,
debates and parties that everyone attended.

While Tom was so prominent in university games, I took little part,
though basking somewhat in his glory, more especially as there were
some who never registered the fact that there were now two (indeed,
three if the Newcastle half of the university was considered) McManners brothers around. This confusion of exploits went on, for when,
long afterwards, Durham generously gave me an honorary degree, the
public orator, before passing on to matters scholarly, decked me out in
the plumes of my brother's sporting prowess – to his consternation as
he sat there in the front row. But there was one day when Father and a
few of his friends came to Newcastle to see a university soccer match in
which the forward line had the three McMannerses all alongside each
other, Joe at centre forward (tough and bustling), Tom at inside left
(very subtle) and myself on the left wing.

For returning servicemen, the university was a matrimonial agency
with a profusion of clever and good-looking young women about, a
sight not to be seen in wartime wanderings. Tom found a delightful girl
reading English, and did his best for me by taking me to tea with one of
his pre-war contemporaries as a student, now back in Durham as a lecturer in geography. 'Jack, Sarah Errington – two left-wingers meeting.'
Sarah had played outside left for the university hockey team. This
turned out to be the moment of my greatest good fortune.

Sarah Errington, 1945

The study of theology, as an intellectual discipline, was fascinating, enjoyable. It meant so much more to me than it had before, as its conundrum-solving aspects receded. Since that day in Tobruk I had thought through and rationalised the impact of the sudden sight of those slaughtered Germans; what had happened was that Christian belief had become intensely personal. Up to then I had followed, in intellectual debates, the *via eminentia* of Christian apologetics: the order and beauty of creation, the working of laws in the universe, spiritual experience, show there must be a God. Then, look around for signs of God's activity in the moral sphere, and we find the story of a good man preaching and healing in Palestine; he is crucified, his followers worship him – but the sight of the dead bodies in the sandbagged post at Tobruk ended that chain of argument. I had seen what men out of their God-given freedom do to each other. This was the face of evil, and I was part of the evil, being glad, even in revulsion, that they were dead. People tell academics and clergy to look at what the 'real world' is like. By this they mean dictating letters, selling and buying shares, instituting manufacturing processes, tapping information into computers. But behind their world is the real world they have forgotten: the battlefield. Here is the ultimate reason of the social order written in letters of lead and shards of steel. In face of this, you cannot believe in God, the God of the deists. But you can, almost in despair, turn to the God who suffers with his creation, accepting the burden of sin that arises from human freedom, and taking it on himself. Religious apologetics begin from Jesus on the cross: the Christian life is allegiance to him.

But it still did not follow that I had to be ordained. I attended chapel every morning and, as far as university affairs allowed, every evening, hoping for the guidance that never came. I was lucky in having as my personal tutor Michael Ramsay, who had just married Joan Hamilton, sister of my old ally Tommy of the Northumberland Fusiliers. Their friendship, and that of Stanley Greenslade, the other canon-professor, and the background influence of my father (a determined Christian believer in a very different intellectual sphere) drew me towards the ministry of the Church in which they all served. We know now, as was not known then, what enervating effects war can have on the minds of combatants: having made life and death decisions and being haunted by them, they lose the capacity for deciding. In fact, there is a sense in which you can never know for sure beforehand if a vocational decision is the right one; until you accept the duties you cannot know they were meant for you – a dilemma which forces a gamble. Ordination, I kept telling myself, meant total allegiance, the willingness to do anything and go anywhere, something I could not feel then and have never felt. Yet I was unable to move off, apply for an academic job in history or a course in law leading to the Bar – there was a constraint defying logical argument.

Half-way through the course of theology at Durham John Kelly wrote to me – my old college at Oxford invited me back as chaplain and history tutor after I had done a year in a parish. So I was ordained just like the port-filled dons of old, to go to a Fellowship. Would I have done so if the invitation had not come? I could not say then and I still do not know.

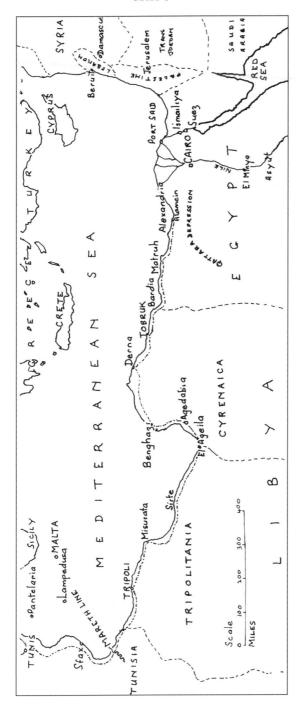

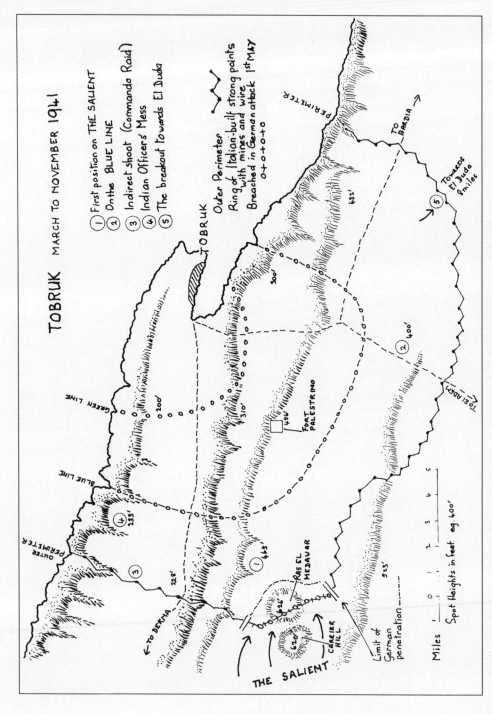

TOBRUK MARCH TO NOVEMBER 1941

(1) First position on THE SALIENT
(2) On the BLUE LINE
(3) Indirect shoot (Commando Raid)
(4) Indian Officers' Mess
(5) The breakout towards El Duda

Outer Perimeter
Ring of Italian-built strong points
with mines and wire
Breached in German attack 1st MAY
o-o-o-o-o

TOBRUK

TO BARDIA →

PERIMETER

Towards
El Duda
9 miles

(5)

431'

500'

(2) 400'

TO EL ADEM →

GREEN LINE

o 200'

310'

450'

FORT
PALESTRINO

BLUE LINE

235'

(4)

OUTER
PERIMETER

(3)

← TO DERNA

320'

445'

(1)

RAS EL
MEDAUAR

620'

CARRIER
HILL

525'

Limit of German
penetration ----------

THE SALIENT

Miles   1   0   1   2   3   4   5

Spot Heights in feet eg. 400'

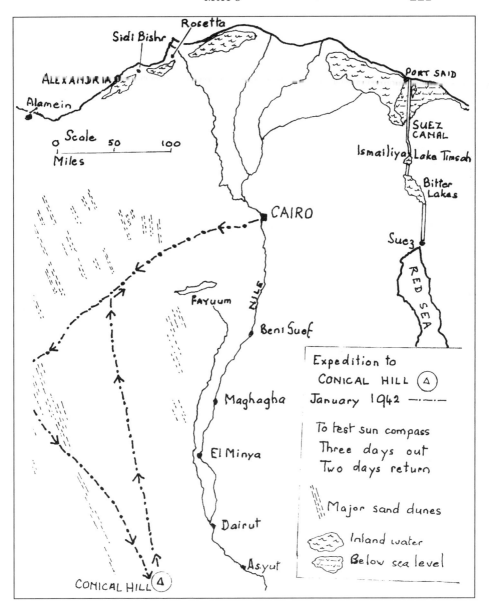

Expedition to
CONICAL HILL △
January 1942 —·—·—

To test sun compass
Three days out
Two days return

Major sand dunes

Inland water

Below sea level

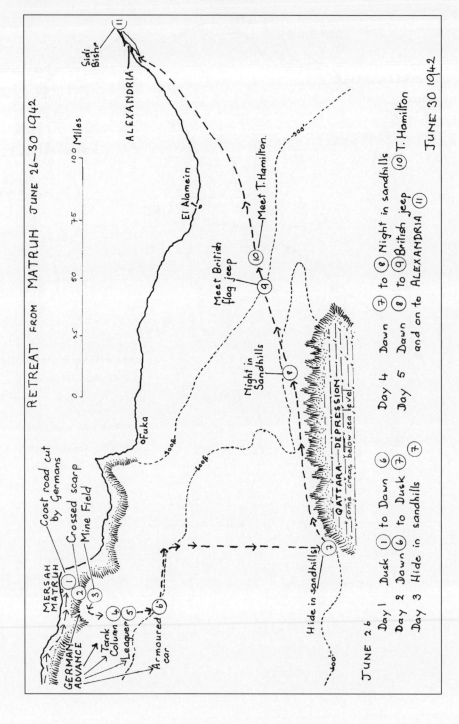

RETREAT FROM MATRUH JUNE 26–30 1942

0   25   50   75   100 Miles

MERSAH MATRUH
Coast road cut by Germans
Crossed scarp
Mine Field
Tank Column
Leaguer
Armoured car
GERMAN ADVANCE

Sidi Bishr
ALEXANDRIA
El Alamein
oFuka

Meet British flag jeep
Meet T.Hamilton.
Night in Sandhills
QATTARA DEPRESSION
some areas below sea level
Hide in sandhills

JUNE 26

Day 1   Dusk   ① to ⑥ Dawn   ⑥ to ⑦ Dawn   ⑦ to ⑧ Night in sandhills
Day 2   Dawn   ⑥ to Dusk   ⑦   ⑧ Dawn ⑨ British jeep
Day 3   Hide in sandhills   ⑦   and on to ALEXANDRIA ⑪
Day 4   Dawn   ⑦ to ⑧ Night in sandhills
Day 5   Dawn   ⑧ to ⑨ British jeep   ⑩ T.Hamilton

JUNE 30 1942

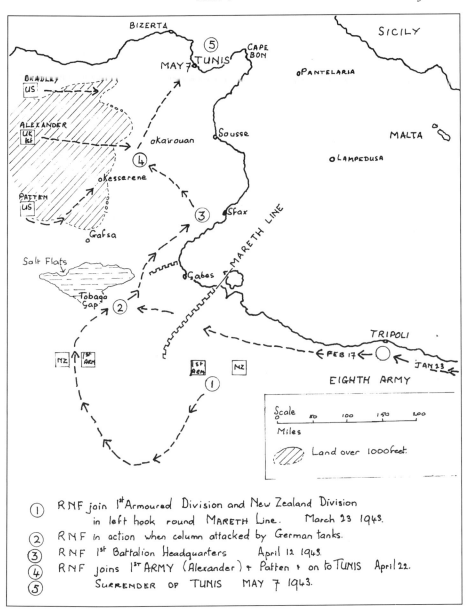

① RNF join 1st Armoured Division and New Zealand Division
   in left hook round MARETH Line.   March 23 1943.
② RNF in action when column attacked by German tanks.
③ RNF 1st Battalion Headquarters   April 12 1943.
④ RNF joins 1st ARMY (Alexander) + Patten + on to TUNIS April 22.
⑤ SURRENDER OF TUNIS   MAY 7 1943.

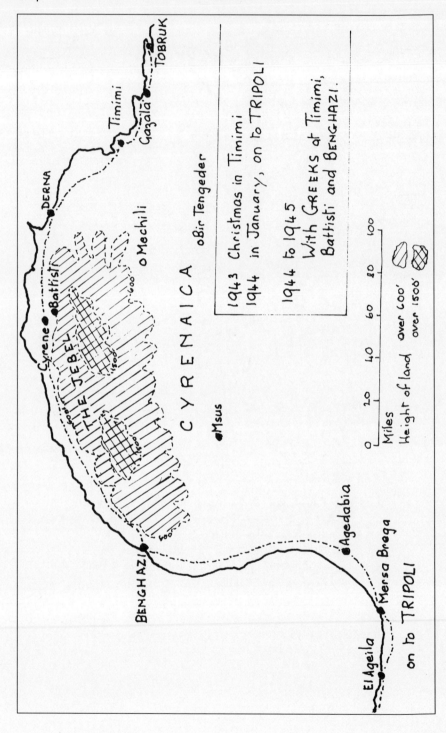

CYRENAICA

oBir Tengeder

TOBRUK

Gazala

Timimi

DERNA

Cyrene
Battisti
THE JEBEL
oMechili

•Msus

BENGHAZI

•Agedabia

Mersa Brega

El Ageila

on to TRIPOLI

1943   Christmas in Timimi
1944   in January, on to TRIPOLI

1944 to 1945
With Greeks at Timimi,
Battisti and Benghazi.

0   20   40   60   80   100
Miles
Height of land   over 600'
                  over 1500'